# MAINL. DENV. R

## The Bombing of Flight 629

ANDREW J. FIELD

JOHNSON BOOKS
*Boulder*

Published by Johnson Books, a division of Big Earth Publishing,
3005 Center Green Drive, Suite 220, Boulder, Colorado 80301.
E-mail: books@bigearthpublishing.com
www.johnsonbooks.com

9   8   7   6   5   4   3   2   1

Library of Congress Cataloging-in-Publication Data
Field, Andrew J.
   Mainliner Denver: the bombing of Flight 629 / Andrew J. Field.
      p.  cm.
   Includes bibliographical references.
   ISBN 1-55566-363-X
   1. Graham, John Gilbert—Trials, litigation, etc.  2. Trials (Murder)—United States.
3. Aircraft accidents—Colorado.  I. Title.
   KF224.G698F54  2005
   364.152'3'0978883—dc22                          2005017211

Printed in the United States of America

# CONTENTS

CHAPTER ONE: *"I may never see any of you again."* 1

CHAPTER TWO: *"My sincere prayer for you."* 13

CHAPTER THREE: *"This one has us worried."* 28

CHAPTER FOUR: *"It all started six months ago."* 43

CHAPTER FIVE: *"I just can't turn from the man."* 66

CHAPTER SIX: *"You're no dummy."* 81

CHAPTER SEVEN: *"I will beat the gas chamber."* 92

CHAPTER EIGHT: *"We are all on the plane."* 102

CHAPTER NINE: *"You couldn't put your arms around her."* 111

CHAPTER TEN: *"The tension has been released."* 123

CHAPTER ELEVEN: *"They won't look at me."* 143

CHAPTER TWELVE: *"Graham—the liar."* 159

CHAPTER THIRTEEN: *"I just want to get gone."* 194

CHAPTER FOURTEEN: *"I expect to see her tonight."* 212

EPILOGUE 228

APPENDICES

    *Appendix A: The Victims* 234

    *Appendix B: U.S. Aviation Security, 1955–2005* 236

    *Appendix C: DC-6B Diagrams* 243

BIBLIOGRAPHY 245

INDEX 248

For J.B.

# ACKNOWLEDGMENTS

FOR ASSISTANCE WITH RESEARCH, I WISH TO THANK: Curtis Anderson and Edward Lehman (*Daily Times-Call*); Florence Aston (Denver District Attorney's Office); Randy Bangert (*Greeley Tribune*); Eric Bittner (National Archives and Records Administration, Rocky Mountain Region); Martha Campbell (Colorado Supreme Court Library); Cindy L. Brown (Wyoming State Archives); Justice Nathan B. Coats, Mac. V. Danford, and Linda F. Roots (Colorado Supreme Court); Peggy Ford (Greeley Municipal Archives); Larry E. Forry (Montgomery County-Norristown Public Library); Miles Flesche and Sabra Millet (Denver District Court); Barbara Hanson (United Airlines Archives); Jim Havercamp and Stephen Sample (National Press Photographers Association); Pat Kant (Museum of Colorado Prisons); Terry Ketelsen and George Orlowski (Colorado State Archives); Dick Kreck and Jeffrey Leib (*Denver Post*); Erik A. Mason (Longmont Museum); Stephanie Matlock (U.S. District Court for the District of Colorado); Phillip R. McCarty (American Air Mail Society); John McWalter (retired DC-6B pilot); Karen Miller (Wilmette Public Library); Paula Meyer (Richmond Memorial Library); Susan Rappaport (Rutherford Public Library); Clark Secrest (former editor of *Colorado Heritage* magazine); Rex Tomb and Susan McKee (Federal Bureau of Investigation); D. Scott Young (Minox Historical Society); and the librarians and curators at the Denver Public Library's Western History Department and the Colorado Historical Society's Stephen H. Hart Library.

For sharing their recollections, I wish to thank: Arlo Boda, Judge Larry Bohning, Judge John Criswell, Charles Dalpra, Richard Downing, Justice William Erickson, Judge Irving Ettenberg, Dorothy Heil, Conrad Hopp, Jerry Kessenich, Dr. John Macdonald, Judge Robert H. McWilliams, Judge George Manerbino, Judge Leonard Plank, Louis and JoAnn Rademacher, Richard M. Schmidt, Jr., Judge Edward Simons, and Bernice Weadick. I am especially grateful to Morey Engle and Zeke Scher for allowing me to interview them about the circumstances of their own interviews with John

Gilbert Graham. In addition to his memories, Morey generously shared his collection of audio recordings, photographs, and film footage.

I wish to express my deepest appreciation to everyone at Johnson Books, particularly Mira Perrizo, who embraced this work as a proposal and shepherded it to completion, and Robert Sheldon and Laura Godt, who worked tirelessly to help me share this story with as many readers as possible. I am also indebted to Polly Christensen for her inspired design work, and to Eric Christensen for his assistance with revisions and his meticulous attention to detail.

I owe special thanks to my sister, Nancy Ringer, who interrupted her work as a freelance editor to review a manuscript for her freeloading brother, and to the three people who read these chapters as they were completed: my mother, Audrey Eldred, whose suggestions were as helpful as her enthusiasm; my colleague, Rich Nielson, whose ideas and words of support were an invaluable source of encouragement at all stages of this project; and my wife, Janet Brown, to whom I dedicate this book as an expression of gratitude for her innumerable contributions.

—ANDREW J. FIELD,
*Denver, Colorado,*
*July 2005*

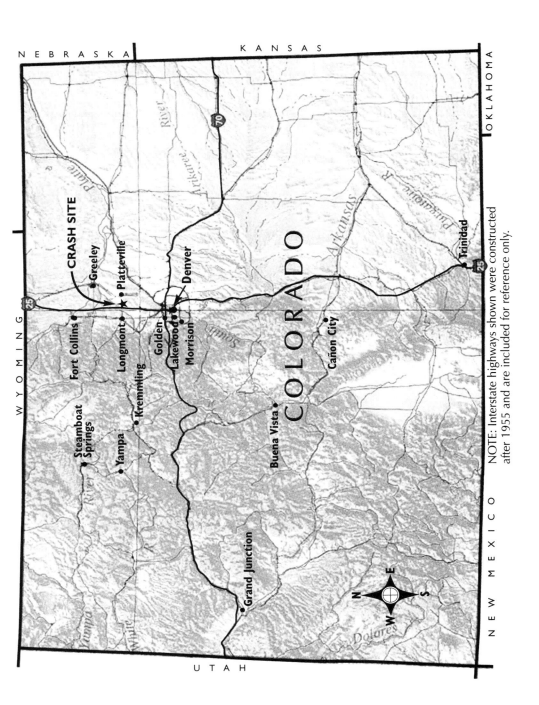

NOTE: Interstate highways shown were constructed after 1955 and are included for reference only.

*"Abominable acts unjustify the man."*

—ALFRED NOBEL,
*inventor of dynamite,*
*1833–96*

CHAPTER ONE

# *"I may never see any of you again."*

IN THE DAYS TO FOLLOW, Martin Bommelyn would tell reporters that he had had a bad feeling about Flight 629, and that he had almost asked his son not to board the plane. However, on the evening of November 1, 1955, he kept this premonition to himself.

Bommelyn, who lived in Denver, was at Stapleton Airfield to see his fifty-three-year-old son, John, who was at the airport on a four-hour layover on his way home to Seattle from a conference in Grand Rapids. With so little time together, the two men decided to eat dinner at the Sky Chef, a restaurant on the second floor of the terminal with a large wall of windows facing east toward the busy runways. They might have chosen to eat there even if they had not been so pressed for time. The Sky Chef was one of Denver's best restaurants in 1955, and residents of the front-range community frequently drove to the eastern edge of the city to celebrate birthdays and other special occasions at the airport.

For Martin Bommelyn, any meal with his son was a special occasion, and he listened proudly as John talked about his work as the superintendent of the Seattle Humane Society. But the brief visit ended too quickly, and soon it was time to go downstairs to the gate where United Air Lines Flight 629 was scheduled for a 6:30 P.M. departure for Portland, with continuing service to Seattle.

The terminal through which they walked was a bustling place. With up to ten thousand travelers each day, Stapleton had become the fifth-busiest airport in the country. It was also one of the most modern. Mayor Quigg Newton's ambitious multi-million dollar expansion project, completed in June of that year, had quintupled the size of the terminal building to almost forty thousand square feet and added a six-story control tower. There were new indoor baggage carousels, so that arriving passengers no longer had to stand in the elements while waiting to retrieve their luggage, though mobile walkways had not yet been invented and departing passengers still had to walk outdoors to board a plane.

© Colorado Historical Society

The terminal at Stapleton Airfield, circa 1955. The Sky Chef restaurant is in the upper level. (Courtesy of Colorado Historical Society, #10032924)

The mid-1950s were a golden age for air travel in America, and on this Tuesday evening the clothing of the passengers waiting at the gate for Flight 629 reflected the grandeur of the experience. The women all wore dresses; the men all wore suits and ties.

Two of the waiting passengers, Carl Deist and James Straud, both senior sales managers for Oldsmobile, were leaving Denver after hosting a regional dealers' meeting at the Brown Palace, the city's most elegant hotel. The meeting had been a success, an opportunity to talk with the local Oldsmobile salesmen about the Starfire Convertible and the Super 88 Holiday Hardtop, two of the chrome-adorned 1956 models featuring the wide white-walled tires so popular at the time. Now the two men were moving on to Portland, where they planned to repeat their sales presentation for the Oldsmobile dealers of that city. Although Straud usually flew home between sales meetings to see his family in Lansing, Michigan, on this occasion he had decided to fly directly from Denver to Portland instead.

James Straud was not the only passenger who had changed travel plans to be on Flight 629. Louise Bunch—the daughter, widow, and mother of Methodist ministers—had spent the previous few days in Colorado Springs attending a conference of the Women's Service Division of the

Above: A 1951 United Air Lines postcard showing the *Mainliner Denver*, aircraft registration number N37559.

Left: Air traffic control tower at Stapleton Airfield, circa 1955. (Courtesy of 1000aircraftphotos.com)

Methodist Church. When the group concluded its business earlier than expected, Mrs. Bunch decided to return a day early to her home in Forest Grove, Oregon, where she lived with her daughter.

Originating in New York, Flight 629 had made one scheduled stop in Chicago, where it had experienced a short ground delay for repair of a malfunctioning propeller deicer. As a result, the DC-6B was eleven minutes behind schedule when it touched down in Denver.

At 6:11 P.M., the aluminum-sheathed plane taxied toward the gate, the roar of its four propeller engines washing across the building. Pilot Hugh Chance parked the aircraft with its wings perpendicular to the terminal and cut power to the piston-driven engines. Ramp men placed blocks under the wheels of the plane and logged the time of its arrival as passengers peering out from the windows located beneath the large "United Air Lines" logo watched the blurred circles on the wings slow to reveal the three individual propeller blades on each rotor. As soon as the blades came to a standstill, the ground crew rolled a large metal staircase forward and aligned it with the door behind the wing nearest the terminal.

Chance completed his post-flight inspections with the assistance of his copilot and readied the plane for the fresh crew that would be taking it onward from Denver. Years later, the aptly-named pilot would recall the DC-6B as "one of the finest airplanes I ever flew. It was very stable. It had a better power-to-weight ratio than anything I'd ever flown up to that time. It was very controllable and easy to fly."

Built by the Douglas Corporation, the DC-6B was a slightly longer version of the DC-6, one of the first commercial airplanes introduced after World War II. Although the family of DC-6 aircraft had a relatively good safety record, they had all been briefly grounded in 1947 when two of the planes experienced in-flight fires. The first fire caused a United Air Lines flight to crash in Bryce Canyon National Park, Utah, killing fifty-two people. Soon thereafter, a fire occurred on an American Airlines flight, though the pilot of that DC-6 was able to land the flaming plane safely at a small airfield in Gallup, New Mexico.

The Civil Aeronautics Board had conducted a thorough investigation of these two incidents and concluded that the fires had started when fuel vented into the cabin heater intakes. The airlines made the necessary changes and, in 1948, the DC-6 class of aircraft—including the *Independence,* the DC-6 used as the presidential aircraft during the Truman administration—was recertified for service.

Three years later, the Douglas Corporation rolled out the first DC-6B. To introduce the new plane to the flying public, the company ran an advertisement in the *Saturday Evening Post* trumpeting the fact that the 117-foot wingspan of the DC-6B was almost as long as the entirety of the Wright brothers' first flight. The advertisement also emphasized the plane's cruising speed—315 miles per hour.

Under optimal conditions, the DC-6B could fly even faster. This capability had been demonstrated only three days earlier when, on October 28, 1955, a United Air Lines DC-6B flying from Portland to Denver had caught the jet stream and set a new record of two hours and forty-eight minutes for the 1,076-mile flight—a trip that normally took four hours.

Although the DC-6Bs were only a few years old, they had already been partially eclipsed by a newer model of propeller-driven aircraft: the DC-7, a faster plane with a greater range that enabled United to offer non-stop flights between the two coasts. Soon, both models would be pushed aside by the arrival of commercial jet aircraft—a development that appeared on the horizon on November 1, 1955.

That morning, the Pratt & Whitney Aircraft Company had run a full-page advertisement in newspapers throughout the country congratulating United for being the first domestic airline to order Douglas DC-8s powered by Pratt & Whitney jet engines. In the announcement, the jet engine manufacturer promised that, when the new planes were delivered to United in 1959, the time for a coast-to-coast journey would be reduced by almost forty percent. However, until those jets arrived, United would continue flying the DC-6Bs on the "Main Line"—the trademarked name it used for its cross-continental route.

Like ocean liners, each of United's DC-6B "Mainliners" was christened with an individual name. These names, which were taken from cities to which United Air Lines offered service, were displayed prominently on the front of the airplanes as part of the red, white, and blue insignias painted directly below the cockpit windows.

The DC-6B Mainliners had another characteristic in common with the ocean liners—comfort. In newspaper and magazine advertisements, United boasted that its DC-6Bs had only fifty-eight seats arranged "two abreast on each side of wide aisles."* The airline also enticed passengers with promises of luxurious service in the "Mainliner Manner," and "delicious meals" prepared by "European-trained chefs." Urging travelers to "Compare The Fare, and You'll Go By Air," United pointed out that tickets for many of its routes now cost "less than first-class rail travel."

These advertising campaigns were effective in luring passengers away from the rails and roads, and there were several first-time flyers on Flight 629. One such passenger was thirty-six-year-old Pittsburgh resident Patricia Lipke, who was flying for the first time in order to see her sister, a resident of Portland. In the seat next to her was her husband, Gerald, a division sales manager for the Hagan Corporation, a Pittsburgh chemical engineering company. Although Gerald Lipke was accustomed to flying, the night before leaving Pennsylvania he had nevertheless taken the precaution of making out a will for the benefit of the couple's three young sons.

Like Mrs. Lipke, James and Sarah Dorey of Whitman, Massachusetts, were also making their first trip by air, flying to Portland to spend time

---

*The DC-6B was designed to carry up to 102 passengers.

Above; The *Mainliner Cleveland*, April 22, 1954, San Francisco Airport. (Courtesy of William T. Larkins, aviation photographer)

with a son, Robert, whom they had not seen for nine years. They had decided to fly because James Dorey's doctors had warned him that his bad arteries might not last long enough to make the trip by car or train. Anticipating the eventual failure of his heart, in advance of this voyage fifty-eight-year-old Dorey had attended a farewell dinner where he told a gathering of friends, "I may never see any of you again."

The door to the plane opened, and chilly air streamed into the cabin. Departing passengers stood to put on their coats and gather their belongings. Many of the nineteen others who were continuing to Portland or Seattle remained in their seats for the short layover. Two of the disembarking passengers, Mr. and Mrs. George Price* of Denver, said farewell to Mrs. Helen Fitzpatrick, who was flying to Seattle to catch another flight for Okinawa, Japan. The Prices had chatted with Fitzpatrick during the flight and learned she was taking her thirteen-month-old son to visit the boy's father, a Navy serviceman who had received his orders to ship out only weeks after the couple's first child had been born. Envisioning the long-awaited reunion, Fitzpatrick had told the Prices, "Papa's going to have to change the baby and get up at night to walk him, and Mama's going to get some rest." The Prices would later recall that, when they left the plane, young James Fitzpatrick II was fast asleep in his mother's lap.

---

• In the 1950s, newspaper reporters often referred to a married woman by using the husband's name. In a few instances, this outdated convention is repeated here when a woman's first name could not be ascertained through research.

Among those traveling on to the next stop were Dr. Ralph Van Valin, a retired Portland dentist who turned seventy-two on this day, and his wife, Minnie, an accomplished genealogist. Lela McClain, also a resident of Portland, was returning home from Glastonberry, Connecticut, where she had spent three weeks visiting her son, Lewis. A sprightly octogenarian who regularly told her friends that she expected to live to be one hundred, Mrs. McClain loved to travel by plane. The year before, she had flown to Pakistan for vacation, an extremely complicated air journey in the 1950s.

Helen Fitzpatrick and James Fitzpatrick II.

As the arriving passengers entered the terminal to meet family and friends, three uniformed crewmen walked past them in the opposite direction. The pilot was thirty-eight-year-old Lee Hall, a father of four who lived in Seattle with his wife, Sally, a former stewardess for the same airline. Hall, who was in his fourteenth year of flying for United, had recently announced plans to retire early and run a sporting goods store in order to spend more time with his family.

The copilot, twenty-six-year-old Don White, had much less experience than Hall, though he had been flying DC-6Bs since they were first introduced. That morning, White, who also lived in Seattle and regularly flew the roundtrip route to Denver, had promised his wife, Maxine, that he would return by midnight to the small rented apartment where the couple lived with their two young children. It was a time of great hope for the Whites. After years of saving their money, they were about to purchase their first home—the culmination of a dream which Don White frequently discussed with his fellow crew members. In a week, after this dream had been dashed by events, Maxine White would tell a *Newsweek* magazine reporter, "Don wasn't due to go out, but the company called to ask if he'd take the flight. I guess they were short a man or something. Don was always ready to go. He loved to fly."

The third member of the crew, Sam Arthur, had also been called in to work as a substitute. A licensed pilot, thirty-eight-year-old Arthur was serving as the flight engineer in charge of operating the engines and keeping a record of the plane's fuel consumption. He was filling the position of flight engineer for Flight 629 because members of the Flight Engineers Union had been out on strike for the preceding eight days. When he had

Left to right: Lee H. Hall, pilot, Donald A. White, copilot, Samuel F. Arthur, flight engineer.

come to work on this evening, Sam Arthur had seen the picket line outside Stapleton Airfield, and he had heard the striking engineers' loud protests against United's requirement that all flight engineers hired in the future also be qualified as pilots.

Earlier in the week, a union spokesman had angrily predicted United's new requirement would eventually cause men holding engineer's licenses to become "the last of the Mohicans." United Air Lines president W. A. Patterson had issued a statement in response explaining that, with the imminent arrival of jet airplanes, "we simply cannot . . . commit ourselves to requirements of the future on aircraft which we do not yet have." The two sides were entrenched in their positions, and United had demonstrated its unwillingness to negotiate by enlisting pilots as replacement engineers.

A few flights had been cancelled due to the strike, including one that Brad and Carol Bynum had planned to take from Denver a few days earlier. The Bynums, who had been in Amarillo to celebrate their first wedding anniversary and Carol's pregnancy, had been forced to extend their stay until they were able to book seats on another flight from Denver. Now, the young couple was relieved that Flight 629 would be taking them on the final leg of their delayed journey home to Portland, where Brad Bynum worked as a geologist for the Sinclair Oil Company.

The striking engineers hoped to cause more disruptions like the one experienced by the Bynums. In an attempt to put more pressure on the airline, the Flight Engineers Union had recently asked the Teamsters Union to support the strike by cutting off all fuel deliveries to United. Tensions between the engineers and the airline were escalating rapidly, and United had stationed a security force from the Burns Detective Agency at Stapleton Airfield to "prevent any violence" and "protect company property."

However, on November 1, the Teamsters had not yet agreed to assist the Flight Engineers Union, and there still was plenty of fuel available for the ground crew refilling the 3,400-gallon tanks of the DC-6B. While the fuel poured into the plane, other members of the ground crew loaded luggage and mail into the rear cargo hold. Against this backdrop of hurried preparations, stewardesses Peggy Peddicord and Jacqueline Hinds strode out from the terminal and climbed the stairs to the plane.

In accordance with the airline's job requirements of the time, the two young women—both of whom were graduates of the United Air Lines Stewardess Training School in nearby Cheyenne, Wyoming—were "between the ages of 21 and 26," "between 5'2" and 5'7" in height," "less than 136 pounds," and "unmarried." *

The two stewardesses wore formal navy-colored uniforms with skirts that hung to midcalf and matching hats with metal wing-shaped pins affixed to the band. Although the uniforms and job requirements were both quite constricting, the image and responsibilities of a stewardess in 1955 had improved substantially since 1930, when United Air Lines (then "Boeing Air Transport") first created the position with an even lower maximum weight limit and an expectation that the young women, all of whom were required to be registered nurses, would occasionally help load baggage, clean the aircraft, and assist with the fueling.

Trouble had plagued United Air Lines' flights to and from Denver during the previous nine years. In 1946, twenty-one lives had been lost when a United DC-3 flying from Boise to Denver veered off course and slammed into the side of Elk Mountain, an 11,125-foot peak in the Medicine Bow mountain range of southeastern Wyoming. Five years later, fifty more people were killed when United Flight 610, a DC-6 flying to Denver from Salt Lake City, inexplicably crashed into Crystal Mountain, eighteen miles west of Fort Collins, Colorado.

If these two accidents had been the only ones, there might not have been reason for the passengers on Flight 629 to worry about the likelihood of a recurrence. However, on November 1, 1955, such concerns would have been nearly impossible to repress in the wake of a third United Air Lines crash that had happened only twenty-six days before.

---

* Although United required its stewardesses to be single, the airline did not apply this rule to its male employees. During this era, gender bias was so pervasive that United even operated special "men only" flights between New York and Chicago featuring "a four-ounce drink before a steak dinner, plus freedom to sit in shirt sleeves and smoke cigars handed out by the stewardesses."

On October 6, 1955, the nation had experienced its deadliest airplane disaster up until that point in time. Sixty-three passengers and three crew members had perished when United Flight 409 from Denver to San Francisco smashed into Medicine Bow Peak, a 12,005-foot mountain only twenty miles from the location of the 1946 disaster on Elk Mountain. The wreckage was strewn just below the summit at the top of a 600-foot cliff and was almost completely inaccessible. An investigative team from the Civil Aeronautics Board had climbed the mountain and set up a base camp above tree line, but they were able to conduct only a cursory examination of the debris before they were forced to retreat due to dangerous weather conditions. In their brief time on the mountain, the investigators were able to determine that the plane had been fully intact when it went down. What they could not understand was why the experienced pilot had deviated several miles from a planned flight path that would have taken the DC-4 safely through a mountain pass at a much lower elevation.

The Medicine Bow crash had been national news, and it had occurred at a time when the entire country's attention was already focused on Colorado due to an even larger news story.

On the afternoon of September 24, Major General Howard Snyder, personal physician to President Dwight D. Eisenhower, had stood outside Fitzsimmons Army Hospital in Aurora, Colorado, and informed the nation that the visiting President had "had a mild coronary thrombosis." While the country waited to learn whether "Ike" would be well enough to serve out the remainder of his term, First Lady Mamie Dowd Eisenhower, a Denver native, moved into the hospital room across the hall from her bedridden husband. By the first week of November, the President was slowly recovering, but he was not yet well enough to return to the White House, and his cabinet officers were still coming to Colorado to brief him on such pressing matters as the upcoming negotiations with the Soviet Union concerning aerial inspections of military facilities.

The progress of the President's recuperation was of particular concern to two passengers on Flight 629. Dr. Harold Sandstead was the Eisenhower administration's Deputy Secretary of the U.S. Public Health Service. A recognized expert in the nutrition problems of developing countries, Dr. Sandstead was traveling to Oregon State College to deliver a speech at the annual Institute of Far East and World Affairs. The second passenger with a connection to Eisenhower was John Des Jardins, the manager of a chain of beauty shops located in Joslin's department stores. A resident of Overland Park, Kansas, Des Jardins was related by marriage to President Eisenhower's chief of staff, Sherman Adams.

A few of the passengers on Flight 629 had purchased one-way tickets, including Thomas Crouch, a young carpenter's apprentice from Wichita who was moving to Seattle for a new job with a large construction firm.

Daisie King was also going to Seattle, but only as a midway stop on her trip to Alaska—at that time still a territory. The widowed owner of a Denver drive-in restaurant, Mrs. King planned to do some caribou hunting with her daughter, a resident of Spenard, a small town on the southern edge of Anchorage.

Along with almost half the other passengers on the plane, Daisie King had purchased flight insurance for the benefit of her relatives. Sold in airports from coin-operated kiosks that looked much like the freestanding ATMs located in airports today, the life insurance policies from Continental Casualty and Mutual of Omaha could be purchased in incremental amounts costing 25¢ for each $6,250 of coverage.*

The most heavily-insured passengers on the plane were Stuart and Suzanne Morgan, a couple in their mid-thirties from Wilmette, Illinois. Before leaving Chicago, the couple had purchased $125,000 of flight insurance—the maximum amount available—for the benefit of their two daughters, fourteen-year-old Sharon and twelve-year-old Susan. Although Stuart Morgan usually traveled alone for his job as a consulting engineer, Suzanne Morgan had decided to accompany her husband on this business trip because his assignment was in their former home city of Vancouver.

Flight 629 had fallen a bit further behind schedule in Denver while waiting for Dr. Sandstead to arrive on a flight from Washington, D.C., but the crew was not anticipating any additional delays once they were aloft. The conditions were good, with light winds out of the southwest and visibility of approximately ten miles.

Sam Arthur flipped a series of switches on the overhead panel and started the number three engine, which was located on the side of the plane away from the boarding stairs. After the last of the passengers had entered the cabin and the door was closed, Arthur started the remaining engines.

---

The interior of the Stapleton terminal, circa 1955. A coin-operated vending machine selling flight insurance can be seen in the foreground on the right. (Courtesy of Colorado Historical Society, #10032925)

At 6:44 P.M., pilot Lee Hall radioed the tower seeking final clearance for departure. The air traffic controller granted the request, directing Hall to fly at 22,000 feet in "Victor Airway 4," an air route running from Denver toward Laramie, Wyoming. Hall revved up the four piston-driven engines. When he released the brake, the plane slowly rolled away from the terminal, its running lights blinking through the darkness.

At the head of the runway, Hall reapplied the brake and brought the engines up to 60 percent power. After checking the tachometer, Hall released the brake and pushed the four synchronized throttles forward, increasing the speed of the engines to full power. The sleek DC-6B responded immediately, hurtling down the lighted runway until Hall eased back the steering yoke and took the plane gently skyward.

Four minutes later, at 6:56 P.M., Hall radioed the tower and reported that he had passed the Denver omnistation, a radio broadcasting beacon located several miles to the northeast of the airport.

In seven minutes, the thirty-nine passengers and five crew members would all be gone.

## CHAPTER TWO

# *"My sincere prayer for you."*

SIX MILES NORTHEAST of Longmont, Colorado, in southwestern
Weld County, the Saint Vrain Creek meanders through a series of
softly rolling fields. A wide ribbon of water, this stretch of the Saint
Vrain is broad enough that it is commonly referred to as a river. Within
sight of its banks, clusters of new homes now sprout from the land. However, in 1955 the only houses in this area were those of a few families who
made their living growing sugar beets.

One of those farmhouses belonged to Harold and Dorothy Heil. Located along State Highway 66 (then a dirt road), the Heils' home sat on the
northern edge of their property, one mile east of the North Washington
Road (now Interstate 25). Like most farms in the area, the Heil farm was a
"quarter section," a 160-acre parcel divided from one of the 640-acre full
sections established under the rectangular survey system used to divide
federal lands deeded to the original settlers.

Throughout October of 1955, Harold Heil had spent long days driving
back and forth on a tractor towing a "digger," a specialized plow for gathering sugar beets. With each pass of the tractor, the digger turned up fresh
rows of rich soil, extracting the thick white roots from the ground and
leaving the broad green leaves behind.

Late on the afternoon of November 1, Heil finished harvesting his beets
and deposited the final load. It was a gratifying sight. Within days the beets
would be taken by train to the Great Western Sugar Company's processing
plant in Longmont, where the extracted syrup would be boiled and converted to crystallized sugar.

By the time Heil completed his other chores and returned to the house for
dinner, it was already growing dark and the nearly full moon was rising in the
east. The temperature—only two degrees above freezing—was falling fast.

High above, Flight 629 was approaching the Heil farm from the southeast.

On the other side of the Saint Vrain Creek, a Union Pacific flagman named Roland Wood was riding in the caboose of a freight train headed to Denver. Looking up at the stars, Wood was taking a moment to rest his eyes when he noticed a "shape moving through the sky, outlined by fire [with] flame . . . dripping off of it like some kind of fireworks." As he watched, the burning object plummeted toward the ground at a thirty-five-degree angle. Wood quickly realized that it was an airplane and pulled out his pocket watch to record the time of impact. Seconds later, he saw a "big mushroom of oily smoke like an atom bomb" and sixty-foot flames that were so bright "it was like four or five haystacks burning all at one time." As the train moved to the south, the flames grew more distant. Wood, assuming he had seen the crash of a military jet, scanned the horizon hoping to see a parachute carrying the pilot to safety.

One mile north of Longmont, Norman Flores was watching television when he heard a car pull into his yard. Stepping outside, he noticed an airplane flying from the southeast:

> It was a real nice moonlight night, just as pretty as it could be. And I
> stood there and I saw this airplane. You could see the lights flickering on
> it. Then all of a sudden there was an explosion, and it was so terrific that
> it shook the house where we lived, and it . . . moved the air when it ex-
> ploded. Then just a little bit after the plane exploded it caught on fire. It
> flew a little ways—I couldn't say how far—kind of hard to judge—I
> don't know how fast they fly per hour—but ... it exploded [and] then
> caught on fire. Just a little while after it caught on fire a flare went up,
> and then it went just a little farther, and then it hit the ground, and when
> it hit the ground a big orange mushroomed affair went up, and from then
> on it just burned.

Closer to the Heil farm, Luella Litzenberger was walking past her east-facing kitchen window when she saw the red sphere of flames. She ran outdoors just as a chunk of the plane hit the ground with a "tremendous thud." According to Litzenberger, the force of the impact was so great that "the house shook and the dishes rattled."

Also looking out an east-facing kitchen window was Mrs. Edwin A. Anderson. At first Mrs. Anderson thought she was "watching the moon come up," but she soon realized that it was an enormous "ball of fire, oval, or odd-shaped." An explosion shook the house, and she "dashed out of the house to see what was going on." Looking up as she heard the second explosion, she saw a "mushroomed . . . ball of smoke and fire."

Another neighbor, Chad Warren, was in his barn milking a cow when he heard the first explosion. Abandoning the cow, Warren moved quickly across the hay-covered floor and slid open the wide door of the barn in time to see a fireball arch toward the ground and explode.

To Tony Route, a twenty-six-year-old Navy veteran who had served in Korea, it sounded as if the plane was in trouble before it exploded. "I heard the plane going over making more noise than it should," he explained. "I've heard planes like that when I was in the Navy—revving up the motors." According to Route, the plane was flying unusually low. From his home in Platteville, nine miles east of the Heil farm, it appeared that the aircraft was only 1,500 to 2,000 feet above the ground and "sputtering" when it exploded into a "big ball of flame like the sun coming up."

Five miles south of the Heil farm, in the small town of Rinn, twelve-year-old Charles Dalpra was unloading grain when he noticed the blinking lights of a plane moving across the sky. Pausing to watch, Dalpra was looking directly at the plane when it burst into flames. Dalpra dropped his grain shovel, ran to the nearby barn, and excitedly told his father what he had seen. At first Gilbert Dalpra thought the boy "was imagining things." But when he stepped outside, he saw the flames on the horizon and ran to his DeSoto. With Charles in the front seat, Gilbert Dalpra sped off in the direction of the fire.

Jake Heil, Harold's father, owned the 160-acre quarter section directly east of his son's parcel. "It looked like a big skyrocket," he said. "It seemed like I could hear those motors for about a minute coming closer and closer, then 'boom!' The motors were still running and there was another explosion when they hit the ground. I thought for a while it would hit our house."

On the quarter section south of Jake Heil's farm, twenty-year-old Bud Lang was in a backyard shop setting out his tools to work on an automobile when he heard an explosion that sounded "like a loud shot." He ran outdoors and saw pieces of debris showering down all around him. "Something fell straight down and when it hit the ground it really exploded," he said, "it looked like a shooting star coming down. . . . Things falling on the ground sounded like heavy hail."

Inside the adjacent two-story white farmhouse, Bud Lang's mother, Bonnie, was finishing the dishes when she heard the explosion. Her first thought was that it had come from the shed where her son was working on his car. Running outside to see if he was injured, she saw a light in the sky and "heard the motors roar and explode . . . when they hit the ground." A large metal bin for food trays fell from the sky and landed on its side at the front gate of the Lang property. A few yards away, on the other side of Weld County Road 11, a tattered plane seat landed right side up, completely intact except for one missing cushion.

Directly beneath the disintegrating plane, Harold and Dorothy Heil thought their farm was under attack. Instinctively, the young couple scooped up their six-week-old son and raced out the door. Once outside, they confronted a bewildering sight—the fields from which Harold had harvested the last sugar beets only hours before were now ablaze.

Harold told his wife to go back inside with the baby and took off running in the direction of the fires, toward the small house the Heils rented out to Jack and Daisy Brubaker. Halfway there, he met up with Jack Brubaker running in the opposite direction with equal speed.

For the Brubakers, it had been an exceedingly close call. They had been eating dinner when they heard the tremendous explosion and ran to the nearest window. Looking up at the flaming sky, they stared in disbelief at a huge object plummeting toward them. "It looked for a minute like the main part of the plane was going to hit our house," said Mrs. Brubaker. "We just stood there scared to death. It landed a few yards away."

Harold Heil and Jack Brubaker headed out to the field together to look for survivors. They soon spotted a man walking from the wreckage but recognized him as Kenneth Hopp, a twenty-two-year-old neighbor who had come to the field from the other direction. The three men strained to hear any faint cries or moans, but the only sounds were the whip of the wind and the loud crackle of the fires. They covered up a few bodies, each of which was "lying beside a hole about a foot deep made by the impact."

James F. Matlack, co-publisher of the *Longmont Times-Call,* was one of the first to arrive at the scene. "There was nothing we could do," said Matlack. "There wasn't a sign of life. I saw the body of a large man, shoeless and wearing serge trousers, white socks, and a T-shirt. He was sprawled on the ground against one of the plane's double seats."

Back near State Road 66, Dorothy Heil was on the telephone. It was a rural party line, and she could hear one of her neighbors reporting what had occurred to the Longmont Police Department. On the other end, patrolman R. W. Cosner, the officer serving as the dispatcher that evening, was struggling to answer a deluge of telephone calls from the many residents who had seen the massive explosions east of the city.

As soon as the neighbor was off the line, Dorothy Heil called her mother in Denver to tell her what had occurred and to assure her that they were uninjured. By the time Dorothy Heil hung up the phone, her yard was crowded with the haphazardly parked cars of the police officers and firemen who had rushed to the scene.

One of those cars belonged to William Trembeth, chief of the Longmont Fire Department. Soon after Trembeth arrived, he directed a Longmont pumper truck onto the field, its revolving red lights illuminating the rows of tilled soil. Two firemen, Charles Shoe and Chuck Maret, leaped from the truck and extinguished the first fire they saw. It was the burning body of a woman. They put out the small fire quickly and then drove on toward a larger fire several hundred yards farther south.

Moving across the field, Shoe and Maret came upon the nose section of the plane. Although it had landed largely intact, it was badly mangled by the force of the impact and the aluminum side panels splayed from the ground at awkward angles, inverting what remained of the crest, which was painted with the words "Mainliner Denver." The bodies of the crewmen were visible inside, and a cap belonging to one of the three men lay upside down on the ground a few feet away.

The two firemen drove several hundred feet farther to the southeast, where the largest section of the fuselage was burning. The entire midsection of the plane had hit the ground in one piece and flattened, its contents compressed within a jumbled mass of torn metal and wires. A black high-heeled shoe could be seen in the midst of the twisted pile, ensnarled along with a battered suitcase and a torn copy of *Time* magazine. Nearby, several bodies were scattered on the ground alongside purses, dinner trays, and torn curtains from the plane's windows. Amid the many recognizable objects, one item stood out due to its utter uselessness: the airplane's first-aid kit.

The firemen set to work dousing the blaze. Soon, other pumper trucks arrived and moved past them toward the two largest fires, twin blazes roaring from vast craters located approximately 150 feet apart. Each of the gaping

The crushed nose section with the crest of the *Mainliner Denver*. The inverted "D" of the word "Denver" is visible in the upper-left corner. (*The Greeley Daily Tribune*, Robert Widlund, reproduced by City of Greeley Museums)

holes was more than twenty feet long, nearly as wide, and six to eight feet deep—giant scars in the earth carved by sections of wing that had struck the ground with the engines still attached. The fires in these broad depressions were fed by the seemingly unlimited supply of fuel leaking out of the tanks housed within the shattered wings. Although the firemen poured water into the pits from all directions, the gasoline-soaked earth continued to burn.

Police officers from half a dozen different jurisdictions walked through the fields looking for bodies. Each time an officer found one of the deceased, he would stay with the body and blink his flashlight to let the others know of the discovery. Within minutes, lights were flashing from all directions.

By 8:30 P.M., all roads leading to the Heil and Lang farms were blocked—choked to a standstill by hundreds of cars carrying the curious. Many of the vehicles were filled with entire families, some of whom had even brought along their pajama-clad children. Others came with a nefarious purpose. Taking advantage of the darkness, chaos, and inadequate number of police officers, a few unseen individuals pocketed wristwatches, pieces of jewelry, and other small valuable items belonging to the dead. Although the police officers succeeded in cordoning off a few areas by running lengths of rope between their patrol cars, they could not gain control of the hundreds of acres covered with wreckage and bodies. More men were needed.

At 9:00 P.M., National Guard Battery B of the 168th Field Artillery Unit moved out from Longmont. Armed with carbines and wearing green fatigues, the guardsmen began clearing the congested roads by sternly directing the gawkers to turn their cars around and drive home. As the roads slowly became passable, the guardsmen set up checkpoints at all of the intersections surrounding the several square miles on which parts of the plane had fallen. Although the guardsmen allowed the reporters to stay, they required them to wear armbands clearly identifying themselves as members of the press.

At 10:10 P.M., a nine-vehicle convoy carrying members of a United Air Lines recovery team passed through the National Guard roadblock on State Road 66 and parked near the wreckage. United employees stepped from a bus carrying armloads of folded canvas sheets. Jack Meyer, the assistant operations manager for United, met with several of the police officers and asked that none of the bodies be moved until the airline's chief medical director arrived at the scene. The officers agreed and led Meyer and the other United employees out into the fields. Moving from one blinking flashlight to another, the members of the United Air Lines recovery team unfurled the large canvas squares and covered the bodies. To keep the brisk wind from carrying the tarps away, they weighted down the corners with suitcases and other loose items thrown from the plane.

Also moving among the dead was Reverend Francis Kappes of Saint John's Catholic Church in Loveland. Accompanied by two men with flashlights, the priest stood over each body and solemnly pronounced conditional absolution—the sacrament given when the religious affiliation of the deceased is unknown. Another priest, Father James Mahrer from Saint John's Catholic Church in Longmont, performed the same rite over those who had come to rest in another section of the field.

At about this time, R. B. Dunbar, the chief postal inspector for Denver, arrived at the scene with five assistants. Flight 629 had been carrying several hundred pounds of mail, and Dunbar and his men were determined to retrieve as much of it as they could. With sacks in hand, the postal inspectors moved through the fields gathering every item of mail they saw. One of the men picked up a singed scrap of paper containing only the words "My sincere prayer for you," and the signature "Anna." Although the postal inspectors retrieved over one hundred pounds of mail, most of the letters had fluttered away in the wind.

An envelope from one of the many pieces of recovered mail. Due to the printed explanation for delayed delivery appearing on the left side, this envelope is known as a "crash cover" by philatelists specializing in the collection of aviation-related items. (Courtesy of Phil McCarty, American Air Mail Society, Interrupted Flight Section)

Darting in between the police officers, priests, and postal inspectors, *Rocky Mountain News* photographers Bill Peery and Bob Talkin rushed to capture as many images as possible for the morning paper. Unlike their counterparts from the *Denver Post*—at that time an afternoon newspaper—Peery and Talkin were working against a tight deadline. The two photographers knew they were taking the pictures for the front page, and they stayed at the scene until the last possible minute before racing back to Denver to develop their film and deliver it to their editors.

In addition to the newspaper photographers, camera crews from Denver's new television stations were on hand filming black-and-white images. Television had arrived in Denver only three years earlier, and the downing of Flight 629 was among the first major disasters to be broadcast over the Denver airways. One of the stations filmed a group of Platteville firemen battling the tall flames that streamed from the deep pits formed by the fallen wings—an inaugural television appearance for the Platteville Fire Protective District that would later be noted with great pride on the front page of the *Platteville Herald*.

Alongside the largest section of the fuselage, Donald McPherson, the fire chief of nearby Fort Lupton, was positioning a trailer with a generator and a large lighting unit. Earlier that evening McPherson had been at his home approximately twelve miles away when his wife, Lucille, yelled for him to "get to a window." Throwing open his front door, McPherson heard

The tail section on the night of November 1, 1955. (*Longmont Times-Call,* Hildreth Studio, reproduced by Colorado Historical Society)

a distant explosion and watched "sparks falling and something that stayed in the sky burning for about three to five minutes." Although McPherson did not know exactly what had occurred, he knew his services would be needed. After calling the Colorado State Patrol dispatcher, McPherson headed to the scene in a fire engine towing the portable lighting unit he was now working to set up.

Once he had the lighting unit in place, McPherson started the generator and threw the switch. In an instant, bright light reflected off the ragged aluminum skin of the plane. The rescue workers, now able to see more of the debris, noticed a pilot's jacket lying on the ground. Because the jacket was undamaged, the men surmised that the owner had not been wearing it at the time the plane went down.

Other portions of the wreckage were illuminated by the headlights of the many cars and trucks that had been driven onto the fields. In addition, an Air Force helicopter equipped with spotlights soon arrived from Lowry Air Force Base in Denver. Captain Edward Brej landed the helicopter and approached a group of United recovery team workers. Taking off his white helmet, Brej asked Frank Crismon, United's manager of flight operations, for direction. "What do you want me to do, fly around and look for survivors with our floodlight?" Upon learning there were no survivors,

Brej took the chopper back into the sky and flew wide circles above the sugar beet fields, maneuvering the eerie beam of light on bodies that had been overlooked by the groups of men working in the fields below.

Near the river, over a mile from the nose section, the entire tail assembly had come to rest in one piece, almost as if it had glided to the ground after separating from the rest of the plane. Both of the horizontal stabilizing fins lay flat against the earth. The vertical stabilizer stood nearly twenty feet straight up in the air, its rudder only slightly askew. The red and blue striping and United logos on either side of the tail were unscratched, though a gash running through the painted script on the starboard side had partially separated the lettering of the words "DC-6B Mainliner." Bodies of the passengers who had been seated in the rear rows of the plane were scattered nearby.

Due to the large number of people who had perished, Weld County Coroner Ross Adamson set up a temporary morgue in the Greeley Armory, a large Mediterranean Revival building located on Eighth Avenue. Built in 1922 as a National Guard training center, the twin-towered brick structure had been used for a variety of other purposes over the years, functioning as a venue for traveling theater performances, Saturday-night boxing matches, and, during World War II, United Service Organization dances. Now it would serve as a repository for the dead.

Another urgent logistical problem was the need for communications. Among the first to recognize this was the manager of the Western Union office in Longmont, who drove to the office and reopened it to provide telegram service for the newsmen filing stories and the emergency workers trying to contact the families of the deceased. In addition, managers at the Mountain States Telephone & Telegraph Company dispatched forty technicians to the crash site with instructions to install whatever phone equipment was needed. Laboring in the bitter cold, the technicians climbed poles and added thirteen new phone circuits and 75,000 feet of phone lines connecting the crash site, the temporary morgue at the Greeley Armory, and the emergency response centers United Air Lines had established at the Camfield Hotel in Greeley and the Imperial Hotel in Longmont.

Working from a list of the passengers, United Air Lines employees began the difficult task of calling family members to deliver the devastating news. In Seattle, a call was received at the home of forty-year-old Elton B. Hickok, a passenger who had been returning to Seattle after attending a Denver conference of the Associated General Contractors (AGC). Similar calls were made to the relatives of three other conference attendees: Frank M. Brennan, Jr., a builder and officer with the Seattle office of the AGC; James Purvis, a Tacoma contractor and president of the organization's chapter in that city; and Clarence W. Todd, manager of the AGC's Tacoma office.

United representatives also contacted relatives of Bror and Irene Beckstrom, the owners of an electrical contracting firm who had been return-

Left: The Greeley Armory. (Courtesy of City of Greeley Museums)

Below: A body being delivered to the temporary morgue at the Greeley Armory. (*The Greeley Daily Tribune,* Robert Widlund, reproduced by City of Greeley Museums)

ing home to Seattle on Flight 629 after visiting their son Howard, a member of the Army stationed in Albuquerque. Another call went out to the family of Virgil and Goldie Herman, the owners of a used-oil reclaiming business located in Vancouver, Washington. The Hermans had just completed their first vacation in several years, a trip to Saint Louis to visit Virgil Herman's sister. For Goldie Herman, the voyage to Missouri was the first time she had ever traveled by airplane.

Several calls were made to families on the East Coast. Gurney Edwards, a prominent Rhode Island attorney and trustee of Brown University, had been on his way to Hawaii with his wife, Elizabeth, to visit a son at the Pearl Harbor Naval Base. Herbert G. Robertson, a New York marine engineer for Gibbs & Cox who had already flown more than twenty-seven thousand miles during 1955, and Marion P. Hobgood, an electrical engineer from Hatfield Pennsylvania who worked for the Philco Corporation, had both been traveling to Portland to supervise engineering projects. Similarly, a third engineer, John Jungels, had been headed to Portland to inspect a heating system that had been installed by the Illinois firm for which he worked.

The United employees made only one international call, which was to the husband of Alma Winsor, a resident of St. John's, Newfoundland, Canada. Mrs. Winsor, who operated a small restaurant with her husband, had been traveling to Tacoma to spend time helping a daughter whose husband had been stricken with polio, a disease still prevalent in 1955 despite the introduction of the Salk vaccine earlier that same year.

Back at the crash site, the temperature had fallen to eighteen degrees and the wind

Alma L. Winsor.

continued to blow. Groups of policemen and United Air Lines employees huddled around the two deep pits, warming their hands over the inextinguishable fires. Out along the road, fifteen ambulance crews sat shivering inside red-and-white station wagons while waiting for permission to transport the bodies to the morgue. Hot coffee was in great demand. The thirty gallons brought to the scene by the men of the Longmont American Legion were gone by midnight. Soon thereafter, members of the Longmont V.F.W. delivered an additional fifteen gallons along with several crates of sandwiches donated by the two local grocery stores.

At 4:00 A.M., Dr. George Kidera, the medical director for United Air Lines, arrived from Chicago and authorized Dale Medland, a senior member of the United recovery team, to begin removing bodies. Medland gathered several of his less experienced colleagues and showed them how to roll a body into a tarpaulin along with whatever personal effects were believed to belong to the deceased. "Altogether now," he exhorted. "Once, twice, three times. Now tuck in the ends. Make sure they're rolled tight." As each body was taken away in an ambulance to the Greeley Armory, the men hammered a metal stake into the frozen ground to mark the spot where the corpse had been recovered, securing a piece of red fabric to the top of each stake and marking it with an "M" or an "F" to signify the gender of the deceased. Several of the stakes were placed next to seats from which dead occupants had had to be unbelted.

At daybreak, Jack Parshall, the regional investigator for the Civil Aeronautics Board's office in Kansas City, arrived and walked the full length of the crash site. As he did so, Parshall approached several newspaper photographers and asked them not to take pictures of the bodies. The camera-wielding men all agreed to the request, though Parshall would soon learn he had not been specific enough in his plea.

That afternoon, the *Denver Post*'s "Picture Page" prominently displayed a photograph of two shoeless feet extending from underneath a plaid horse blanket and a second photograph with a superimposed large white arrow helpfully pointing to a detached hand perched atop a pile of twisted metal. Similarly, the *Longmont Times-Call* included a photograph of a man's leg protruding from the wreckage with a caption noting the attached shoe.

In addition to the grisly pictures of the dead, the newspapers used aerial photographs to help readers understand the great distance between the nose and tail sections. The *Longmont Ledger* sent photographer Neal Miller over the crash site with a private pilot from the Longmont airstrip, while the *Denver Post* used its greater resources to charter a helicopter for photographer Albert Moldvay and reporter Harmon Kallman.

From his vantage point in the helicopter, Moldvay photographed the debris, the still-smoldering fires, and the many trucks and passenger cars parked in the fields. The pilot held the helicopter in position low to the ground so that Moldvay and Kallman could watch as three United employees wrapped the body of a woman who had landed on top of a haystack. The United employees stopped for a moment and looked up, their angry expressions conveying their disdain for the low-flying newsmen.

By 7:00 A.M., the workers had located most of the bodies. A United Air Lines employee working near the fuselage emerged from behind a pile of mangled plane siding with a small object in his arms. "Is that a doll?" asked a photographer. The United employee ignored the question and carefully placed the small lifeless body on a canvas sheet. It was thirteen-month-old James Fitzpatrick II, the only child on Flight 629. Other United employees working nearby came over and helped wrap the canvas tarp around the dead child. Delicately securing the canvas with rope, they placed the small package in the back of a nearby Air Force vehicle and stood together watching as the makeshift hearse drove away. Returning to their gruesome work, the members of the United recovery team sifted through the debris near where the boy had been found. A short time later, they discovered the infant's tiny blue coat.

Two National Guardsmen inspect the tail section of the DC-6B on November 2, 1955. (*The Greeley Daily Tribune,* Jerry Kessenech, reproduced by City of Greeley Museums)

Although an airplane falling from the sky was an extraordinary event, the farmers living nearby still needed to complete their daily chores. One mile south of the wreckage, Louis Rademacher, a sugar beet grower, pulled his truck up to a National Guard checkpoint and explained that he needed to get to the other side to feed a herd of cattle. The guardsmen were unsympathetic; they had strict orders not to let any civilians through. Rademacher could not conceal his exasperation with the unnecessary display of authority. "I know you boys don't have bullets in those guns," he said, shifting the truck into gear to emphasize his firmness of purpose. The Guardsmen—realizing they were no match for such a determined farmer—stepped to the side and allowed Rademacher to proceed up the road.

## CHAPTER THREE

# *"This one has us worried."*

JACK PARSHALL HAD BEEN INVESTIGATING commercial aircraft disasters for the Civil Aeronautics Board (CAB) since the agency was created in 1940. Most of those tragedies involved airplanes that had hit the ground in one piece, though on a few occasions Parshall had examined the remnants of planes that had exploded in midair due to mechanical problems. However, in his fifteen years with the CAB, Parshall had never seen anything like this.

The main area of the crash site encompassed six square miles, and smaller parts of the plane were littered over an area nearly twice that size. It was obvious the DC-6B had been shredded by a massive blast.

There were several plausible explanations. First, it was possible that gas fumes had accumulated in a closed compartment of the plane due to a design defect like the one that had resulted in the grounding of all DC-6 aircraft in 1947. However, Parshall thought it unlikely that a sufficient quantity of fuel vapor could have accumulated during the short time the plane had been in the air. Another possibility was that one of the engines had overheated and blown loose from the plane. This hypothesis also seemed doubtful due to the brevity of the flight, but Parshall could not discount the idea until all four engines were located—work that could not begin until the flames burning in the two craters were extinguished. It was also conceivable a structural failure in the fuselage had caused the aircraft to tear apart and explode, though Parshall judged this idea improbable as well due to the enormous size of the debris field. A more likely explanation for the explosion was that it had been caused by a combustible item of cargo or luggage negligently put aboard the plane.

During the early stages of the investigation, the idea that someone might have deliberately destroyed the plane was considered far-fetched. At United Air Lines' corporate headquarters in Chicago, a spokesman went so far as to state that the possibility of sabotage was not even being considered.

There had never been a confirmed case of sabotage committed against a commercial aircraft in the United States. In 1933, foul play had been suspected when a United Air Lines plane heading for Chicago exploded over Chesterton, Indiana, killing all four passengers, the lone stewardess, and both crewmen. The Aeronautics Branch of the Department of Commerce—the agency then charged with oversight of the nascent aviation industry—had conducted an inquiry in conjunction with United Air Lines, the Army Ordnance Department, and the Department of Justice. The probe was exhaustive, but the results were inconclusive. The investigators did determine that there had been an explosion in the aft section of the plane, and they found traces of a substance resembling nitroglycerin. However, the Department of Justice never identified a person with a motive to destroy the plane.*

There had been one unsuccessful attempt to sabotage a plane in the United States. In 1950, a suitcase had burst into flames as it was being loaded onto a United Air Lines plane bound from Los Angeles to San Diego. A quick-thinking baggage handler doused the piece of luggage with a fire extinguisher and carried it back to the terminal for inspection. Moments later, thirty-one-year-old John Henry Grant rushed into the baggage storage room shouting frantically, "Don't let the plane go!" Grant grabbed the scorched bag and fled the terminal, but he was quickly apprehended and charged with the attempted murder of his wife and two young children, passengers on the plane who were covered by $25,000 worth of life insurance the debt-ridden Grant had purchased from an airport vending machine after packing his wife's suitcase with gasoline-filled inner tubes and a crude timing device attached to a book of paper matches. He was convicted at trial and sentenced to twenty years in prison.

Outside of the United States, there had been several incidents of aircraft sabotage. In 1949, thirteen people had died when a Philippine airliner traveling from Manila was blown up by a bomb intended to kill one of the passengers—a theater owner whose wife had planned the murder with the assistance of her lover.

In September of that same year, twenty-three people aboard a Canadian Pacific DC-3 had died when an explosive device detonated in the cargo hold minutes after the plane lifted off from Quebec City. The Royal Canadian Mounted Police charged three individuals with the murders: J. Albert

---

* United Air Lines concluded that the explosive material had likely been brought on board the plane by one of the passengers, a marksman traveling to a shooting competition who liked to make his own ammunition.

Guay, a jeweler involved in an extra-marital affair whose wife had been a passenger on the plane; Generaux Reust, a watchmaker who had built the bomb in exchange for a promised share of the $10,000 in life insurance proceeds Guay expected to collect upon his wife's death; and Marie Pitre, a housewife who had delivered the bomb to the airport at the request of Reust, her older brother. All three conspirators were convicted and hanged.

The following year, a powerful bomb tore a large hole in the side of a British European Airways plane traveling to Paris. Miraculously, the pilot managed to return to England and land the heavily damaged aircraft. The person responsible for that bombing was never apprehended.

In 1952, two men had planted a bomb aboard a Mexican Airways DC-3 headed from Mexico City to Oaxaca in hopes of collecting $208,000 worth of life insurance they had purchased on behalf of seven passengers. Although the bomb exploded shortly after takeoff, it caused only minimal damage and the pilot was able to bring the plane down at a nearby military base.

Most recently, in April 1955 sixteen people had been killed by a bomb hidden in the wheel well of an Air India plane chartered to transport a delegation of Chinese government officials from Hong Kong to a conference in Indonesia. However, the saboteur's intended target, Chinese Premier Zhou Enlai, had learned of the bombing plot beforehand and secretly changed his travel plans. The assassination attempt had provoked an international controversy in May 1955 when an Indonesian board of inquiry uncovered credible evidence suggesting that the bomber—a plane cleaner working at the Hong Kong airport who later fled to Taiwan and obtained asylum—had been recruited by the CIA as part of the agency's covert campaign to curb the expansion of Communism in Asia.

Jack Parshall was familiar with the details of these earlier bombings, and he knew the field of debris sprawled around him resembled the scene of the 1949 bombing in Canada. However, Parshall was a methodical investigator who did not jump to conclusions. Speaking to reporters, he explained his cautious approach: "[This is] the first . . . mid-air explosion we've encountered in some time, and we're exploring it from every angle [and examining] any possible clue."

Parshall was soon joined at the scene by James N. Peyton, the chief of the CAB's investigation division, and William Mentzer, the general manager of engineering for United Air Lines. Walking through the wreckage together, the three men devised an ambitious plan to learn the origin of the

A crane removes parts of the wreckage. (*The Greeley Daily Tribune,* Jerry Kessenich, reproduced by City of Greeley Museums)

explosion—they would collect the parts of the plane and rebuild it inside a warehouse at Stapleton Airfield. It would be a mammoth undertaking. The DC-6B weighed more than fifty-eight thousand pounds, and the body of the plane was more than one hundred feet long.

Parshall, Peyton, and Mentzer agreed that, before a single piece of debris could be removed from the scene, they needed a system for recording the location where each part of the plane had fallen. Looking around, they realized there were virtually no landmarks in the sugar beet fields other than a few trees and an irrigation ditch. To overcome this problem, they hired a surveying firm to plat the entire area and create reference points.

Led by William A. Parker, the three-man team of surveyors from nearby Arvada first established a two-mile baseline through the debris field running from the southeast to the northwest—the approximate direction the plane had been traveling when it exploded. Along this line, at one-thousand-foot intervals, the men next laid out perpendicular lines extending one thousand feet. The surveyors then connected these lines with additional lines running parallel to the baseline. Repeating this process as they moved outward from the center, Parker and his colleagues divided the sugar beet fields into a grid of large numbered squares.

While the surveyors worked on the outskirts of the crash site, a crane equipped with a block and tackle moved to the center of the field. United Air

Lines workers and CAB investigators threaded the crane's cable between two bent cross members attached to a section of the fuselage. Once the cable was secure, the crane operator hoisted the crumpled side panel into the air, slowly untangling it from the rest of the pile. As the powerful winch groaned under the stress of the great weight, the hunk of torn metal was loaded onto one of the many flatbed trucks hired to haul debris to Denver.

Several miles to the north, two members of the National Guard stood at the front door of the Greeley Armory sternly rebuffing the morbidly curious individuals who wanted to peek inside. Within the armory, Dr. George Kidera of United Air Lines and Coroner Ross Adamson directed the efforts of a dozen United employees who were attempting to match bodies with names from the lists of passengers and crew. They were not having much success. By midmorning, they had only identified nine of the bodies.

Assistance arrived that afternoon when Quinn Tamm, the head of the FBI's fingerprint identification division in Washington, D.C., walked into the armory accompanied by three other fingerprint experts and Webb W. Burke, the FBI special agent-in-charge of the Denver field office. The FBI agents unpacked their ink pads and quickly fingerprinted the thirty-five bodies that had not yet been identified. The agents then sat down with magnifying glasses and began the tedious work of comparing the gathered fingerprints with those in the personnel records United Air Lines had delivered from its Chicago headquarters, and with other prints contained in FBI files the agents had brought with them from Washington.

For various reasons, the fingerprints of almost half the passengers were on file with the FBI. Several passengers had been fingerprinted upon enlisting in the military during World War II, including Brad Bynum, who had been decorated with the Flying Cross after surviving seventy-four combat missions as a combat pilot in the European theater. Other passengers had been fingerprinted as a condition of their employment in defense plants during the war, and one couple had been fingerprinted when they applied to become United States citizens. Curiously, one passenger had submitted his fingerprints to the FBI in 1941 and asked that they be kept on file for purposes of personal identification.

As the FBI agents continued their painstaking task, Adamson fielded several calls from reporters inquiring about rumors that some of the passengers—particularly the woman who had landed on top of the haystack— might have survived the crash and died some time afterward. Seeking to provide some measure of comfort to the relatives of the deceased, Adamson told the reporters that the bodies were so "badly battered" as to "preclude any thoughts that some of the victims might have lived any length of time." When asked about the progress in the temporary morgue, Adamson said that the bodies that had been identified were being transported to one of three local mortuaries: the Secord Funeral Home, the Macy Undertaking Company, or Adamson's Mortuary (operated by the coroner and his brother). Adamson explained that he would begin shipping bodies home to the grieving families as soon as United Air Lines delivered the forty-four metal sealer caskets the company had ordered from the Batesville Casket Company in Indiana.

Although the CAB was the agency in charge of investigating aircraft accidents in the mid-1950s, a second federal agency, the Civil Aeronautics Administration (CAA), had authority over many other aspects of commercial aviation, including air traffic control operations, safety enforcement, development of airports, approval of routes, and the certification of pilots, flight engineers, and aircraft. The CAA rarely participated in accident investigations. Nevertheless, on November 2, a CAA spokesman in Washington, D.C., made a highly unusual announcement: Fred. B. Lee, the agency's chief administrator, was traveling to Colorado "to find out if any type of immediate remedial action is necessary." "This one has us worried," the spokesman added.

Lee arrived at Stapleton Airfield accompanied by Ward Madsen, the agency's deputy director; W. H. Weeks, the chief of the agency's aircraft engineering division; and G. C. Waysbeer, the chief crash investigator for the Netherlands, who happened to be in Washington, D.C., at the time. The CAA officials set to work immediately, meeting with their counterparts from the CAB for a briefing concerning the progress of the investigation.

The first topic for discussion was whether the pilot or copilot had deployed emergency flares before the plane disintegrated. A few of the CAB investigators were convinced the bright lights the eyewitnesses had seen lingering in the sky were burning pieces of lightweight debris drifting to the ground. However, most of the investigators discounted this theory, believing instead that the lights had emanated from two long-duration parachute flares located in compartments tucked behind the DC-6B's wings—emergency equipment provided to illuminate the ground in the event of an unplanned landing. All the investigators agreed on one thing: even if the remnants of burned flares were eventually discovered, it would likely be impossible to determine whether the flares had been activated by the force of the explosion or remotely deployed from the cockpit by a member of the crew.

As the CAA and CAB officials discussed the many mysteries surrounding the crash, United Air Lines issued a statement from its headquarters in Chicago:

> All evidence now strongly indicates this accident resulted from an explosion in the air. Determination of responsibility for the accident is beyond the authority of United Air Lines alone. Federal and local officials are now working at the scene. United has retained the services of Charles Wilson, an outstanding authority in the field of explosives, who is affiliated with the crime laboratory of the State of Wisconsin. Experts from our own organization and the Douglas Company are cooperating with all Federal agencies in the most vigorous investigation. We will search out every possibility, however remote.

The decision to bring in Charles Wilson was a clear indication that the airline no longer was ruling out the possibility of sabotage. Wilson was one of the most respected forensic investigators in the country. Before being appointed to run the Wisconsin crime laboratory in 1947, he had been the chief of the Chicago Police Department's crime detection laboratory at Northwestern University. During World War II, he had investigated plane crashes for the Air Force and served as an explosives advisor to the Army.

On the evening of November 2, Wilson met with reporters at the Madison Airport while waiting to board a flight to Denver. "All I know about the crash is what I've been told and what I've read," he said. "What I've heard indicates there was an explosion, so I naturally will attempt to determine if there was an explosion and, if so, what caused it." Wilson explained that when investigating an airplane bombing, "you look for the same things you do in the bombing of a car." However, he cautioned he would not "anticipate a thing in this case until we've made a complete examination."

One person who was anticipating things was William "Pat" Patterson, the president of United Air Lines. Speaking to reporters in Los Angeles—where he was finalizing United's order for twenty-eight Douglas jet airliners—Patterson predicted that "certain sources will make claims casting reflections on the qualifications of our flight engineer, Samuel F. Arthur. The facts are, he was only recently promoted to flight officer status after a highly satisfactory record of seven years of flight engineer duty between

William A. "Pat" Patterson, 1955. (Courtesy of United Airlines)

1948 and 1955, and he had considerably more experience as a flight engineer than the average."

William Kent, the president of the Flight Engineers Union, quickly issued a statement in response:

> We cast no reflections on Mr. Sam Arthur or his ability, but we do think that this incident does bring into focus the terrific tension under which these strike-breaking pilots do their jobs. All flight engineers are seriously concerned about the strike-breaking activity of the United pilots during the flight engineer strike. We know the stresses, both physical and mental, which are required of flight crews during normal operations and it seems to us to impose an impossible burden on these pilots who are ask[ed] to sit in as scab flight engineers during our strike.

Kent also announced that the union had provided CAB investigators with several unspecified "leads" concerning the cause of the crash.

In telegrams sent to the CAB and the CAA, the leaders of the Air Transport Division of the Transport Workers Union—one of the unions supporting the striking flight engineers—demanded that all United Air Lines DC-6 and DC-6B aircraft be grounded until the strike was settled and "qualified personnel" were again available. The union even went so far as to suggest that United might be criminally liable for the forty-four deaths and asked that "all information developed by the investigation be referred to the grand jury for possible manslaughter charges."

Despite the heated rhetoric, on November 3 the leaders of the Flight Engineers Union sent representatives to a meeting at Stapleton Airfield with United Air Lines managers, CAB investigators, and CAA officials. The meeting was also attended by members of the Air Line Pilots Association and managers from the other four airlines then providing service to Denver: Braniff, Continental, Western, and Frontier. All of the participants recognized how much was riding on the CAB's investigation. In a single month, one hundred and ten people had died on two separate flights from Stapleton Airfield, and the CAB had not made any progress in determining the cause of the Medicine Bow crash. United Air Lines had already experienced a measurable decrease in reservations, and there was good reason to wonder whether a second unexplained disaster would permanently destroy the public's newly developed confidence in the safety of air travel. With so much at stake, the airline managers and union representatives promised to put aside their differences and help the investigators in any way possible.

The leaders of the Flight Engineers Union followed through on their pledge, assigning two senior flight engineers with experience in crash investigations to assist the CAB investigators. The union leaders also stopped issuing inflammatory press releases and instructed the picketers at Stapleton Airfield not to obstruct the United Air Lines vehicles hauling debris from the crash site for the CAB.

By Thursday night, only forty-eight hours after the plane went down, a steady procession of trucks began delivering plane fragments to the warehouse where the rebuilding was to take place. Each piece came with a paper tag detailing where it had been found, as well as the exact distances to other parts found within the same square of the survey grid. Using this information, the CAB investigators and United Air Lines engineers positioned the pieces of wreckage on the floor of the warehouse inside a scaled-down grid of painted squares replicating the much larger grid at the crash site. The investigators carefully studied the relative positions of the parts, looking for clues that would help them understand the source and force of the blast.

On the far side of the warehouse, other investigators and engineers were constructing sturdy frames that could bear the weight of the exterior parts of the plane. Built of wood and sheathed with wire fencing material, the structures looked like enormous chicken coops.

Nearby, in a United Air Lines cargo hangar, hearses from the three Greeley mortuaries began delivering caskets to be flown home to waiting relatives. Several of the coffins had already been shipped home by train, a method of conveyance apparently selected by relatives who, for understandable reasons, were unwilling to have the remains of their loved ones put aboard another plane.

On the morning of Friday, November 5, Ross Adamson closed the temporary morgue at the Greeley Armory. It had taken three exhausting days and nights, but his work was finally at an end. There would be no coroner's inquest. Adamson had decided that a local inquiry would merely interfere with the federal investigation.

As life began to return to normal in Greeley, the level of activity at the Heil farm increased. The fires in the craters had burned out the night before, and dozens of men with shovels were now digging through the many feet of charred earth covering the motors. One by one, the four motors and propellers were excavated, attached to a special crane brought in from the Warren Air Force Base in Wyoming, and hoisted from the deep holes. The discovery of all four mangled assemblies allowed Jack Parshall and the other CAB investigators to eliminate one possible cause of the explosion: it was clear that the motors had not detached from the wings before plunging into the ground.

Later that day, the CAB investigators found fragments from the two burned-out parachute flares. News of the discovery distorted as it spread, and reporters soon began inquiring about the nitroglycerin residue that had been located in the debris. Jack Parshall adamantly denied the reports, saying, "That's a ridiculous rumor. We have found absolutely no evidence of nitroglycerin. In fact, no particular explosive is under special suspicion." Although Parshall admitted that the CAB was now receiving assistance from the FBI's criminalistics laboratory, he emphasized that the FBI was not yet involved in the field investigation: "Frankly, we're going to have to await the results of the laboratory examination." Webb Burke of the FBI supported Parshall's remarks, explaining that his agency was not "conducting an active investigation" and was without "jurisdiction unless there is an indication of sabotage."

On Saturday, D. R. Petty, United's vice president in charge of flight operations, stated that the company's investigation had confirmed that "there was no malfunctioning of the aircraft prior to the accident." Charles Wilson went even further, telling reporters that he had reached an "inferential conclusion" of sabotage.

The next day, United Air Lines president Pat Patterson arrived at Stapleton Airfield and met with Wilson to view the partially reconstructed DC-6B. Patterson was heartsick. He could not fathom how someone could deliberately destroy an airplane.

Pat Patterson was not just an airline executive; he was a pioneer in the field of commercial aviation. In 1919, while a young clerical worker at the Wells Fargo bank, Patterson had spent two weeks' worth of his meager salary to become one of the first passengers to fly in an airplane. The sightseeing flight over the San Francisco Bay lasted only twenty minutes, but it left Patterson with a passionate belief in the revolutionary potential of air travel.

Ten years later, having worked his way up to the level of bank vice president, Patterson averted bankruptcy for a Wells Fargo client—a fledgling airline known as Pacific Air Transport—by negotiating its merger with a much larger entity, the Boeing Air Transport Corporation. The new company was named United Aircraft and Transport Corporation. Not long afterward, Patterson shocked his colleagues by walking away from his secure position at the bank to join the upstart airline.

In 1934, the company was reincorporated as United Air Lines and spun off from Boeing with Pat Patterson as its new president. Under Patterson's leadership, United expanded its routes across the country, constantly replacing its fleet with the newest aircraft produced by the Boeing and Douglas corporations. Throughout this period of rapid growth, Patterson used his legendary capacity for remembering names to maintain a personal connection with the increasing number of United employees, all of whom he encouraged to address him simply as "Pat." A short avuncular figure known for his small acts of kindness, Patterson always made sure that a blue or pink baby blanket was delivered whenever a United employee had a child.

Over the years, Patterson had mourned for many dedicated employees killed in plane crashes. Each loss was a wrenching experience, but the

Flight 629 disaster was especially hard. In addition to the three crewmen and two stewardesses, three other United employees had been traveling on the plane as passengers.

Thirty-eight-year-old Fay E. "Jack" Ambrose, the company's senior reservations clerk in Seattle, had been with the company since 1946. A former semiprofessional baseball player, Ambrose had been returning home to his wife and fourteen-year-old daughter after making an exploratory trip to Colorado to learn more about a position he had been offered in United's Denver office.

Sally Ann Scofield and Barbara Cruse, two United Air Lines stewardesses stationed in Denver, were traveling to the West Coast together to share a few days of vacation in advance of Scofield's upcoming December wedding to a United Air Lines pilot. As part of the trip, Scofield intended to visit her future in-laws, select a wedding dress, and sit for a photograph to be used for the newspaper announcement of her marriage. Although the two young women originally planned to depart on November 2, they changed their plans

Sally Ann Scofield.

at the last minute when they learned seats were available on Flight 629. Marjorie Scofield, Sally Ann's mother, would later recall that her twenty-three-year-old daughter had kissed her on the cheek and "walked out of the house as excited, thrilled, and pretty as any expectant bride."

On Monday, November 7, *American Aviation Daily,* an industry newsletter published in Washington, D.C., reported that the CAB investigators had found evidence conclusively establishing that "a bomb-type explosion" had occurred in the DC-6B's number four cargo compartment. According to the article, the side walls of the compartment were pushed out and pulverized, and "gunpowder-type odors" had been detected "on sections of the compartment." However, the accuracy of the article was called into question when Webb Burke issued another statement indicating that the FBI had not yet launched a criminal investigation.

Things changed the next day. James Peyton of the CAB admitted that the *American Aviation Daily* article was accurate and that a smell "like gunpowder or an exploding firecracker" had been detected in the number four cargo hold. Although Peyton would not definitively state that the plane had been brought down by a bomb, he told reporters that the explosion had clearly been caused by something other than "a part of the plane." And, for the first time, Webb Burke verified that FBI agents were actively investigating.

On Wednesday, November 9, Pat Patterson issued a statement explaining that the airline would no longer respond to inquiries from reporters:

> As indicated by officials of the Civil Aeronautics Board, the Longmont accident was caused by an explosion while the aircraft was at normal altitude on its assigned course of flight. The investigation to fix responsibility for this act is being directed by the Federal Bureau of Investigation. To avoid hampering the work of these agents, no further details can now be provided.

The revelation that Flight 629 might have been bombed led to speculation that the culprit was a disgruntled flight engineer.*

William Kent, the president of the Flight Engineers Union, sought to quell suspicions of union involvement by announcing a $1,000 reward for the arrest and conviction of the person or persons responsible for the "alleged explosion." The reward offer produced immediate results, though not the kind Kent had hoped for. Within hours, United Air Lines responded by posting its own reward of $25,000 for aid in producing "information which will lead to an early solution of this air industry tragedy and lead to the arrest and conviction of the person or persons responsible for the explosion."

As the public relations battle between the union and the airline continued, CAB investigators stopped speaking with the press, explaining that FBI agents had directed them not to discuss the inquiry. The FBI agents were equally reticent. Webb Burke began referring reporters' questions to the FBI's headquarters in Washington, D.C., where J. Edgar Hoover's personal assistant made it clear that no further information would be forthcoming until the case was solved.

A veil of secrecy had descended over the investigation.

---

* It would not have been the first time a striking union had bombed a Colorado transportation system in order to kill "scab" replacement workers. In 1904, gold miners in the small town of Cripple Creek had gone on strike in support of their fellow workers at a nearby smeltering company whose managers had been aggressively interfering with attempts to unionize the plant's workforce. When the mining company responded by bringing in nonunion workers, a union activist using the assumed name "Harry Orchard" decided to take matters into his own hands. Early one morning, as a group of the replacement workers waited for a train in the town of Independence, Orchard detonated more than one hundred pounds of dynamite hidden beneath the platform. The massive explosion leveled the station, killing thirteen men and injuring several others.

Friday was Veterans Day, and the most famous veteran in the United States was finally well enough to return to the White House. During his lengthy recuperation, President Eisenhower had taken a keen interest in the Flight 629 tragedy and, according to an aide, "followed the story very carefully."

As the motorcade drove the short distance from the Fitzsimmons Army Hospital to Lowry Air Force Base, the President and First Lady waved to the thousands of people lining the streets. Arriving at Lowry, the black limousine parked in front of the presidential plane, *Columbine III,* a Lockheed Constellation named after Colorado's state flower in recognition of Mrs. Eisenhower's close ties to the state.

The President bounded up the stairs with unexpected energy and shook hands with the many dignitaries gathered on the platform. More than three hundred members of the public stood behind a rope barrier listening as Eisenhower delivered a radio-broadcast speech, his first since the heart attack:

> My friends, it is again time for me to say goodbye to Denver after a summer stay. This time we leave under somewhat unusual circumstances. As you know, I have spent time in the hospital. Such a time is not fully a loss. Misfortune, and particularly the misfortune of illness, brings to all of us an understanding of how good people are. . . . So, I leave with my heart unusually filled with gratefulness to Denver, to the people here, to the locality. . . . Goodbye, and good luck.

After thanking the medical staff at the hospital and the thousands of well-wishers who had sent cards and gifts, the President walked to the top of the boarding stairs, waved farewell, and ducked inside the cabin.

Thirty-two miles to the north, a more somber Veterans Day observance was being held on the Heil farm. The Longmont chapter of the Jaycees (the Junior Chamber of Commerce) erected a flagpole at the crash site and raised one of the American flags the group had been selling as part of its annual "Americanism" fundraiser. This particular flag had been purchased from the Jaycees by United Air Lines as an expression of gratitude to the Longmont community for the service of its many police officers, firemen, and volunteers. The airline had donated the flag back to the organization for use in a raffle, but the Jaycees had decided it would be more appropriate to fly the flag at the crash site on Veterans Day in honor of twenty-four-year-old Jesse Sizemore, the only active-duty serviceman killed on Flight 629.

An Airman Second Class, Sizemore had been traveling to Seattle on his way to an overseas assignment after spending a period of leave with his fiancée in his hometown of Munford, Alabama. He had previously been attached to the Student Squadron at the Francis E. Warren Air Force Base in Cheyenne, Wyoming—only sixty miles north of the flag that now rippled in the wind as a tribute to his service.

Jesse T. Sizemore.

Throughout the rest of the holiday weekend, FBI agents and CAB investigators continued to maintain their silence. Despite the official news blackout, reports began to surface indicating that FBI agents around the country were conducting detailed background investigations on all of the passengers, especially those who had purchased flight insurance policies.

On Monday morning, the CAB convened a public hearing in Denver's Cosmopolitan Hotel to hear testimony about the October 6 crash of United Air Lines Flight 409, the Douglas C-54B that had veered off course and taken sixty-six people to their deaths on top of Medicine Bow Peak. The cause of the disaster was still undetermined, and there was little reason to hope anything new would be learned from the two dozen witnesses scheduled to testify before the investigative panel. Nevertheless, CAB investigator James Peyton and his colleagues were visibly exuberant as they took their seats behind the table at the front of the Century Ballroom. They had good reason to be cheerful. Earlier that morning, they had received word that the FBI had arrested a suspect in the bombing of Flight 629.

CHAPTER FOUR

# *"It all started about six months ago."*

HISTORY HAS NOT BEEN KIND to the reputation of J. Edgar Hoover. But in the 1950s, Hoover was a national celebrity, a public figure widely admired for his considerable accomplishments. In 1924, he had been appointed as the director of a moribund agency with an ill-defined mission and a payroll larded with inept bureaucrats. By 1955, he had thoroughly transformed the FBI by clearing out the deadwood, establishing field offices in every major city, opening a criminalistics laboratory in Washington, and starting a training academy for the hundreds of new agents he recruited, all of whom were required to have college degrees.

Roy K. Moore was the quintessential example of Hoover's new "G-man." A former Marine who was one of few men to achieve a perfect score at the agency's firing range, Moore also had an accounting degree from the University of Miami. Since joining the FBI in 1940, Moore had worked on a variety of criminal investigations in field offices throughout the country, including a stint in Chicago, at that time one of the frontlines in the FBI's fight against organized crime.

In January 1955, Hoover sent Moore to Denver and made him the assistant special agent-in-charge, the second in command under Webb Burke. Although Moore had no way of knowing it at the time, the move to Colorado had put him in position for the most important assignment of his career.

On November 7, James Peyton of the CAB called Webb Burke and told him that he and Jack Parshall were convinced Flight 629 had been sabotaged. The reconstruction of the fuselage had revealed the source of the explosion:

The mockup showed that the pieces were progressively smaller from all directions to a point in the number four baggage compartment. Many pieces were mere fragments or were entirely missing in that area. This reconstruction and examination showed very conclusively that the aft fuselage disintegrated from extremely violent forces which originated in a very concentrated area within the baggage compartment below the aft buffet and just slightly left of the centerline of the aircraft. The forces were shown to have acted out in all directions from this point. These blew the cabin floor upward, the fuselage bottom shell outward, the aft bulkhead of the baggage compartment rearward, and its forward bulkhead forward.

There were no fuel lines located near the origin of the blast, and there was no innocuous explanation for the odor of explosives lingering on the luggage and mail sacks that had been stored in the number four baggage compartment.

Nevertheless, Peyton qualified his opinion slightly, telling Burke that the CAB would not make its official determination until the FBI's forensic experts in Washington finished analyzing the black sooty substance covering the eleven small fragments of red and blue sheet metal that had been shipped to the FBI laboratory on November 5. Peyton suspected that those bits of badly burned metal—one of which was embossed with the letters "OT"—were remnants of a bomb, but he could not prove it without the results of the chemical tests.

By nightfall, the FBI had launched one of the largest investigations in its history. From Alaska to Alabama, hundreds of agents working in more than twenty field offices fanned out to interview friends and relatives of the deceased. In the search for a motive, no possibility was considered too remote. Among other things, the agents probed for hints of financial difficulties, marital troubles, mental illness, enemies, suicide attempts, or recent unusual behavior.

In Los Angeles, two FBI agents interviewed John Henry Grant—the man who had attempted to blow up an airplane in 1950 by placing a bomb in his wife's suitcase. Grant, who had been living with his parents since his release from prison in January 1955, told the agents that he had assumed he would be contacted as a suspect after reading a newspaper article which stated that the Flight 629 disaster might have been caused by a bomb. Grant insisted he had not left California during his parole—a claim the agents quickly verified by speaking with his parents. The agents then quizzed Grant to find out whether any of the inmates he had served time with had shown an unusual interest in learning the details of his insurance-related crime. Grant was eager to help, but he was unable to provide the agents with any leads, explaining that he was so ashamed of his offense that he had not discussed it with anyone while serving his sentence.

In Colorado, Webb Burke charged Roy Moore with heading up the local aspects of the investigation. Moore quickly as-

Special Assistant Agent-in-Charge Roy K. Moore. (Courtesy of Federal Bureau of Investigation)

sembled a team of thirty agents, most of whom had aviation experience from their service during World War II. He dispatched several of these men to the airport with instructions to examine the shipping documents for the cargo that had been loaded in Denver. He sent other agents to interview the passengers and crew who had disembarked in Denver, as well as the handful of ticketed passengers who had not followed through with their plans to travel on Flight 629.

One such passenger, Russ Cowger of Ketchikan, Alaska, had a good explanation for why he had missed Flight 629. Cowger, who had been in Colorado for a hunting trip, was scheduled to take a November 1 Frontier Airlines flight from Montrose to Denver, where he was to connect with United Air Lines Flight 629 for Seattle. However, due to bad weather, the Frontier plane had been unable to land in Montrose. As a result, Cowger was forced to spend an extra night on Colorado's Western Slope—a most fortunate inconvenience.

The FBI agents continued interviewing other ticketed passengers who had missed Flight 629. It was a series of dead ends. Like Cowger, all of the absent passengers had credible reasons for changing their plans.

The interviews of the passengers who had deplaned in Denver were not fruitful either. Dr. and Mrs. Frank Gassner described an uneventful trip from New York, recalling nothing more significant than some light turbulence over Omaha, Nebraska. Though, while driving from Stapleton Air-

field toward their home in Fort Collins, the couple had seen a strange "or-
ange-red cone of light" off to the east. At the time, they had no idea they
were seeing the burning wreckage of the plane in which they had just
flown. It was not until the next morning that the Gassners learned "that
those very nice . . . passengers with whom we had become acquainted on
our flight had died."

Other FBI agents interviewed the workers at Stapleton Airfield who
had had access to the DC-6B during its brief time in Denver. The mechanics
and fuel men who had serviced the plane told the agents they had not seen
anything out of the ordinary, and they were certain that none of the picket-
ing flight engineers had been near the plane during its brief time in Denver.
The ramp men had not noticed anything unusual either, though they did
provide the agents with one useful piece of information: after Flight 629
had landed in Denver, they had unloaded everything from the number four
baggage compartment and moved the contents to the forward baggage
compartment. The move had had nothing to do with redistributing the
load—they had been searching the hold at the request of a ramp man in
Chicago who had called ahead to Denver to report that he had lost his keys
while loading the number four cargo compartment. After emptying the
compartment and failing to find the man's keys, the ramp men had refilled
the hold with the luggage, cargo, and mail originating in Denver.

Armed with this knowledge, the FBI agents narrowed the scope of their
investigation to the passengers who had boarded in Denver.

The only Colorado resident who had boarded the flight as a paying passenger was Daisie E. King. The widowed restaurateur seemed like an unlikely target, especially since her name was not on the two lists of insured
passengers provided to the FBI by the companies that sold flight insurance
policies from vending machines located in the Stapleton terminal. However,
as the FBI agents would later learn, Mrs. King had purchased flight insurance, but, due to misplaced paperwork, her name had been inadvertently
omitted from the lists of insured passengers.

Daisie Eldora King was born in Buena Vista, Colorado, on March 9, 1902,
the youngest child of Gilbert A. Walker and Debbie Mosher Walker, two
teachers who had come to Buena Vista from Kansas in 1892. By the time she
was born, Daisie's father had left teaching and become an attorney. In addi-

tion to his legal practice, Gilbert Walker was an active participant in Republican party politics, serving as editor of the *Colorado Republican* before being
elected as county superintendent of schools. In 1910, he was elected to the
Colorado House of Representatives.

Two years later, Gilbert Walker was elected as the district attorney for
the judicial district encompassing Chaffee and Fremont counties. In his single term as district attorney, Walker achieved statewide prominence for
prosecuting a group of miners charged with a fatal shooting that had occurred during a mining strike in the small town of Chandler.

Daisie enjoyed her early years of rural living, later describing herself as a
"tomboy" who spent most of her childhood engaging in outdoor pursuits such
as fishing and riding. However, in 1916 her surroundings changed when the
Walkers left Buena Vista and moved to Denver's Capitol Hill neighborhood.

Daisie graduated from high school in Denver and continued living with
her parents when they moved from Denver and bought a ranch in Yampa,
near Steamboat Springs. In 1921, Gilbert Walker was elected as a district
court judge—thus making him one of the first Coloradoans to hold elected
office in all three branches of state government.

At about this same time, Daisie married a man named Tom Gallagher. In
1923, the couple had a daughter, Helen Ruth. Soon thereafter, the marriage
ended in divorce.

Daisie next married William Henry Graham, a mining engineer. Over
the next few years, the couple lived in several small Colorado mountain
towns, their frequent moves dictated by the location of William Graham's
various mining projects. On January 23, 1932, Daisie gave birth to her second child. She and her husband named the boy John Gilbert, his middle
name taken from that of his illustrious grandfather.

William Graham's mining ventures never panned out. In the depths of
the Great Depression, he died of pneumonia. Daisie was destitute.

To make ends meet, Daisie took a job at the phone company; her divorced
mother took care of John and Helen. When her mother died in 1938, Daisie
enrolled Helen at Saint Scholastica's, a Benedictine college-preparatory
boarding school in Cañon City. She placed six-year-old John in the Clayton
College of Denver.

Located at the intersection of Thirty-Second Avenue and Colorado
Boulevard, Clayton College was an orphanage established by a 1911 be-
quest from George W. Clayton—one of the city's leaders—for the benefit of "poor white male orphans . . . born of reputable parents." Offering

instruction in the "building trades, farming and other manual occupations," the school required that half of each day "be devoted to the industrial pursuit which the child may choose, and half to acquiring the elements of an English education." Although John Gilbert Graham's mother was alive, he was eligible for admission because the school defined an "orphan" as "one who has lost both parents or the father."

In 1941, Daisie married for the third time, to Earl King, a wealthy rancher living in the town of Toponas, approximately ten miles from Yampa. Despite the improvement in her economic circumstances, she did not retrieve her son from the orphanage.

On October 16, 1954, Daisie King became a widow again. However, this time her financial situation was considerably better. Under the terms of Earl King's will, his entire estate went to Daisie as a "life estate."* Combined with the money she had inherited when her father died two years before, Daisie King had a net worth of approximately $150,000.

By this point in time, John Gilbert Graham—known by his nickname, "Jack"—was twenty-two years old, married, and living in Grand Junction, on Colorado's Western Slope. He and his wife, Gloria, had an eleven-month-old boy named Allen, and they were expecting a second child in less than two months.

Using an offer to purchase a house as leverage, Daisie King persuaded her son to move back to Denver and reenroll in the evening program at the University of Denver's downtown campus (where he had previously completed two quarters of classes). Although the timing of Daisie's offer was opportune, it came with a significant condition—the house had to have separate quarters where she could live whenever she was in Denver.

The young couple found a newly built home located in southwest Denver. It was a single-floor ranch, with ornamental shutters mounted on painted siding above a skirt of brick veneer. Although the main floor was only 875 square feet, it had an efficient floor plan that squeezed in two bedrooms, a living room, a kitchen with dinette, and a bathroom. There was a second bathroom in the basement, as well as an extra bedroom, a den, and a laundry area. In a testament to the quality of the construction, the builder, G. C. McClendon, lived in the house next door.

---

* A life estate is an interest in property with a duration limited to the natural life of the party holding it.

The former home of John and Gloria Graham.

Daisie met with McClendon and offered to buy the house for $14,500, telling him of her plan to give the house to her son as a gift. McClendon agreed to the selling price, but he suggested that Jack would not fully appreciate the magnitude of her generosity if she paid for all of it. Persuaded by McClendon's reasoning, Daisie made a $5,500 down payment and helped her son and daughter-in-law obtain a mortgage for the balance.

In mid-December, the Grahams moved into their new home and Daisie set up her living quarters in the basement. After Christmas, she flew to Marco Island, Florida.

On February 10, 1955, Suzanne Graham was born by cesarean section. Gloria experienced serious complications. Upon hearing the news, Daisie immediately flew back to Colorado to help care for her grandchildren.

During Gloria's recuperation, Daisie approached her son with a second offer to assist him financially. Explaining that she wanted to invest some of her money, Daisie offered to provide the capital for a drive-in restaurant if Jack would agree to work as the manager. Although neither of them had any experience in the restaurant business, Jack agreed to go to work for his mother.

The Crown-A drive-in. (*Denver Post*, Reproduced by Colorado Historical Society)

In Colorado—unlike in California, the birthplace of the drive-in restaurant craze—most drive-ins closed for the winter due to the weather. In spite of this seasonal limitation, by 1955 there were more than sixty-five drive-in restaurants operating in Denver. For the many teenage cruisers who frequented these establishments, one of the most popular strips was Federal Boulevard, located only five blocks west of the Grahams' new home.

In March, Daisie bought a vacant parcel of land at 581 South Federal Boulevard for $12,000. She spent another $30,000 to construct a building, erect signage, and pave the lot. In late May, she and her son opened the Crown-A drive-in, offering foot-long hotdogs, hamburgers, ice cream, malts, shakes, and "broasted" chicken.*

As FBI agents were preparing to contact Jack Graham to learn more about his deceased mother, they received a telephone call from Bishop Richard Hanson of the Church of Jesus Christ of Latter-Day Saints. Bishop Hanson in-

---

* Broasting, a cooking process trademarked by the Broaster Company in 1954, requires a Broaster, a large stainless-steel pressure fryer made for the restaurant industry and not available for home use.

formed the agents that one of his parishioners, Lou Messervy of Edgewater, wanted to meet with them to provide information relevant to the bombing investigation.

On Tuesday, November 8, two FBI agents met with Messervy, a former potato-chip salesman whose accounts had included the Crown-A drive-in restaurant. In addition to his work in the snack-food business, Messervy had a proven track record as a police informant. In December 1953, he had helped solve a sensational Denver murder case—the strangling death of twenty-six-year-old Evelyn Leick. The day after the murder occurred, Messervy had called the Denver police and informed them that the victim's husband, LeRoy Leick, had previously asked him to kill his wife in exchange for a portion of the life insurance proceeds. Based on Messervy's testimony, Leick had been convicted of murdering his wife during a staged robbery. Although Leick had been sentenced to death, in early 1955 the Colorado Supreme Court had reversed his conviction due to an error in the jury instructions relating to insanity. Messervy was scheduled to testify a second time at the retrial set for later in November.

Messervy began by telling the agents that Daisie King was a "fine person," but that her son was "a little odd." Messervy then revealed his suspicion that Graham was responsible for a gas explosion in September that had damaged the Crown-A drive-in. Although Messervy admitted that he had no proof to support his hunch, he told the FBI agents that Graham might have caused the explosion as part of an insurance scheme.

Unbeknownst to Messervy, the agents had already heard a secondhand report about the explosion at the Crown-A drive-in. Richard Conley, an insurance adjuster for the General Adjustment Bureau—an agency where Jack Graham had worked as an office assistant the year before—had been assigned to investigate the drive-in explosion. Conley suspected Graham had caused the explosion, but he had not been able to prove it, and he had reluctantly recommended the insurance company pay the $1,200 claim. Word of Conley's misgivings had reached the FBI through John C. Morgan, a fellow insurance adjuster who was following the Flight 629 investigation on behalf of the company that had supplied the fuel for the plane.

On November 9, the FBI agents learned of yet another person with suspicions about the cause of the blast at the Crown-A. Charles McErlean, the director of United Air Lines' legal department, contacted the agents and told them he had received information from Samuel M. Morris, a United Air Lines flight kitchen employee who owned a Denver drive-in. Morris, who had sold Jack Graham several pieces of restaurant equipment, was convinced that Graham was responsible for the gas leak that damaged the Crown-A. However, Morris was unwilling to speak with the FBI directly because he was afraid Graham might sue him for slander.

Several agents drove to the Denver Police Department headquarters to look at the file. According to the incident reports, at 1:36 A.M. on Monday, September 5, 1955 (the final day of the Labor Day weekend), a motorist driving on Federal Boulevard had seen an explosion blow out the windows of the Crown-A drive-in. By the time the fire department responded to the scene, there were no flames for them to extinguish—the vacuum caused by the explosion had put out the fire.

Assistant Fire Chief Franklin Soper quickly determined that someone had forced open the back door of the restaurant and disconnected a copper gas line near the chicken broaster. The leaking gas had ignited when it reached the pilot light of the hot-water heater.

Patrolmen John Meeker and Cecil Curtis had called Jack Graham at home and told him what had occurred. When Graham arrived a few minutes later, he inspected the cash register and told the officers that only three dollars in loose change was missing. He also said that he was certain the gas line had been connected when he left the restaurant at midnight. Graham told the officers that he had not had any "trouble" and knew "of no one whom he would suspect in the offense."

After arson investigators concluded that the gas line could not have been disconnected without a wrench, Graham volunteered that several of his former employees had kept keys to the back door. However, the officers interviewed the former employees and concluded that they were not involved. The final report stated that burglars had "attempted to blow up and burn down the restaurant, apparently in retaliation for their bad luck."

Looking back on the incident later, Detective Charles Clark conceded that "it was a screwy idea. . . . We had no other lead to go on. . . . The whole thing didn't seem right." Patrolman Meeker agreed. "A burglar doesn't take that kind of revenge. . . . Burglars are not generally interested in blowing anything up—unless it is a grudge deal."

Based on the discoveries about the Crown-A drive-in, Roy Moore sent several agents to Stapleton Airfield with instructions to comb through Daisie King's personal effects. Arriving at the warehouse that housed the reconstructed fuselage, the agents walked to the area set aside for the passengers' belongings. Nearby, the battered seats from the DC-6B sat on the floor, arranged in even rows with an aisle in between, a haunting reminder of the men and women whose property was now stored in cardboard boxes marked with their names.

Several items belonging to Daisie King had been found in the purse that landed near her body. There were a few handwritten letters, $1,000 in traveler's checks, an address list, the keys and receipts for two safety deposit boxes, and a yellowed copy of a 1951 newspaper article identifying John Gilbert Graham as one of the Denver district attorney's "six most wanted men." According to the article, Graham had forged $4,305.34 in checks while working as a bookkeeper for the Timpte Brothers Automobile Company in east Denver. Over the course of three days, he had cashed more than forty checks at Denver banks and businesses before skipping town.

When the FBI agents contacted the Denver district attorney's office, they learned that Graham had used the money from the bogus checks to finance a road trip around the country. Among other places, Graham had visited Salt Lake City, Seattle, Kansas City, and St. Louis.

On September 11, 1951, Graham's journey had come to an end when a police officer in Lubbock, Texas, attempted to stop Graham for a traffic violation. The Denver fugitive refused to pull over, crashing through a police roadblock at a speed of almost one hundred miles per hour. After veering into a ditch, Graham steered back onto the road, and he did not surrender until the officers began shooting. At the time of his arrest, Graham's car was filled with cases of whiskey he was bootlegging into one of Texas's dry counties; he also had a gun.

Graham served sixty days in the county jail for illegal possession of a firearm and "hauling whiskey in violation of Texas laws." In November 1951, he was extradited back to Denver, where he pleaded guilty to the pending forgery charges.

The pre-sentencing report from the 1951 conviction provided the FBI with a wealth of information about the life of John Gilbert Graham. Among other things, the agents learned that, after completing ninth grade at Kremmling High School, Graham had left home in April 1948 and enlisted in the Coast Guard using forged identification papers that added two years to his age. He had completed training at the Avery Point Training Center in Groton, Connecticut, achieving the rank of Motorman Third Class, but later went absent without leave for forty-three days. When he eventually reappeared, the Coast Guard discharged him as a minor.

In 1949, Graham returned to Colorado and lived on his stepfather's ranch. In May of that year, he moved to Alaska to stay with his sister and her family. Working alongside his brother-in-law, Riney Hablutzel, Graham spent half a year with the Army Corps of Engineers doing construction at Elmendorf Air Force Base.

In January 1950, Graham moved back to Colorado to live with an uncle, Verne A. Walker of Englewood. He received his high-school equivalency certificate and passed the entrance exams at Denver University, though he decided to defer admission in favor of the bookkeeping position with the Timpte Brothers Automobile Company.

The probation officer who had prepared the pre-sentencing report observed that Graham "shows very little concern over this present offense. For the past couple of years he led a wild life—spen[ding] most of his money on drinking parties and women." The report included Graham's statement that his spree was merely "one last fling" that he allowed himself because he assumed he would soon be drafted to fight in Korea. Of Daisie, the probation officer wrote that she "appears to be a type that has overprotected her son. She feels he has learned a serious lesson from this offense and his experience down in Texas."

At the sentencing hearing, Daisie asked for leniency and made an initial restitution payment of $2,500. In addition, Sheriff William McFarlane of Routt County, who had known Graham for several years, appeared in court and offered his opinion that the young man was a "good risk" for probation. Based on this recommendation, the judge suspended a prison sentence on the condition that Graham complete five years of probation and pay full restitution.

Graham's probation officer, James R. Scott, described him as a "model probationer" who never missed a restitution payment. In October 1952, Graham approached Scott and asked for permission to marry Gloria Ann Elson of Lakewood. The probation officer denied the request, telling Graham he should wait until he was financially secure. For nine months, Graham worked hard and saved his money. On June 14, 1953, he and Gloria were married.

Soon afterward, the Grahams moved to Grand Junction. Despite his earlier troubles, Graham was granted a security clearance by the Atomic Energy Commission, a prerequisite for his job as a mechanic for the Walker-Lyberger Construction Company, a subcontractor. At the end of each month, he dutifully mailed a restitution payment to Scott.

When the Grahams returned to Denver in 1954 at Daisie's request, Jack began hand-delivering the restitution checks to Scott, apparently using the appointments as an excuse to visit with one of his few friends. Scott told the FBI agents that Graham had made his most recent $40 payment on November 3, reducing the outstanding balance to only $105.34. "He appeared quite broken up over the death of his mother," Scott said. "He couldn't seem to reconcile himself to his mother's death." At Graham's request, Scott had attended Daisie King's burial ceremony at the Fairmount Cemetery.

On November 10, FBI agents Roy Mischke and William Broderick met with Jack Graham and his sister, Helen Hablutzel, who had flown to Denver to attend her mother's funeral and help settle the estate.

Helen Hablutzel carried herself with a sense of self-sufficiency, a trait developed during her many years of living in Alaska. Since dropping out of Saint Scholastica's and moving north, she had worked as a photographer, a sled-dog trainer, and a builder of log cabins. The mother of four children, she would later tell reporters that she spent what little spare time she had educating herself by reading "half of Anchorage's library."

Helen would also later tell reporters that Daisie had developed a fear of flying because of the recent Medicine Bow crash. "She had already planned to come visit us, but she wrote that the Wyoming accident had frightened her. She said she was fearful the same thing would happen to the plane she was on. If I hadn't kept begging Daisie to visit us, she wouldn't have been on that plane—she'd be alive today."

Helen held an unvarnished opinion of her mother. "No matter how the cards seemed to fall, Daisie never found happiness. She and Earl were happy in many ways, but she was the kind of woman who could never find real happiness. I don't know how best to describe Daisie. In a word I guess you could say she was temperamental. She was never calm. She was easily hurt, and she pouted a lot. She was wonderful when she was relaxed, but you never knew when that was going to happen."

The agents—both professionally trained to observe personal characteristics—made a quick assessment of Jack Graham. He was approximately six feet tall and weighed just over two hundred pounds. The short cut of his black hair accentuated the adolescent roundness of his face. He was articulate, and Mischke and Broderick judged his affect appropriate for a person who had recently suffered the unexpected loss of a parent. The two agents noticed that, like his sister, Jack consistently referred to Mrs. King by her first name, never once calling her "mother" or "mom."

When Mischke asked Graham about his ownership interest in the Crown-A drive-in, Graham explained that, shortly before opening the business, he had insisted that Daisie place the title in his name because he did not want to work long hours building up the business as the manager only to lose it "when she died." After consulting with an attorney, Daisie had transferred the deed, but she had retained a life estate in the business in order to maintain managerial control. According to Graham, Daisie had exercised this authority by strictly overseeing the finances of the business, forbidding him from writing any checks other than for small amounts owed to suppliers.

When asked about the disposition of Daisie's estate, Graham explained that, under the terms of Earl and Daisie King's joint will, half the property would now go to Earl King's brother-in-law, Charles Garland of Pueblo; the other half would be divided between Graham and his sister.

Mischke brought the conversation back to the subject of the Crown-A, asking whether it was a lucrative business. Although Graham admitted that the business was "not entirely a financial success," he attributed this to the fact that "he could not be on the premises and actively manage the business at all times." He denied any involvement in the September gas explosion, telling the agents it had been caused by disgruntled burglars. He also told the agents that the windows of the drive-in had been shot out in May.

Without any prompting, Graham mentioned another recent insurance claim. In August, his new Chevrolet half-ton pickup truck had stalled on a set of railroad tracks just as a fast-moving train was approaching. Graham claimed that he barely escaped with his life by jumping out of the truck before it was struck by the train. Although Graham was convinced the truck was a total loss, the adjuster for the General Insurance Company of America had disagreed and had had the vehicle repaired.*

Mischke changed the topic again, this time asking for a detailed description of Daisie's preparations for her trip. Graham said that his mother had

---

* According to court records, the truck—which had not run out of gas—stalled at an Englewood crossing adjacent to the intersection of South Santa Fe Boulevard and West Dartmouth Avenue shortly before 2 A.M. on the morning of August 22, 1955. The Englewood police officer who responded to the scene determined that Graham was at fault and issued him a summons for careless driving. On September 6, Graham appeared before the Englewood justice of the peace and refused to pay the $50 fine, protesting that he would not have allowed a "1955 truck [to] get wrecked on purpose." After spending a night in the county jail for contempt of court, Graham was released when Gloria paid the fine.

first mentioned the Alaska trip in early September. He and Gloria had tried to persuade her to stay in Colorado through November, but Daisie wanted to get to Alaska in time for the caribou hunting season.

Broderick asked Graham if he knew of anyone with a motive to harm his mother. Graham said he did not, though he suggested that the agents investigate the former manager of a second drive-in restaurant Daisie had opened in Steamboat Springs. According to Graham, Daisie had suspected the manager was embezzling. Graham also said that there was "animosity" between Daisie and her brother-in-law, Charles Garland.

Mischke shifted the questioning and asked about Daisie's activities on the day before she departed. Graham told the agent that he and his mother had gone shopping together and that Daisie had bought him a pair of shoes as a gift. She had also purchased a number of toys as Christmas presents for her four grandchildren in Alaska. Later that afternoon, she had wrapped the gifts, packed them in two crates purchased from the Denver Dry Goods Company, and shipped them to Alaska from the Air Express office at Stapleton.

Graham remembered that a family friend, Dr. Earl Miller, had joined them for dinner. Dr. Miller was still there at 11:00 P.M. when Graham left for his new job as a nightshift mechanic for the Hertz Rent-A-Car Company.

Graham said that he had arrived home at 8:00 A.M. the next morning and slept the entire day. At 5:00 P.M., Daisie, Gloria, and Allen left together to take Daisie's Chevrolet to the Denver Motor Hotel, a long-term parking garage located at Fourteenth and Stout streets. Graham——who was supposed to meet them at the Motor Hotel and drive them to the airport——hurriedly shaved, showered, and dressed. Before leaving, he went across the street and asked a neighbor to look in on his daughter occasionally and make sure she was still sleeping in her crib.

Graham told the agents that he then returned to his house and loaded Daisie's three suitcases into the trunk of his 1951 Plymouth. At this point, Mischke interrupted and asked for a description of the luggage. Graham said that the largest bag was thirty inches long, twenty-eight inches wide, and ten inches deep, and that it was made of a light tan fabric. The second suitcase was slightly smaller than the first, dark brown, and monogrammed with the initials "GAW," a reminder of the years when it had belonged to Graham's grandfather, Judge Walker. The smallest suitcase, a Samsonite, had a broken hinge that had been only partially repaired. Graham said Daisie had bound it closed with several strands of clothesline. He told Mischke that he had been concerned the rope might break, and that he had therefore stopped on his way downtown and purchased two olive-colored straps from a military surplus store near the intersection of Federal Boulevard and Alameda Avenue.

Mischke interrupted again, asking whether Graham had helped Daisie pack her bags. Graham said he had not. "I don't know what she put in her luggage. Daisie liked to pack things herself and she never let anyone help her. I do know she took some shotgun shells and rifle ammunition with her."

Graham continued, telling the agents he had been delayed by rush-hour traffic and had been late arriving at the Denver Motor Hotel. Daisie was "quite perturbed" and worried she might miss her flight. Graham said he had rushed to the airport, deposited his family at the terminal, and then parked in the lot. After securing the damaged suitcase with the straps he had bought, he carried all three bags into the terminal.

According to Graham, Daisie had handed him a handful of quarters and asked him to buy three flight insurance policies: one with himself as the beneficiary, a second for the benefit of Helen, and a third for Daisie's sister, Mrs. Helen Smith of Saint Genevieve, Missouri. Jack said there had been some "confusion" at the vending machine when they were filling out the policies, but he was quite sure Daisie had signed all three policies before they walked her to the gate. He could not answer Mischke's questions about the exact amounts of the policies, stating that he thought they were for the minimum, "about $12,000."

Graham remembered that they had had only a couple of minutes to chat at the gate before the boarding call had begun. Daisie then kissed them all goodbye, said farewell, and walked out to the plane. Graham told the agents he had watched her board before carrying Allen to the Administration Building, depositing a dime in the turnstile, and climbing the stairs to the second-floor observation deck.

Graham said he and his son had watched the plane take off and had stayed on the observation deck until it disappeared from sight. Returning inside, they rejoined Gloria for a light dinner at the first-floor coffee shop. As they were finishing their meal, they overheard the cashier say that another United plane had crashed. They could not find anyone in the airport who knew any details, so they drove home. Because the Plymouth was not equipped with a radio, they did not learn that it was Daisie's flight until they got back to the house and listened to the news on the radio.

Graham told Mischke that he had immediately called United Air Lines and spoken with a person who was unsure whether there were any survivors. An hour later, he called United again and learned that everyone on the plane was presumed dead.

On November 11, two FBI agents met with Gloria Graham, an attractive brunette who wore fashionable glasses—aluminum "cat's eye" frames with ornate etchings on the tips and arms. She was a heavy smoker, though she had not had the habit long enough to lose the softness in her voice.

Gloria corroborated her husband's description of Daisie's packing habits, recalling that her mother-in-law never allowed anyone to help and always stuffed her bags "so full." Her account of Daisie's departure was consistent too, though she mentioned that she had seen Jack holding a box wrapped with Christmas paper just before she and Daisie left the house to drive to the parking garage. The gift was approximately eighteen inches long, fourteen inches wide, and three inches deep. Gloria told the agents she did not know what was inside, but she assumed it was a set of X-acto tools because Jack had talked about buying such a gift for Daisie, who enjoyed carving costume jewelry out of sea shells. Gloria said she had seen Jack take the gift to the basement, though she claimed not to know whether he had actually given it to his mother.

After speaking with Gloria, the FBI agents called the Denver-area stores that stocked X-acto tool kits. There were only two such shops, and neither of them had sold a tool set during the previous month.

For several days, a small group of women living in Lakewood, a suburb west of Denver, had been discreetly debating whether to go to the FBI. On November 3, their neighbor, Christine Elson, had told them that her son-in-law, Jack Graham, had hidden a gift in his mother's luggage. As related by Mrs. Elson, Jack was "heartbroken" and "despondent" because he had failed "to make his mother's last hours happy by . . . giving her the present before she left Denver." Mrs. Elson also revealed that Jack Graham had claimed to have had a premonition of his mother's death and, while eating at the airport, had gone to the men's room to "throw up."

The husband of one of the women insisted that his wife call the FBI, arguing that "if there was sabotage and it goes unpunished, crackpots all over the country would be bombing planes." The woman refused, explaining that she "simply could not," because the Elsons were "wonderful people" and she was "the last person on earth" who would "do anything that might harm them." On the morning of Friday, November 11, the husband took matters into his own hands and called the FBI. "You should talk to my wife," he said.

Based on this tip, FBI agents contacted Mrs. Elson and learned that Gloria had called her mother on November 3. "Jack is cracking up," she had said. "None of us seem to be able to get close to him." Gloria had also told her mother that her husband was unable to sleep and that he was pacing constantly.

On Saturday, November 12, agent James Wagoner called Gloria to see if she and Jack would come to the FBI office, ostensibly for the purpose of identifying some luggage. Gloria asked if it could wait until the next day. Wagoner said that would be fine.

After attending Sunday services at the Lakewood Community Methodist Church, Jack and Gloria Graham drove downtown to the Customs House, located at the intersection of Nineteenth and Stout streets. An imposing structure covered with Colorado Yule marble, the five-story Italian Renaissance Revival building had been designed to inspire respect for the authority of the federal agencies housed inside.

At 12:45 P.M., the young couple entered the FBI office on the second floor and met with agents Roy Moore, Lloyd Hasman and Donald Sebesta. The agents showed the Grahams several scraps of leather and pieces of clothesline arranged on a table and asked if they recognized them. Both Jack and Gloria thought the items had likely come from Daisie's small Samsonite suitcase. They also examined a small photograph in a gold frame and identified it as a picture of Earl King.

As the Grahams were preparing to leave, Wagoner asked Jack if he would be willing to answer a few more questions, assuring him that they would give him a ride home when they were finished. Jack agreed to stay, and Gloria went home to look after their children.

Once Gloria was gone, Wagoner and Sebesta escorted Graham to an interview room and asked him about the ammunition his mother had taken to Alaska. Graham listed the calibers of the shells, estimating that Daisie had packed several hundred rounds.

Wagoner also asked Graham whether he had purchased a Christmas gift for his mother. Graham said that he had planned to buy her an X-acto tool set he had seen in a newspaper advertisement for the Dave Cook Sporting Goods Store. He said that he had shown the advertisement to Daisie and she had told him the $30 tool set was inadequate for cutting shells—the tool set she wanted cost almost $150. As a result of this conversation, Graham said, he had abandoned the idea of buying Daisie a Christmas present.

The agents asked Graham for a step-by-step account of his actions on November 1. Graham complied, reciting the chronology of events he had previously provided for agents Mischke and Broderick. In his account of the day, Graham added a few details, describing how the flight insurance vending machine had failed to stamp two of the three policies. He also said that, because he had not yet received the one policy he had addressed to himself, he thought he might have accidentally placed the policies in a trash can instead of a mailbox.

Graham also verified that he had become sick while eating at the airport coffee shop. When asked about the cause of his illness, Graham blamed the poor quality of the food he had eaten and his excitement about Daisie's departure.

Graham contradicted his previous statement when he told Wagoner that, after walking Gloria to the car, he had reentered the terminal building and obtained additional information about the plane crash. According to Graham, the cashier had told him that a plane went down somewhere near Longmont. Graham said this information was reassuring because he was confident Daisie's plane would have been farther away from Denver at the time the accident occurred. In addition, although he had not mentioned it before, Graham told Wagoner that he and Gloria had driven to Longmont on November 3 and attempted—unsuccessfully—to gain access to the crash site.

At 3:40 P.M., Wagoner asked Graham if he could stay a bit longer. Graham said he would, accepting the agent's invitation to continue the conversation over steak sandwiches at the Albany Hotel, located nearby at Seventeenth and Stout streets.

After finishing their meal, the agents brought Graham back across the street to the FBI office. Wagoner began to sharpen the focus of his questions, asking Graham whether he had any experience working with dynamite. Graham said he did, explaining that he had used fuse-lit dynamite to remove beaver dams on his stepfather's ranch in Toponas. Wagoner asked Graham whether he had ever detonated dynamite with electric blasting caps. Graham said he had once used blasting caps while working on a construction project in Alaska.

At 6:30 P.M., Wagoner excused himself from the interview room and walked down the hall to brief Roy Moore.

Based on the information provided by Wagoner, Moore called the FBI's criminalistics laboratory in Washington to find out whether the technicians had finished their analysis of the black sooty substance found on the metal fragments. A technician told Moore they had just completed the final tests: the powdery residue contained traces of sodium carbonate, sodium nitrate, and sulphur-bearing compounds—conclusive evidence of a dynamite explosion.

It was not until 1966 that the United States Supreme Court announced its landmark decision in *Miranda v. Arizona* requiring police officers to provide arrestees with an advisement of their "Miranda rights." However, in the early 1950s J. Edgar Hoover had issued a directive requiring FBI agents to provide an advisement of rights to any suspect before conducting an interrogation. Thus, when Roy Moore entered the interview room at 6:40 P.M., he advised Graham that:

> he did not have to answer any questions, that if he did they could be used against him in a court of law at a later date, and that he could call an attorney of his own choosing, . . . that the door of the interview room would remain open, [and] that he was privileged to walk out of the interview room and out of the [FBI] office any time he felt the questions were not to his liking.

Moore further explained that he and the other agents would not make any threats or promises, and if at "any time [Graham] cared to go to the men's room, if he wanted anything to eat or drink, he had only to request it."

After verifying that Graham understood these rights, Moore leaned across the table, looked him squarely in the eyes, and addressed him in a calm tone of voice. "Jack," he said, "I accuse you of blowing up the plane. Did you do it?"

"No, I did not," Graham replied, speaking in an equally composed manner.

"In that event," Moore asked, "do you have any objection to signing waivers allowing us to search your automobiles, your home, your business, and your mother's ranch?" Graham said he would consent to the searches.

Although Moore did not have a polygraph machine in the office, he wanted to see how Graham would react to a request that he submit to the "lie detector" test. To Moore's surprise, Graham agreed without hesitation.

At approximately 8:00 P.M., Gloria answered a knock at the door to the Graham home expecting to see her husband. Instead, she encountered half a dozen FBI agents with a signed consent form authorizing them to search the premises. As Gloria watched in bewilderment, the agents began scouring every nook and cranny of her small house.

While the search was proceeding, Jack Graham continued to answer a barrage of questions posed by the many FBI agents who were moving in and out of the interview room. Agent Wagoner was the first to extract a major concession, getting Graham to admit that he had purchased an X-acto tool set as a gift for his mother. According to Graham, he had bought the $30 tool set for $10 during the early morning hours of October 30 from a man who occasionally peddled stolen merchandise at the Hertz garage. Graham provided a detailed description of the man and drew a sketch of the tools. Graham said he had hidden the wooden box containing the tool set in his car until the morning of November 1, at which time he had driven to a Rexall Drugstore and purchased a single sheet of red and green striped Christmas paper. Sitting in his car outside the store, he had wrapped the gift using a roll of Scotch tape he kept in the glove compartment. On the upper corner of the package he had written, "From Us." Graham said that he had told Gloria about the hidden present, but he claimed she had no advance knowledge of his plan to conceal the gift in Daisie's suitcase.

When Roy Moore learned of Graham's revelation, he called the agents who were searching the house and directed them to advise Gloria that she had committed a federal crime by lying in her November 11 interview.

Confronted with proof of her deception, Gloria recanted. "Well," she admitted, "I have been lying to you. Jack told me not to tell you about the Christmas present." She then signed a written statement indicating that she had "seen and handled the Christmas present," and that her husband had told her "he would put it in his mother's luggage." She said she had known of Jack's plan to hide a Christmas gift in Daisie's luggage since the last week of October, explaining that she had lied because Jack later told her the X-acto set may have been stolen.

As Gloria was signing the statement, an agent searching in the basement found several boxes of rifle bullets and shotgun shells—items Jack claimed Daisie had taken with her to Alaska. The agent brought the ammunition up from the basement, collected Gloria's signed statement, and drove downtown to deliver the items to Roy Moore.

At 11:06 P.M., Moore reentered the interrogation room, dropped the heavy boxes of ammunition on the table, and asked Graham why his mother would have left them behind. Graham said he must have been mistaken concerning how much ammunition Daisie had packed.

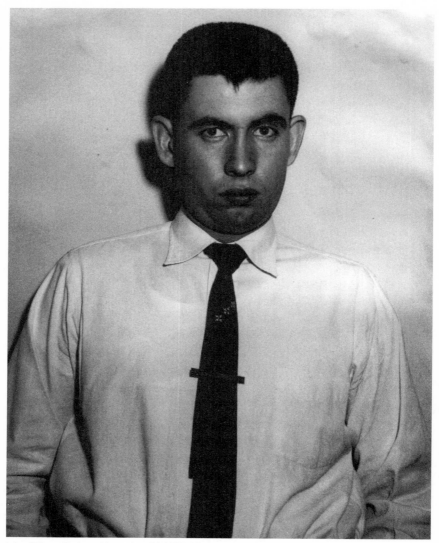

John Gilbert Graham, November 14, 1955. (Coutesy of the Federal Bureau of Investigation Denver Field Office)

Unsatisfied with this response, Moore showed Graham his wife's written statement, pointing out that Gloria had contradicted his own account with respect to the date when she had first learned about the plan to hide the Christmas present. Without directly threatening to do so, Moore made it clear that he could charge Gloria with making a false statement to a federal law enforcement officer.

As Graham tried to convince Moore that Gloria was simply mistaken, another agent entered the interview room holding a $37,500 flight insurance policy he had found hidden inside a cedar chest located in the Grahams' bedroom. The policy was dated November 1, it was signed by Daisie E. King, and the listed beneficiary was Jack Graham.

Graham disavowed any knowledge of the policy, claiming that he had never seen it before. Moore ignored the denial and pressed on, informing Graham that the agents who had searched his car had not found any Scotch tape in the glove box. Graham said the agents must have overlooked it, and he suggested Moore have the agents look again.

At 11:57 P.M., Moore confronted Graham with two strands of yellow wire an agent had found in the buttoned pocket of one of Graham's shirts. Graham examined the wire and told Moore it did not appear to be the type that could be used to detonate dynamite.

Four minutes later, agent John McCullough entered the room and informed Moore that he had interviewed Graham's coworkers at the Hertz garage. None of the other mechanics had ever seen the man Graham claimed had sold him the X-acto tool set.

Roy Moore had had enough. "You've been lying to us all night, Jack," he said. "We are going to charge you with the crime. Why not make it easy for us?"

Graham took a drink of water and set the glass on the table. "Okay," he said, "where do you want me to start?"

"Wherever you want to," Moore replied.

After thinking for a moment, Graham began to speak. "It all started about six months ago. Daisie had been raising hell about the drive-in. I had been working long hours. She wasn't satisfied. . . ."

## CHAPTER FIVE

# *"I just can't turn from the man."*

FIFTEEN MILES AWAY from the crash site, in a field just west of Brighton, John Martin was hunting with his grandson. Although the area was usually thick with pheasant, on this morning they had not flushed a single bird and Martin was weary from all the walking. Stopping to rest by a large bush, Martin glanced down and noticed a folded piece of paper tangled in the branches. A self-described collector of "any damned thing" he happened to find, Martin picked up the slip of paper and examined it. It was a ticket from United Air Lines Flight 629.

Squinting to read the small print, Martin saw that the ticket had been issued to a Mrs. King traveling from Denver to Seattle. In the section of the document reserved for baggage information, a handwritten entry indicated that Mrs. King had paid a $27.82 surcharge because her luggage exceeded the weight limit by thirty-seven pounds.

Martin refolded the piece of paper, tucked it in the pocket of his hunting jacket, and set out across the field in search of birds.

Gloria Graham was inconsolable. She had been sobbing for hours, ever since FBI agent Mischke called her at 5:00 A.M. to tell her that her husband had confessed to placing a timer and twenty-five sticks of dynamite in his mother's suitcase. One of her neighbors, fearing Gloria might be having a "complete breakdown," summoned Dr. Earl Miller, the family physician who had dined with the Grahams the night before Daisie departed. Dr. Miller rushed to the house and administered a sedative. As the narcotic began to take effect, members of the Elson family whisked Gloria and the children away, escaping only moments ahead of the onslaught of reporters.

Dr. Miller was still at the house when the first members of the press arrived. Although he stated that he "knew of no reason for Jack to do such a thing," he admitted that Graham had the ability, describing him as "a mechanical genius." Dr. Miller also mentioned an October 25 incident in which he, Daisie, and Jack were deer hunting on the King ranch near Yampa. According to Dr. Miller, Graham had pointed at an old shed and told him, "If you want some action, shoot that shack," later telling the doctor the building was used to store dynamite. "But," added Dr. Miller, "Jack wasn't out of my sight, and he never went near that shack."

After Dr. Miller drove away, the swarm of reporters canvassed the neighborhood to learn more about Graham and elicit reactions to the news of his arrest.

Lexie McClendon, the Grahams' next-door neighbor to the west, recalled a lunch she had shared with Daisie on the Saturday before the ill-fated flight. "Daisie told me her son was quick on the trigger, and what a bad temper he had," said Mrs. McClendon, "but he never showed it in front of me." The other next-door neighbor, Delores Torres, remembered how "all of us went over on a sympathy call after Mrs. King died. Mr. Graham seemed all broken up. He just sat staring at the floor. He looked like he'd been crying, but he didn't when we were there, and he didn't say anything." Across the street, Mrs. Helene West was worried about Gloria. "I went over as soon as I heard the news," she said. "Gloria didn't say a word, she cried all morning. I just hope she is all right now."

Donald E. Kelley, the United States attorney for Colorado, was experiencing a different kind of shock. After combing through the federal statute books looking for the provision that made it a crime to blow up an airplane, Kelley was astonished to discover there was no such law. The only statute that came close was Section 2155 of Title 18 of the United States Code, which prohibited interference with a "national defense utility." Although it was a bit of a stretch, Kelley concluded that he could charge Graham under this section because Flight 629 had been transporting Jesse Sizemore, an active-duty serviceman. Reviewing the statute's penalty provision, Kelley was surprised a second time—the maximum punishment for interfering with a national defense utility was only ten years in prison and a $10,000 fine.

By 10:00 A.M., reporters, photographers, and onlookers had gathered on Nineteenth Street, waiting in front of the U.S. Customs House for FBI agents to bring Graham outside for the short walk across the street to court. "Here he comes!" a man yelled, triggering a synchronized turning of heads toward the top of the granite steps leading up from the sidewalk. When the heavy metal doors swung open, flashbulbs began popping.

Graham was still dressed in the clothes he had worn to church the day before: a bluish gray double-breasted suit, a white shirt, and black wing-tip shoes. The only items missing were his belt and tie, both of which had been removed to protect him from himself. His wrists were in handcuffs attached to a metal chain wrapped around his waist. He kept his eyes fixed on the ground, relying on the two FBI agents grasping his arms to steer him through the pack of jostling reporters, a scene one member of the press corps likened to "a football team executing a trick play." As the agents cut through the crowd, Pat Patterson, the president of United Air Lines, hurried behind in their wake.

A woman on the sidewalk shouted at Graham, calling him a "dirty dog!" She did not succeed in getting his attention.

The agents escorted their prisoner across Stout Street and led him up the wide steps of the Post Office Building toward the entryway set back from the building's sixteen towering Ionic columns. Halfway up the stairs, Graham raised his head and looked around to locate the source of a whirring sound. He quickly tucked his chin back into his chest when he realized the noise was coming from the camera of a photographer shooting footage for a newsreel, a weekly film summary of current events to be shown in movie houses throughout the country.

Entering the building, the agents moved Graham through the ornate lobby and guided him into the elevator. One of the agents pushed the button for the third floor. A moment later, the trio emerged into a second throng of reporters waiting outside the office of United States Commissioner Harold S. Oakes.* Sidestepping the raucous press corps, the agents ignored the reporters' many shouted questions and deposited Graham in the detention cell adjacent to Oakes's small office.

Graham was soon joined in the cell by Oscar A. Crist, the deputy United States marshal. Crist walked Graham next door and stood him in front of Commissioner Oakes, who was sitting at his desk typing out the complaint charging Graham with a single count of interfering with a na-

* Until 1968, commissioners assisted federal judges with administrative matters such as initial advisements. The position of commissioner was eliminated in 1968 through enactment of the Federal Magistrates Act.

tional defense utility. United States Attorney Donald Kelley stood next to Graham, along with Denver District Attorney Bert M. Keating and Weld County District Attorney Marc Smith.

When Oakes finished preparing the complaint, he asked Graham whether he was represented by an attorney, admonishing him to "look at me when I'm talking to you." Graham raised his eyes slightly and sullenly replied, "No." Just then, Jerome R. Strickland entered the room, accompanied by Helen Hablutzel.

Strickland, a Denver attorney who had previously handled several business matters for Daisie King, had agreed to represent Graham temporarily until the family located an attorney specializing in criminal law. "I have not accepted the case," he explained. "I am not in criminal law practice—in fact, I've never tried a criminal case. But I promised Mrs. Hablutzel that for the interim I would appear." Oakes declared a five-minute recess to give Strickland an opportunity to confer with Graham in the detention cell.

In addition to his lack of experience in the field of criminal law, Jerome Strickland had another reason why he could not defend Graham—he was a potential witness. On the evening of November 1, Strickland had driven to Stapleton Airfield to meet his brother, an engineer with Boeing's guided missile division who was returning to Seattle from Chicago on Flight 629. Although the engineer had no plans to extend his brief layover in Denver, Jerome Strickland had been determined to persuade his brother to stay for dinner. While waiting for the delayed flight to arrive, Strickland had visited briefly with Daisie King and the Grahams. Thinking back on the evening and the coincidental encounter, Strickland would later recall how he had "practically dragged" his brother "over to the reservations counter to cancel out and get confirmation on a later flight," a memory he said gave him "goose pimples."

When the proceeding reconvened, Strickland informed Oakes that Graham was willing to waive his right to a preliminary hearing. The commissioner verified the waiver with Graham, set bail in the amount of $100,000, and adjourned the hearing.

As Crist and another deputy U.S. marshal led Graham from the room for transportation to the Denver County Jail, Helen called out after her brother, "Goodbye, Jack, we'll see you later." Graham did not reply.

After the arraignment, the three prosecutors met to discuss the filing of state murder charges. At the conclusion of the one-hour conference, Kelley informed the press that district attorneys Keating and Smith were both "willing to accept jurisdiction" and that if Justice Department officials in Washington, D.C., could "find no federal laws covering the case with more severe penalties," the case would have to be "turned over to the state for prosecution."

Across town, United Air Lines president Pat Patterson was also speaking to reporters at an impromptu press conference in a meeting room of the Brown Palace Hotel. "There is a tendency to regard a company like United as a great impersonal organization without feelings in matters of this sort," he said. "But I can't convey the shock and sorrow of such a tragedy as it affected every man and woman in our organization. We lost seven wonderful employees on that plane. If we hadn't found out about this one, it would have been hanging over our heads for all time."

Patterson went on to describe the reconstruction of the fuselage, emphasizing how the work of the United Air Lines employees had advanced the FBI's investigation. He also pointed out that the rebuilding would not have been possible if Flight 629 had departed on time because the explosion would have scattered the debris "in the exact same spot" as the earlier crash on Medicine Bow Peak, thus preventing any recovery of the parts until the spring.

The reporters were intensely interested in the $25,000 reward, peppering the airline president with questions about the likely recipient. Patterson refused to speculate, stating that he had referred the matter to United Air Lines' legal department. Patterson closed the session by reading a prepared statement:

> On behalf of the management and the wonderful employees of our company who work so conscientiously and with such great sincerity in providing safety to the traveling public, I want to express my appreciation to those agencies who assisted in the investigation of the cause of this accident, and particularly to the Federal Bureau of Investigation who did such a remarkable job solving this great tragedy. We again extend our very deepest sympathy to the families of our employees and passengers who were victims of this terrible crime.

After finishing his remarks, the senior executive went upstairs to his hotel suite, where he followed the orders of a physician who had been warning him all week that he needed to get some sleep or "face the risk of collapse."

Shortly after 6:00 P.M., a man phoned the city desk editor of the *Denver Post* and reported that a mob of "sixty-five guys are going to take Graham out of the county jail tonight." The editor tried to call Warden Gordon Dolliver

The old Denver County Jail. (Courtesy of Denver Public Library, Western History Collection, Call # X-20608)

at home, but Dolliver was already on his way to the jail, having just received an anonymous call telling him a lynch mob of "one hundred and twenty-five men would try to take the jail."

Arriving at the jail at the intersection of Kalamath Street and Colfax Avenue, Dolliver met with Dan Stills, the division chief of police, who had also been warned of the threats. In making their preparations for the fortification of the jail, Dolliver and Stills agreed that the mob might attempt to disrupt the police department's radio communications. To prevent this from occurring, Stills dispatched two officers to stand guard at the base of the radio transmission tower located across the street from the Denver Botanic Gardens.

As the off-duty guards summoned to the jail began to arrive, Dolliver gave them their assignments. He stationed several men outside the door of

Graham's solitary-confinement cell. He directed the others to arm themselves and surround the jail.

Minutes later, a car filled with armed men pulled up by the front entrance. Oscar Crist and four deputy U.S. marshals climbed out of the vehicle and began distributing extra pistols, shotguns, and ammunition. The guard stationed closest to the front gate was given the one available tear-gas gun.

For several hours, the guards, marshals, and policemen stood at their positions nervously waiting for the vigilantes to arrive. Throughout Denver, police officers patrolled the streets scanning the sidewalks for unusual gatherings.

The mob never materialized.

On Tuesday morning, the story of Graham's arrest was on the front page of newspapers from coast to coast. In the *New York Times,* President Eisenhower was quoted as saying he was "shocked" to learn of Graham's confession. The story was also international news, as were the reports of the threats against the jail. In London, a reporter for the *Daily Sketch*—apparently envisioning Denver as a frontier outpost on the "Wild West"—began calling the jail at regular intervals to find out whether Graham had yet been hung.

In Washington, D.C., J. Edgar Hoover and CAA Administrator Fred Lee met behind closed doors to discuss how best to prevent future airplane bombings. In addition, the CAB convened an emergency session to consider safety measures such as:

> actual inspection of all luggage and air freight, fluoroscopic machines to
> X-ray suspicious packages, posting of guards in uniform to discourage
> "crackpots," and posters above flight insurance windows or automatic
> policy-vending machines pointing out the certainty of discovery if anybody
> tries to sabotage a plane to collect insurance.

However, when discussing these options, many federal officials worried that a governmental overreaction might scare the traveling public away from airports and damage the airline industry.

Farther down Pennsylvania Avenue, Colorado Senator Gordon Allott announced that he would introduce a bill making sabotage of a commercial aircraft a federal crime punishable by death. There was no shortage of willing cosponsors for the legislation. Many other senators had lost constituents on Flight 629.

At Justice Department headquarters, attorneys in the criminal section completed their own legal analysis and concluded that their counterparts in

Colorado were correct—there was no applicable federal statute carrying the death penalty. Assistant Attorney General Warren Olney III called U.S. Attorney Kelley and authorized him to transfer the case to one of the state prosecutors.

Later that morning, Kelley met with reporters and announced that he would be relinquishing responsibility, stating that he would hold the federal charge in abeyance pending trial on the "more serious charges in state court." Kelley explained that, although murder charges could be filed in either Denver County or Weld County, he and the two state prosecutors had agreed the case should be filed in Denver. Kelley enumerated the factors supporting his decision:

> the primary victim was a resident of Denver, she boarded the plane at Denver, the suspect is a Denver resident, his preparation for the crime and all acts for carrying out the crime were committed in Denver, personnel of United Air Lines are more accessible in Denver, and FBI agents working on the case are also based in Denver.

Kelley's list of reasons justifying the choice of venue was persuasive, but it was deliberately incomplete. Out of consideration for the Weld County district attorney, Kelley did not mention the fact that the Denver district attorney was one of the most respected prosecutors in the country.

Stocky, balding, and bespectacled, Bert M. Keating was not a tall man. However, he was a giant in the courtroom, a talented trial lawyer who personally handled many of the most important cases he filed. He was equally skilled as a politician.

In 1932, two years after graduating from the Westminster Law School,* Keating was elected to the state legislature as a Democrat. During his two terms in the state house, he helped establish a pension program for policemen and firemen, a favor the firefighters and police officers repaid by assisting him in his successful campaign for the post of election commissioner in Denver.

Keating managed to stay in that office for four consecutive terms by craftily circumventing a provision of the Denver city charter that prohibited the election commissioner from succeeding himself. His solution was ingenuously simple: two months before the end of each term, he resigned.

---

\* A night law school that has since merged with the University of Denver.

He then persuaded the voters of Denver that he was the best-qualified candidate to fill the vacancy he had just created.

In 1948, Keating was easily elected district attorney. During his first term in office, he received national recognition for his innovative juvenile justice initiatives, his prosecution of "fadeaway fathers" who shirked their child support responsibilities, and a crackdown on check forgers he dubbed "Operation Checkmate." In 1952, he was reelected by an overwhelming margin—no small feat in a year when most Republican candidates rode Eisenhower's coattails to victory. In 1953, he was elected president of the National Association of County and Prosecuting Attorneys.

The following year, Denver came perilously close to losing its district attorney when Keating dropped a lighted cigarette on the floor of his Buick, reached down to recover it, and drove his car off the side of a road in the foothills west of the city. Keating spent a full hour pinned beneath the car and nearly died from his injuries.

By the spring of 1955, Keating had recovered sufficiently to launch his campaign to succeed Quigg Newton as mayor. Although favored to win, the district attorney conceded defeat a month after the polls closed when the first recount of a mayoral election in city history established that Will F. Nicholson had won by a mere 820 votes.

The Denver electorate's decision to retain the services of Bert Keating as chief prosecutor would soon prove to be a prescient one.

Following Kelley's press conference, Keating returned to his office in the West Side Court Building, located at the intersection of Speer Boulevard and Colfax Avenue, where he drafted a criminal information. The one-page document revealed the district attorney's first tactical move—his decision to prosecute the simplest possible case of premeditated murder committed against a single victim:

> Bert M. Keating, District Attorney within and for the Second Judicial
> District of the State of Colorado, in the name and by the authority of the
> People of the State of Colorado, informs the Court that on the 1st day of
> November, A.D. 1955, at the City and County of Denver, and State of
> Colorado, John Gilbert Graham, feloniously, willfully, and of his premed-
> itated malice aforethought, committed an offense in the City and County
> of Denver, State of Colorado, for the deliberate purpose of causing, and

which offense did deliberately cause, the death of DAISIE E. KING in the County of Weld, State of Colorado, and thereby killed and murdered said DAISIE E. KING on said November 1, 1955; contrary to the form of the statute in such case made and provided, and against the peace and dignity of the People of the State of Colorado.

By narrowly tailoring the charge in this manner, Keating hoped to avoid cluttering the trial with evidence concerning the question of whether or not Graham knew the other passengers would be on the plane.

Pursuant to Colorado law, Keating was required to support the charging document with an affidavit signed by an individual having personal knowledge of the facts alleged. As a practical matter, it would have made sense for him to use Roy Moore or one of the other FBI agents who had taken Graham's detailed confession. However, the district attorney made a symbolic statement in his choice of an affiant, selecting the one individual who could best serve as a representative for the forty-three other victims not named in the charging document: Pat Patterson.

With a handful of reporters looking on, the United Air Lines President strode into Keating's office, sat down at the large oak desk, removed a pen from the breast pocket of his jacket, and signed the document, attesting "that the facts stated in the foregoing information hereto attached are true." After a notary applied her seal, Keating handed the papers to one of his deputies and instructed him to file it in the Denver District Court and obtain a "no bond" hold.

In brief remarks following the signing ceremony, Keating announced that he would ask the jury to impose a sentence of death in the gas chamber. He also said he would press the court to "try the case as early as possible" due to the "long chain of evidence which must be established through witnesses." Before dismissing the reporters from his office, Keating read the telegram he had received that afternoon from J. Edgar Hoover:

> I want to assure you that the complete investigative and scientific facilities of the FBI are available to you in the handling of the prosecution of John Gilbert Graham. I am asking my personal representative in Denver to immediately contact you to go over all facts developed to date and render such assistance as is necessary to insure the fulfillment of justice.

After the reporters were gone, Keating and Patterson lingered in the office talking about the case. Outside the glass door, a group of deputy district attorneys hovered in the hope that their physical proximity might result in an invitation to work on the biggest mass murder case in U.S.

history. Keating pointed at one particularly eager-looking young man and gestured for him to come into the office. The deputy bounded into the room anticipating the important assignment he was about to receive. "I need you to go downstairs," Keating said, fishing some change out of his pocket, "and get me a pack of Pall Malls from the vending machine."

The *Denver Post* and the *Rocky Mountain News* soon began reporting every conceivable detail of Graham's daily routine: what he was reading (dime novels with titles such as *The Shadows, Naked Are Mine Enemies,* and *Nature Child*); what he was eating (oatmeal for breakfast, a cheese sandwich and tomato-rice soup for lunch, and a dinner of pork, beans, corn bread, and chocolate pudding); what time he went to bed (8:30 P.M.); his first visitor (Reverend Lloyd C. Kellams, his pastor from the Lakewood Methodist Church); how he slept (on his left side, beneath a wool army blanket, with his head resting on his forearm); and what time he awoke (at 4:30 A.M., when the guards roused the other prisoners to perform the morning chores).

Neither newspaper demonstrated any great concern about prejudicing the pool of potential jurors. The *Denver Post* repeatedly referred to Graham as "pouty-faced" or as a "baby-faced playboy," comparing him to the most "infamous . . . mass murderers of history," such "monsters" as German serial killer Fritz Haarman and—closer to home—Alfred "the Cannibal" Packer, the nineteenth-century Colorado mountain guide convicted of manslaughter for killing and eating members of his expedition party. Not to be outdone, the *Rocky Mountain News* reminded its readers of the Lizzie Borden parricide prosecution and bolstered its own comparison of Graham and Packer with gruesome details of half a dozen other crimes committed by Colorado murderers and an ominous prediction that, of these many culprits, Graham would be "the one you'll find occasion to tell the grandchildren [about] on some cold winter night when the television show is no good."

Predictably, the newspapers compared Graham to J. Albert Guay, the ringleader of the 1949 insurance-related bombing of a Canadian airplane. The *Denver Post,* attempting to demonstrate a Colorado connection to the earlier bombing, reported:

> One of the victims of the Canadian plane crash was Russell J. Parker, a Kennecott Copper Corporation executive whose son, Patrick Parker, a student at the Colorado School of Mines, tried to avenge his father's death but was stopped by police before he could carry out his plan to kill Guay.

Beyond this regional angle, the earlier bombing was an irresistible opportunity to contrast a son whose parent had been murdered on an airplane with a son charged with murdering a parent on an airplane.*

In the days following Graham's arrest, a more complete picture began to emerge of the financial difficulties afflicting the Crown-A drive-in. Paul Steinberg, the owner of another drive-in located near the Crown-A, considered himself a "friendly competitor" with Graham who often swapped "ideas about operations, and even borrow[ed] food supplies back and forth." Steinberg said he was surprised Graham had not reopened the Crown-A after the explosion because the windows had been repaired in time to capitalize on the remaining weeks of the cruising season. Steinberg also said he had heard rumors Graham had not been paying his food suppliers.

Eighteen-year-old Eleanor Schrader, who had worked at the Crown-A as a carhop delivering trays of food to car windows from May to July, said she often worked with Graham on the night shift and thought him to be "changeable—he could be just as nice one moment, and then bite your head off the next." Schrader had heard that the business might have been "in some kind of financial trouble," though she was unconcerned because her "paychecks always came regularly." She had seen Daisie only occasionally, but those few visits were memorable. "[She and] Mr. Graham argued frequently over all kinds of things. When the arguments would start in front of the girls, they would go to the back room and finish it. When Mrs. King came out you could see she had been crying."

Fifteen-year-old Naomi Harger, another Crown-A carhop, had also observed the many arguments. "He used to fly off the handle at her even if she made just the littlest mistake. He used dirty and foul language at her too." Harger had lost her job in August when, "for no good reason," Graham converted the restaurant to self-service. According to Harger, once the customers discovered they would have to pick up their food at the counter, the restaurant "started losing money and business fell off pretty badly."

However, not all the losses were attributable to bad business decisions. Ira Turner, the operator of a nearby gas station, reported that Graham "sure

---

*The article was slightly inaccurate. In fact, it was the elder Parker, a native of Colorado, who had attended the School of Mines; his son was a student at Brown University in Rhode Island when he robbed a liquor store and told police he had planned to use the proceeds from the holdup to finance a trip to Canada to "kill the man responsible for my father's death."

was popular with the kids around here. He used to sell them ten-cent ice cream cones for a nickel."

Additional information came to light suggesting that Daisie King had not been happy with her son's performance as manager. Late in the summer, on the way back from one of her frequent trips to Steamboat Springs to check on her other drive-in, the Dairy King,* Daisie had stopped in the town of Kremmling to visit a friend who owned a diner. When the friend asked Daisie how her Denver business was doing, Daisie had confided that sales were "pretty good, but the kid is taking it out as fast as we get it."

After the Crown-A was damaged by the gas explosion, Daisie had given up on the business and listed it for sale with a real estate broker.

By Wednesday, Gloria was well enough to speak with reporters at her parents' home in Lakewood. Dressed in a gray skirt, a printed blouse, and a red leather belt threaded through a metallic buckle embossed with her name, she began by apologizing for her earlier unavailability. "I'm sorry I couldn't take your calls on Monday. I was too ill to see anybody. I've been under the care of a doctor." Asked about developments in the case, she voiced her frustration. "They haven't allowed me to see him. I can't find out anything except what I read in the papers, and I know some of that isn't the truth. Thank God the children are too young to realize what is happening."

She told the reporters she had first met Jack in the fall of 1951 when they had attended Denver University together. "He was studying business administration and I was taking secretarial science. Jack was going to take an engineering sales course, but engineering aptitude tests showed it wasn't his line."

She flatly rejected the idea that her husband could have killed his own mother. "He was so good to her, and she, in return, did everything for us— paid for our home and helped Jack in his business. Oh, they occasionally argued over the operation of their restaurant, but what business partnership doesn't have differences like that?" She insisted that Jack and his mother had been getting along "beautifully . . . for the past few months," and she refused to believe the accounts of his confession. "It doesn't seem possible," she said. "I've lived with him so long and I know him. That is why I just can't grasp this. I just can't turn from the man."

---

*The name of the restaurant was apparently a play off that of the popular Dairy Queen chain, as well as Daisie's own name, which, according to the *Steamboat Pilot,* was "one of the most widely known [in] Routt County."

When describing the trip to Stapleton Airfield with her mother-in-law, Gloria remembered the other passengers on the plane. "I'll never forget some of their faces," she said. "I had known Sally Ann Scofield from a Methodist Church summer camp several years ago. There were two or three gentlemen who were quite inebriated and we got quite a kick out of that."

The only questions she refused to answer were those having to do with the hidden Christmas present, a subject she did not want to talk about "because the FBI made so much out of that." "I can't believe Jack really did this," she said, her voice trailing off. "I must talk to him."

That afternoon, Warden Dolliver granted Gloria's wish, calling to inform her that she could come to the jail after the regular visiting hours for a thirty-minute meeting with her husband. Dolliver instructed her to be there at 8:00 P.M.

Arriving at the jail in a car driven by her aunt, Gloria walked across the snow-covered yard toward the metal gate topped with barbed wire. She tried to shield her face from the cameramen with a sheaf of papers. It didn't work. The photographers moved to the side and captured the images they needed, the glare of their flashbulbs enhancing the confused expression of a sad-looking young woman wearing a heavy wool jacket and a white scarf wrapped around her head.

After obtaining her visitor's pass, Gloria followed a guard into a small room divided by a metal grate. There was only one piece of furniture, a small wooden bench. Lighting a cigarette to calm her nerves, she sat on the bench, clutched her purse, and waited.

When the door on the other side of the partition opened, Graham shuffled into the room sandwiched between two burly guards. Gloria immediately burst into tears, choking out the same question again and again. "Jack," she asked, "why did you ever sign that confession?" Graham mumbled an inaudible reply and looked away, shivering in his light cotton prisoner's garb as a gust of cold air blew into the room from between the bars of an open window. Gloria continued to weep, bemoaning the hopelessness of the situation. "No matter what happens, we'll be penniless and unable to support the children."

A guard standing behind her soon interrupted the one-sided conversation. Trembling as she stood to leave, Gloria looked back through the metal screen and watched as the guards led her husband away.

Although she left the jail without receiving an answer to her question about the confession, Gloria had unwittingly planted the seed of an idea that would grow to become the focal point of the entire case.

In 1955, Colorado's death penalty statute prohibited the execution of any person convicted "on circumstantial evidence alone." In a string of decisions interpreting this provision, the Colorado Supreme Court had consistently ruled that the ultimate penalty could be imposed only when a conviction was based on eyewitness testimony or evidence of the accused's confession.

Bert Keating had already publicly acknowledged that he did not have an eyewitness. Despite the best efforts of Roy Moore and the other FBI agents, not a single person had been located who could testify that Graham had placed a bomb in his mother's suitcase.

Without Graham's confession, the maximum possible penalty would be life imprisonment.

## CHAPTER SIX

# *"You're no dummy."*

B Y 8:30 A.M. ON THE MORNING of Thursday, November 17, more than two hundred people were waiting on the fourth floor of the Denver City and County Building, "the biggest crowd in Denver District Court history," according to the *Rocky Mountain News*. Those who had arrived early—mostly women, elderly men, and college students—stood within view of the frosted glass doors leading to the courtroom. Those who had underestimated the demand for seats were relegated to the far end of a line that snaked back around the corner to the center of the building. As the appointed hour drew near, the murmured exchange of predictions and theories increased in volume, echoing off the marble-lined walls of the broad corridor.

When at last the bailiff opened the doors, the spectators streamed into the courtroom. Men and women scrambled for the wooden pews closest to the front, abandoning all decorum and ignoring the bailiff's shouted pleas to "fill up the seats on the far side first." In less than a minute, there was not a single vacant space in the gallery. The bailiff ushered those who had been left standing back out into the hallway.

A few blocks away, John Gilbert Graham was shaving with the jail's communal electric razor in the "holding tank," a special cell reserved for inmates traveling to court. When he finished, a sheriff's deputy handed him his suit, shirt, shoes, and—despite concerns that Graham might be entertaining thoughts of suicide—a navy necktie embroidered with three small florets.* At 8:45 A.M., four plainclothes deputies escorted Graham from the jail and helped him into the backseat of a county vehicle for the short drive along Colfax Avenue.

---

* The day before, Warden Dolliver had told a *New York Times* reporter that Graham "hasn't been out of our sight one minute since they brought him here—we want to make sure he doesn't take the easy way out."

Arriving at the City and County Building a few minutes later, the deputies parked in front of the entrance on the west side and helped the shackled prisoner to his feet. In a replay of the scene that had occurred earlier in the week outside the federal courthouse, photographers swarmed around as the deputies directed Graham toward the elevator.

When the deputies stepped from the elevator onto the fourth floor, they gestured at the crowd to clear a path. The spectators obediently moved to the sides of the hallway, staring in silence as Graham slowly shuffled down the long corridor.

By drawing of lots, the case had been assigned to Judge Edward M. Keating.* However, because Judge Keating was home recovering from an illness, Judge James M. Noland was presiding in his place.

At 9:03 A.M., Judge Noland took the bench for his cameo appearance. He began by cautioning the onlookers against "any display of emotion whatsoever," warning that he would take "disciplinary action" against anyone who disobeyed his order. He then picked up the file and called the lone matter on the docket: "We have set for this morning case number 42604— the People of the State of Colorado versus John Gilbert Graham." Graham stared at the court reporter's stenographic machine, apparently more interested in the gadget than in the proceedings it was being used to record.

Jerome Strickland spoke first, explaining his interim status and asking for a thirty-day continuance to allow Graham time to retain the services of an experienced criminal defense attorney. Bert Keating objected, arguing that a delay of that length would be inappropriate for such an important case. Judge Noland agreed with the prosecutor and granted an eleven-day continuance, informing Graham that he should "be prepared to enter a plea at that time." To the great disappointment of the spectators, Judge Noland adjourned the hearing at 9:07 A.M.

As the deputies were preparing to lead Graham away, Strickland cupped a hand and leaned down toward his client's ear. "Don't make any statements to the press," he whispered.

---

* Judge Keating was not related to District Attorney Bert Keating.

In eleven years as a crime reporter for the *Rocky Mountain News,* Al "Nak" Nakkula had established his reputation as a tenacious investigator with a knack for breaking the unbreakable stories and obtaining the unobtainable interviews. He had also cemented his reputation as a difficult man with whom to work. Irascible and famously intolerant of superiors, Nakkula was a master of creative invective, including threats of posthumous revenge. "When I die," he once warned a city desk editor, "I'm going to be cremated and have my ashes thrown in

Al Nakkula. (Courtesy of *Rocky Mountain News*)

your face. There will be one piece that gets stuck, and you'll walk around for the rest of your life with a piece of Al Nakkula in your eye."

On the afternoon of Thursday, November 17, the editors of the *Rocky Mountain News* were once again reminded why it was that they tolerated Nakkula's cantankerousness. Through means that remain unclear to this day, the quarrelsome reporter had trumped his competitors at the *Post*—as well as all of the reporters from national publications who had descended on Denver—by landing the biggest scoop in the city: the first interview with John Gilbert Graham.

The meeting took place in Warden Dolliver's private office on the second floor of the jail. When the guards brought Graham into the room, he was wearing gray denim coveralls with the word *CAPIAS* conspicuously stenciled in several places.*

Graham sat in a chair across from the reporter and folded his cuffed hands in his lap. Nakkula did not waste any time with pleasantries. "Jack," he said, "I understand the FBI obtained a signed statement from you admitting you placed a bomb on that plane."

---

* A Latin term authorizing law enforcement officers "to take into custody the body."

Graham acknowledged the accuracy of the reporter's sources. "Yes, I signed a statement," he replied, "but it's not true. They told me they were going to put my wife in jail, and I'd better get it straightened out myself." Graham claimed that he had acted out of exhaustion and duress, complaining that the interview "started at about noon that Sunday and didn't stop until I signed that confession about 4 A.M. the next morning." He denied hiding a present in his mother's suitcase, explaining that he had "only bought some straps to put around the luggage because the hinges on the suitcase were breaking."

Graham told Nakkula that Daisie had had a premonition of her own death, and that she had "called everybody she could think of before she left."

"Do you mean," Nakkula asked, "your mother might have planted the dynamite in her own suitcase to take her own life? Has your mother ever mentioned taking her own life?"

"I won't answer that," Graham snapped.

"Well," Nakkula continued, "was your mother in ill health?"

"She was in the hospital a couple of times last summer," Graham replied, "but I don't know what for."

Nakkula, who had researched the family history in preparation for the interview, asked whether Daisie might have been "despondent over the deaths of her two previous husbands—your father and stepfather?"

Graham agreed that was a possibility, recalling that "she'd been sort of depressed or nervous since Earl died."

The veteran crime reporter could not conceal his annoyance. "Look, Jack," he said, "you've had a couple of years of college, you're no dummy. Do you think the FBI is lying? Do you realize there are forty-four people dead? The FBI said you caused their deaths. You've been charged with murder."

Graham was unruffled. "Sure," he said, "but I didn't do it and I don't know how it happened."

On Friday morning, the *Rocky Mountain News* trumpeted Nakkula's exclusive interview with a banner headline: "DYNAMITER CHANGES HIS STORY."

Reading the morning paper, Bert Keating realized that the recantation was a double-edged sword. By providing such a detailed repudiation of his confession, Graham had undermined his own best defense. At a press conference, Keating announced that he would call Al Nakkula to testify as a witness at trial, explaining that "any insanity plea now will be inconsistent with the statements Graham made to the reporter."

To Al Nakkula, the news of the forthcoming subpoena was, in all likelihood, as welcome as a nomination for a journalism award—a delightfully public validation of his skill as a reporter.

In the 1950s, the competition between the *Rocky Mountain News* and the *Denver Post* resembled a blood feud, a daily battle for readers fought with such ferocity that reporters from the two papers rarely socialized with members of the opposing camp. The editors of the *Denver Post*, a broadsheet billing itself as the "Voice of the Rocky Mountain Empire," regarded the *Rocky Mountain News* as an inferior publication, and their disdain for the tabloid-style competitor undoubtedly compounded their sense of indignation at Al Nakkula's triumph. The editors needed a similar

Isaac "Zeke" Scher. (Courtesy of Zeke Scher)

interview for the afternoon edition of the *Post* to prevent the *Rocky* from establishing itself as the newspaper with the better coverage of the Graham case. With only a few hours remaining before the noon deadline, they were counting on their talented reporter who covered the Denver courts—Zeke Scher.

He had been born as Isaac Scher, and many who knew this assumed the name "Zeke" was a hard pronunciation of the second syllable of his given name. In fact, the nickname had been bestowed upon him in 1939 by childhood playmates who compared his skills as a baseball player to those of Zeke Bonura, at that time the first baseman for the New York Giants. Later, as a journalism student at Washington & Lee University, Scher resurrected the nickname and began using it for his byline as a reporter. He was still using the name two years later when—after a stint writing for a newspaper in Lewiston, Montana—he landed a position with the *Denver Post*. And it was this same name, more than that of any other reporter, that would ultimately become intertwined with the Graham case.

At their first meeting that Friday morning, Scher asked Graham about the confession. Graham denied any responsibility for the bombing, again asserting that he had not "put anything into my mother's luggage." Repeating the claim he had made to Nakkula, Graham said he had confessed because he was "so confused," telling Scher that "they had something Gloria signed, and they said would put her in jail for lying to a federal officer if I did not sign the confession." At one point, Graham said he did not even recall signing the written confession.

Scher posed a hypothetical, asking Graham what punishment he would like to see imposed against the bomber.

"Death, I suppose," Graham replied, "but I'm not in that spot."

In his confession to the FBI agents, Graham had said that he obtained the parts for the bomb from a man he knew only as "Karl." Graham had described Karl as being "about twenty-eight to thirty-five years old," "six feet tall," and a "flashy dresser." He had "light brown or blond hair" that he "combed straight back in a wave," "perfect teeth," and "large hands." He "spoke with a German accent," he "did not smoke," and he "knew a lot about explosives."

Graham claimed he had first met Karl in September at Saliman's, a bar on Larimer Street in lower downtown Denver. According to Graham, on October 7, the day after the United Air Lines plane crashed on Medicine Bow Peak, he and Karl discussed the recent air disaster while drinking a few beers. Karl thought the plane might have been brought down by a bomb, and he told Graham how such a device could be constructed.

Graham said he next met with Karl at Saliman's on October 11. According to Graham, he had told Karl that he "wanted to kill someone that was on a plane that he didn't like." Karl offered to sell him the necessary components, and the two men agreed to meet the next day at the Crown-A drive-in.

Graham said Karl had arrived for the meeting in a "1950 green Buick two-door sedan" carrying a "small army-type ditty bag" containing twenty-five sticks of dynamite, a timer, three primer caps, and a battery. Graham also said he and Karl had tested the timer by hooking the battery to one of the primer caps and wrapping it in several towels. They placed the bundle in a metal trash can and detonated the cap using the timer and battery. Karl instructed Graham to "take out all the trip insurance policies that he could" and purportedly demanded "fifty percent of any of the money he obtained." Graham said Karl had "threatened to turn me in if I didn't pay him this money."

At their final meeting, which Graham claimed took place on October 29, "Karl told me that he was not sure the bomb would work in a suitcase." Graham said Karl had told him he would "get in touch with me concerning his share of the insurance money." According to Graham, he never heard from Karl again.

None of the FBI agents believed this tale, particularly since Graham's physical description of the mysterious Karl was strikingly similar to his earlier description of the merchandise peddler who had supposedly sold him the stolen X-acto tool kit. The agents were convinced Graham had acted alone. However, they could not prove it until they learned where he had obtained all of the components for the bomb.

The first break had come within hours of Graham's arrest. Joseph Grande, a salesman at the Ryall Electrical Supply Company, a wholesale distributor located at 500 Lincoln Street in Denver, saw Graham's photograph in the *Denver Post* and immediately recognized him as the recent purchaser of an electric timer. Within minutes of receiving Grande's call, several FBI agents were at the front counter of the Ryall Electrical store listening to the salesman's account of his first meeting with Graham.

On October 17, a man identifying himself as "Jack" had come in and said "that he was an employee of the Colorado-Texas Pump Company, and that he was in Denver to buy a timing device for a six-volt pump circuit" for a project in Utah. Grande showed the young man a catalog from the M. H. Rhodes Company in Hartford, Connecticut, and helped him select "a one-hour, hand-wound timer that he thought would do the job." Because the man said he needed the timer immediately, Grande telegrammed his order for the $5.12 item with instructions to ship it by air parcel post.

On October 19, a timer arrived, but it was not the one Grande had ordered. Grande had requested an "on" timer that could be set to close a circuit and activate an electrical device after a period of time; the timer the Rhodes Company had shipped was an "off" timer that would open a circuit and deactivate an appliance when the time expired. Grande sent a second telegram to correct the order and called Jack at the phone number listed on the invoice to apologize for the delay. Grande offered to pay to have the timer shipped to the job site, but the young man explained that his living expenses were being paid by the Colorado-Texas Pump Company and that "it was not a personal hardship for him to stay in Denver" until the new timer arrived.

On October 24, Grande received the correct timer and called again. To his surprise, a woman answered the phone and informed him that Jack had gone hunting. "Well," asked Grande, "would you tell him his timer has arrived?" The woman agreed to pass along the message.

On Wednesday, October 26, the man Grande knew only as "Jack" came to Ryall Electrical and picked up the timer. However, he returned two days later and asked to swap it for the sixty-minute "off" timer that had originally been shipped by mistake. Grande thought it was an odd request, but he exchanged the two timers and put the "on" timer back in his inventory.

Grande was positive that "Jack" was John Gilbert Graham, and he showed the agents the sales slip for the timer he sold to the Colorado-Texas Pump Company. The phone number on the invoice was West 5-7332—the home telephone number of John and Gloria Graham.

The agents were encouraged by the discovery, but they were also perplexed. In his confession, Graham had said he set the timer to close the circuit between the battery and the blasting caps after ninety minutes. The agents asked Grande about these discrepancies. Grande explained that a person with mechanical aptitude could easily convert an "off" timer to an "on" timer with a screwdriver and a pair of pliers. He also told the agents that these same tools could be used to extend the amount of time on the clock.

For the next five days, the FBI agents kept the information about the Ryall Electrical Supply Company from leaking to the newspapers. However, on Saturday, November 19, the front page of the *Rocky Mountain News* featured a large photograph of a sixty-minute timer beneath a banner headline announcing another scoop by Al Nakkula: "SOURCE FOUND FOR PLANE BOMB CLOCK." In the accompanying article describing the timer purchase, Nakkula tantalized his readers by posing the "still unanswered" question: where did Graham get the twenty-five sticks of dynamite?

Not long after the Saturday edition of the *Rocky Mountain News* landed on doorsteps throughout the city, Zeke Scher was at his desk in the newsroom of the *Denver Post* dividing up a stack of Colorado phone books with his colleague,

George McWilliams. Scanning through the yellow pages, the two reporters made up a list of every business in the state that might possibly stock explosives. Then they began making calls. Throughout the day, Scher and McWilliams repeatedly heard the same thing—the employees had already spoken with the FBI agents and had told them they had not sold any dynamite to Graham. The two reporters were about to give up when McWilliams called the Brown Mercantile Store in Kremmling and spoke with the owner, Lyman Brown.

McWilliams asked Brown whether his business sold dynamite.

Brown said he stocked the DuPont brand in three different concentrations of nitroglycerin.

"Have you spoken with the FBI?" asked McWilliams.

Brown said he had not.

"Well," asked McWilliams, "have you seen the photographs of John Gilbert Graham in the newspaper?"

Brown said he had, and that he had also met Graham a few times when Graham was attending school in Kremmling.

"Have you ever sold him any dynamite?" McWilliams asked.

"No," replied Brown, "but if you'll hold the line for a moment or two I'll check with my clerks."

Brown returned to the phone a few minutes later. "I checked with my clerks and no one recalls the sale of any dynamite, but I have one clerk who is out to supper, and when he comes back, I'll check with him."

McWilliams asked Brown to call him collect and gave him the telephone number of the *Denver Post* newsroom.

Fifteen minutes later, Brown called McWilliams back. "I reconstructed it in my mind," he said, "and I did sell Graham some dynamite. It never dawned on me that he was the man I sold the dynamite to until you called." Brown's recovered recollections were quite detailed:

> He came into the store on a Saturday night in late October. He was dressed in an olive-drab khaki suit, very similar to what a hunter would wear, or a prospector. He walked up to the counter and I said, "May I help you?" He asked me if I sold dynamite. And I said, "Yes, would you like regular or ditching?" He said, "Regular," and I asked him, "How much?" I believe he said twenty sticks, though it could have been twenty-five. I went into the back room, opened the magazine, took out the dynamite with 45 percent nitroglycerin, brought it back to the scales, which is approximately in the middle of the sales room, put the dynamite on the scales, and went up to the front of the store and retrieved a small

cardboard box. I brought the box back to the check stand, noted the
amount of the sale of the dynamite, and put it in the box.

He asked me, "Do you have any blasting caps? And I said, "Yes, we do."
We ordinarily don't sell them except in box lots of fifty, but I happened
to have a box of caps that we had broken open before. I informed him
that I had an open box of caps with sixteen-foot wires, and if he wanted
them he might have them. I asked him how many he wanted, and he said,
"Two." I went back to a different part of the store in the back where we
kept the caps, opened the box, took out two blasting caps, brought them
back, and wrapped them up in a piece of paper very gently. I handed
them to him and said, "Be careful with these, they're dangerous. Don't
carry them with the dynamite." He put them in the pocket.

"What are you doing," I asked, "some prospecting?" He said, "Yeah,"
paid me for his purchases, and left the store.

McWilliams thanked the shopkeeper for the information and assured
him he would pass it along to the FBI.

On Sunday, it was the *Post*'s turn to crow. Scher and McWilliams had
scooped the *Rocky Mountain News,* the national press, and—even more im-
pressively—the FBI. In a front page article describing Graham's dynamite
purchase, Bert Keating was quoted complimenting the two *Post* reporters
for providing "the telling link in the state's case which will send the mass
killer to the lethal chamber."

Despite the mounting evidence, Gloria Graham was standing by her husband. She would not accept the idea that he could have put a bomb on the
plane. "I'll believe he is innocent unless he is proven guilty," she said, pledg-
ing she would remain "loyal to him, as every wife should be toward her
husband." In an interview broadcast on radio station KIMN, she pleaded
with the listeners not to believe everything they were reading in the *Denver
Post* and the *Rocky Mountain News*. "The newspapers have made my husband
look like a mad dog wandering the streets," she protested, "[but] he's been
very good to me, and he has been a good father to the children."

On Sunday evening, she made her second trip to the jail and gave her husband a photograph of herself to keep in his cell. She also delivered news
about the couple's two children. For the first time, Warden Dolliver saw Jack
Graham smile.

Patricia Lipke,
Gerald G. Lipke.

There was no smile on the face of Father Lawrence O'Connell, the priest for the Saint Gabriel Church of Pittsburgh. Three students in his parish school had lost both of their parents on Flight 629. The Lipke brothers— ages eleven, nine, and seven—had no other family in Pennsylvania, and they were about to be sent to Portland, Oregon, to live with their uncle.

Earlier in the week, several students at the Saint Gabriel school had approached Father O'Connell and asked whether there was anything they could do for their departing classmates. The priest had told the youths he would speak with the oldest of the three brothers and propose a rosary service for the souls of Mr. and Mrs. Lipke.

When Father O'Connell approached Jerry Lipke, the boy had only one question. "Father," he asked, "couldn't we say the rosary, too, for the man who put the dynamite on the plane and killed my mother and father? Maybe God might forgive this man and make him a saint someday to be in heaven with my dad and mom."

## CHAPTER SEVEN

# *"I will beat the gas chamber."*

IF DONALD O. RAUSCH HAD AGREED to help the *Denver Post* reporters with their ill-conceived idea, the photograph would have been extraordinary—an image that undoubtedly would have appeared on the front page of the paper as the reporters had hoped. But it was not to be. Rausch, an explosives expert who taught at the Colorado School of Mines in Golden, apologetically informed the *Post* reporters who had contacted him that detonating twenty-five sticks of dynamite on one of the mesas towering high above the Coors brewery "would create consternation for miles around." He did, however, agree to educate the reporters about explosives.

Rausch explained that blasting caps—small explosive devices used to detonate sticks of dynamite—were the cause of many serious accidents. The tiny tin tubes, one-quarter inch in diameter and one and one-half inches long, contained a base load of mercury fulminate that could easily detonate if mishandled—even "a slight jolt might do the trick." Rausch told the reporters that dynamite was far more stable, and that it could take a "tremendous jar without going off." The half-pound cylindrical sticks of explosive, each of which was eight inches long and one and one-quarter inches in diameter, were produced by packing nitroglycerin in a filling of wood pulp, a technology first developed by Alfred Nobel, the Swedish inventor who discovered how to stabilize nitroglycerin and patented the idea in 1867.*

When detonated, the explosive force was tremendous—a single stick would be more than enough to destroy an aircraft. Twenty-five sticks was, in the parlance of the Cold War, overkill.

---

* Nobel called his invention dynamite, after the Greek word "dynamis," meaning "power."

On Monday morning, Lyman Brown was in the basement of the Denver County Jail anxiously waiting to view a lineup put together by Ray Humphreys, the chief investigator for the Denver District Attorney's Office who had filed the 1951 check forgery case against Graham. When Brown entered the small room, he saw seven dark-haired prisoners in jail clothing. All of the men were approximately the same age, height, and weight. One by one, the inmates stepped from the lineup and walked back and forth in front of the Kremmling merchant. Brown carefully examined each of the men before telling Humphreys he was positive the dynamite purchaser was the person standing in the middle of the lineup: John Gilbert Graham.

After participating in the identification procedure, Graham was no longer loquacious, answering all press inquiries with some variation of "I don't know," "I don't remember," or "you'll have to see my attorney about that." Warden Dolliver was not surprised by Graham's reticence. "I imagine he recognized Brown," he told the reporters.

Although Brown was certain about his identification of Graham, it soon became apparent there was a problem: Brown was equally certain the sale had occurred on the night of October 29. However, Graham had an airtight alibi for that evening—he and Gloria had been in Denver eating dinner with another couple, a claim the FBI agents had already verified. There were only two possibilities: either Lyman Brown was confused about the date of the sale, or he had misidentified Graham as the purchaser.

On Tuesday, Bert Keating drove to Stapleton Airfield to make a "thorough inspection" of a United Air Lines DC-6B and become "completely familiar with the terms, and with areas of the plane referred to by the expert witnesses who will testify at trial." Accompanying the district attorney was Gregory Mueller, the thirty-nine-year-old chief deputy whom Keating had selected to help him prepare the case.

Like Keating, Greg Mueller was a talented trial lawyer who enjoyed working in a courtroom. He had begun his legal career as a trial judge advocate in the U.S. Army before joining the Denver District Attorney's Office in 1950. Mueller had been with the office only three years when Keating promoted him to chief deputy. Since that time, the two men had worked together on several high-profile trials, including the case against LeRoy Leick, the man convicted for the insurance-related murder of his wife based on information provided by Lou Messervy, the potato-chip salesman who had given the FBI information about the suspicious explosion at the Crown-A drive-in.

Looking up at the gleaming plane, Mueller and Keating tried to envision the explosion that had felled Flight 629. The two prosecutors paid close attention as United Air Lines representatives pointed out the different parts of the aircraft and explained how baggage was loaded into the two lower holds. Keating and Mueller took turns climbing a ladder to examine the inside of the number four baggage compartment, where the bomb had detonated. After completing their inspection of the intact DC-6B, the two men walked to the nearby warehouse and examined the reassembled fuselage, their understanding of the giant jigsaw puzzle greatly improved by having viewed an undamaged aircraft.

On Wednesday, Lyman Brown concluded that it was "conceivable" he had sold Graham the dynamite on Saturday, October 22. Brown said he had checked his records and determined that he did not have an invoice for the sale. However, he was "almost sure" the sale had occurred on October 29 because he had been in the back room preparing his end-of-the-month payroll when Graham came into the store. Brown thought Graham had paid him $4.40, "and, if I recall correctly—but I'm not sure—he gave me a $5 bill."

Bert Keating said he remained "convinced Brown sold Graham the dynamite." "We didn't push him to try to refresh his memory or try to alter his identification in any respect—we only asked him to recall what he could." The discrepancy concerning the dates was a complication, but it was one the jury could sort out at trial.

Keating's more immediate problem was the fact that Jerome Strickland still had not found a lawyer who was willing to represent Graham. Strickland had approached several prominent criminal defense attorneys, but the lawyers—whom Strickland did not want to identify because it "could be touchy as far as the kid's chances are concerned"—had all declined the case. The stumbling block was money. Under Colorado law, Graham would not be entitled to any share of his mother's estate if he was convicted, and it was unclear whether any of his relatives had the ability, or the inclination, to fund his legal defense. Until Graham was properly represented, the case would remain at a standstill.

Frank Hays—another lawyer who had agreed to help Strickland in the search for replacement counsel—was concerned that Graham might not be competent to stand trial. "We told him not to make any statements because they could be used against him," Hays said. "Yet he signed waivers in county jail to permit interviews and pictures. I don't know if he knew what he was doing." Hays petitioned Judge Keating to allow a psychiatrist to examine Graham "to determine whether he is mentally alert enough to talk to reporters, and also on his general conduct since being in jail. We have serious questions about his ability to understand and comprehend, and we are trying to protect his rights."

Bert Keating thought Hays's motion was "rather irregular because no plea has been entered in the case," but he was unwilling to object. "We are not going to interfere with the preparation of his defense in any way." Nevertheless, Judge Keating refused the request. "The two attorneys have entered the case for one special purpose only," he explained, "and that is to obtain adequate counsel for Graham. Their actions are to be confined to that purpose only."

Thursday was Thanksgiving. Although Graham remained in an isolation cell, he received the same meal as the other 650 inmates: two pieces of fried chicken, dressing and cranberry sauce, mashed potatoes and gravy, string beans, butter, two slices of bread, coffee, and a wedge of pumpkin pie. Warden Dolliver assumed that Graham would enjoy the holiday dinner since nothing had "ever been taken out of his cell uneaten" before. However, for the first time Graham had no appetite. After nibbling at the heaping servings of holiday food, he slid the tray back out into the hallway. "I'm not a heavy eater," he told the guard. The deputy, who had seen Graham consume "all his previous meals with apparent relish," took the tray away without questioning the explanation.

The following morning, a columnist writing in the *Rocky Mountain News* wondered whether the accused mass murderer was unable to eat because he was "thinking of the empty dinner plates in homes across the country—empty places representing the forty-three persons who died aboard the plane along with his mother?"

It would be several more months before the FBI disclosed that Daisie King had refused her son's request to stay in Denver for Thanksgiving.

Because Graham had an ironclad alibi for October 29, the FBI agents continued looking for other witnesses who might be able to connect him with dynamite purchased elsewhere. In an interview with Mr. and Mrs. Roy Bray, owners of the Morrison Uranium Company, the agents learned that a young man had stored twenty sticks of dynamite at the Brays' mining business in early September, only three days before the gas explosion that had damaged the Crown-A drive-in. Although the young man had said he would return and retrieve the dynamite, he never did, and the Brays had used the explosives for their mining operation.

On Friday morning, investigators reassembled the seven-man lineup in the basement of the county jail "to check out the possibility that Graham may have had another source of dynamite." However, after viewing the lineup, the Brays said they did not know if Graham was the same young man who had stored the explosives at their mine. It was a loose end—either a coincidence or a missed clue that would never be satisfactorily explained.

Later that day, at the conclusion of a lengthy closed-door meeting with attorneys Strickland and Hays, Judge Keating announced that "after an exhaustive inventory of the finances of Graham, the court is satisfied from the report of the attorneys that Graham is an indigent person within the meaning of the law." Graham's only unencumbered assets were his wrecked truck and his 1951 Plymouth. "He has some equity in his home," the judge acknowledged, "but this is in joint tenancy with his wife." Graham's sister did not have the ability to pay her brother's legal expenses, and Judge Keating did not have the authority to order her to borrow against her anticipated inheritance. The State of Colorado would have to bear the expense of Graham's defense.

Due to the complexity of the case and the substantial resources of the prosecution team, Judge Keating wanted to appoint more than one experienced attorney for Graham. It was a prudent precaution. However, in making his selections, the jurist neglected to consider the importance of choosing lawyers with compatible personalities and practice styles.

The first attorney Judge Keating recruited was John J. Gibbons, a forty-one-year-old resident of Cherry Hills who had represented hundreds of criminal defendants since graduating from Westminster Law School in 1938. Although Gibbons had an extremely successful practice, he was a controversial figure in the Denver legal community. Behind his back, other lawyers derisively referred to him as "Chesty" due to his swaggering gait and bombastic ways—and this was one of the kinder things they said. He was also described as a "poseur," a "pompous son-of-a-bitch," and a "vain man" who was "enamored with himself" and his appearance. At a time when Colorado attorneys favored conservative suits and haircuts, the flamboyant Gibbons styled his hair and outfitted himself with a colorful wardrobe of designer clothing. When he appeared in front of a jury, he would emphasize his points by stabbing at the air with his glasses, waving the spectacles professorially to project a false air of intellectualism.

Prior to his appointment to the Graham case, Gibbons's most high-profile client had been Gene Dukes, the twenty-year-old Georgia farmhand LeRoy Leick had enlisted to help kill his wife after he was turned down by Lou Messervy. At the March 1954 trial, Bert Keating and Greg Mueller had presented strong evidence proving Leick and Dukes staged a robbery and took turns strangling Evelyn Leick until she was dead, and in his closing remarks Keating had urged the jury to impose the death penalty, referring to Dukes as the "merchant of murder" and a "mad-dog killer." However, Gibbons and another attorney portrayed Dukes as a "quiet and submissive youth"—a "little country boy who came to town" and was "talked into" committing the crime by the diabolical Leick. It was an effective defense strategy: the jurors found Dukes guilty, but they recommended a sentence of life imprisonment. Speaking with reporters afterward, Gibbons made no mention of his co-counsel. "I saved the boy's life," he immodestly proclaimed.

Within hours of his appointment to the Graham case, Gibbons made another brash statement, a prediction clearly intended to needle Bert Keating and Greg Mueller. "I will beat the gas chamber," Gibbons confidently predicted, "just as I did in the Dukes case."

In contrast, Charles S. Vigil accepted his appointment to the Graham case without making any grand pronouncements. "I know nothing about the matter except what I have read in the papers," he said, humbly characterizing his representation of the most reviled man in the state as "a duty one must take as a practicing attorney before the Colorado Bar."

Like Bert Keating, Vigil was an active participant in Democratic party politics who had spent much of his career as a prosecutor. After graduating from law school at the University of Colorado in 1935, Vigil had worked as a deputy district attorney in his hometown of Trinidad, Colorado, a small city near the New Mexico border. In 1951, President Truman had appointed him United

States Attorney for the District of Colorado—the first Hispanic ever to hold the position. Vigil was well regarded during his time as Colorado's chief federal prosecutor, acquiring the nickname "Gangbuster" for his aggressive prosecution of two brothers with even more colorful nicknames: "Checkers" and "Flip Flop" Smaldone, the leaders of Denver's most renowned organized crime family.*

Although Judge Keating was willing to appoint only two attorneys at state expense, Vigil—who divided his time between law offices in Trinidad and Denver—obtained the judge's permission to use part of his own fee to pay for the services of Paul Weadick, a younger lawyer who had assisted Vigil with several other cases, most notably a recent murder trial in which the two lawyers had persuaded the jury to find their client not guilty by reason of insanity despite contrary testimony from both of the psychiatrists who had examined the man.

On Saturday morning, Judge Keating met with the three defense attorneys in his chambers, praising them as "the best defense team I could think of, and as outstanding lawyers as there are in Denver." The judge handed the attorneys a copy of the information charging Graham with a single count of murder. He also gave them one piece of advice: "avoid any unnecessary delays."

Taking the judge's instruction to heart, Gibbons, Vigil, and Weadick went directly to the county jail to see their client. In a conference room adjacent to the main lobby, the three lawyers sat across from Graham at a long wooden table divided by a partition rising about a foot from the surface. Speaking in a hushed tone so as not to be overheard by the guards, Vigil asked Graham several questions, including whether he had ever been treated for mental disorders. Graham said he had not, though he indicated he would be willing to submit to a psychiatric examination. After only twenty-two minutes, the attorneys departed, reassuring Graham that they would be with him when he appeared in court the following morning.

As the trio walked from the jail, John Gibbons could not resist the urge to speak with reporters. "I don't believe he's guilty," he said, explaining that the brief conversation with Graham had "convinced" him that "the boy is innocent of this charge."

---

* When President Eisenhower took office in 1953, Vigil refused to resign as United States attorney, arguing that he should be allowed to finish prosecuting the Smaldone brothers before he was replaced with a Republican appointee. President Eisenhower ousted him from office, and the Senate Judiciary Committee held a special full-day hearing to investigate Vigil's complaint that FBI agents in the Denver field office had penalized him for overstaying his welcome by refusing to help investigate an incident in which the Smaldone brothers tried to bribe one of the jurors hearing an income tax evasion case Vigil had filed against Checkers. The Senate hearing ended inconclusively.

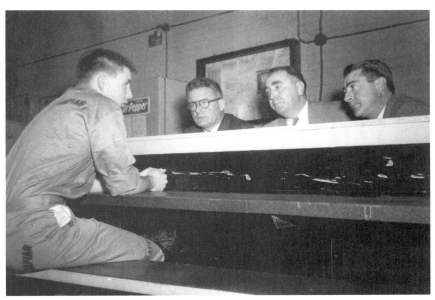

Graham meets with his attorneys. From left to right: John Gibbons, Charles Vigil, and Paul Weadick. (Courtesy of Denver Public Library, Western History Collection)

In a sign of the divisions that would later develop, Charles Vigil and Paul Weadick declined to comment.

The defense attorneys were not the only ones working through the weekend. On Sunday, Bert Keating visited the crash site northeast of Longmont. Wearing a Western shirt, bolo tie, and Stetson hat—an outfit that made him look more like the Greeley sheriff than the Denver district attorney—Keating walked through the sugar beet fields with two representatives of United Air Lines, who pointed out where the different sections of the plane had fallen. The prosecutor also inspected the parts of the plane that had not been removed, remnants encircled by a temporary fence that had been erected by the National Guardsmen who were still protecting the site twenty-four hours a day. At the conclusion of the tour, Keating spoke with reporters. "It's just as I expected," he said. "I just wanted to get the feel of the ground before we moved on in our preparation of the case."

In addition to readying the case for trial, Bert Keating was spending a great deal of his time juggling the many requests for television interviews. Since filing the charge against Graham, Keating had appeared several times on NBC and CBS news programs, national exposure that had prompted hundreds of people to write letters addressed to "Mr. Keating, District

Attorney, Denver." One man suggested the prosecutor seek a life sentence, insisting that the death penalty
would unfairly allow Graham to
"have his troubles over." However,
most of the letters expressed sentiments closer to those of a woman
who urged Keating to "relieve the
state of its worry by tying him to
twenty-five sticks of dynamite and
giving him ninety minutes to live."
Other letters communicated grief

Brad and Carol Bynum.

with no accompanying recommendation as to the appropriate punishment.
Writing from Amarillo, Texas, the parents of Brad Bynum struggled to describe their immeasurable loss: "We had our son and daughter-in-law with
us the last two weeks of their lives. We had the pleasure of knowing our
daughter-in-law for only two weeks, and we were, of course, looking forward to our grandchild as we had waited so long for our son to marry and
raise a family after having his life disrupted by two wars."

Graham was receiving letters, too. More than a dozen clerics from
around the country had written urging him to turn to prayer. Reverend
Robert S. Lutz, pastor of the Corona Presbyterian Church—the church
President Eisenhower attended when in Denver—wrote offering to visit
with Graham in jail and "lead him in prayer for the salvation of his soul." Although Graham did not accept the offer, he did continue his regular meetings
with Reverend Kellams, his minister from the Lakewood Methodist Church.

On Monday, Graham and his attorneys appeared before Judge Keating.
Once again, the courtroom was packed with spectators and reporters. And
once again, the hearing was a disappointment to the observers. Judge Keating took the bench, warned the crowd he would "not tolerate any demonstrations, sighing or outcries," granted the defense lawyers' request to
continue the case until December 9, and adjourned the proceeding only
seven minutes after it had begun. As the crowd filed out of the courtroom,
Judge Keating instructed Bert Keating and Greg Mueller to return at 2:00
P.M. to begin selecting the jury for the retrial of LeRoy Leick.

Speaking with reporters as Graham was led away for the return trip to the
jail, John Gibbons tipped his hand slightly, stating that he planned to file motions "attacking the information against Graham." However, in a rare moment
of taciturnity, he refused to elaborate on the grounds for the challenge.

That afternoon, the November 28 issues of *Time, Newsweek,* and *Life* magazines were delivered to homes and newsstands throughout the country. All three magazines featured stories on the Graham case. A *Time* article titled the "The Christmas Present" summarized the evidence against the "husky man" with the "perpetual hangdog look." In *Life*, the preeminent magazine of news photography, the incident was called "A Case of 44 Mid-air Murders." The magnitude of the crime was starkly illustrated with passport-size photographs of all forty-four victims, and an accompanying article poignantly comparing the deceased's "chance fellowship of travel" to that of the five fictional characters in Thornton Wilder's book *The Bridge of San Luis Rey.* *

*Newsweek* focused on the families of the victims. In a piece captioned "This Was Left Behind," Maxine White, the widow of copilot Don White, was quoted as saying that her husband had "died doing something he loved. That's one consolation." In answer to a question about how the loss was affecting her children, Mrs. White said two-year-old Cynthia was "too young to realize what happened, but Gerald is seven. He is in the second grade and he's taking it awful hard. He was a daddy's boy." The article also described the scene in Munford, Alabama, where Airman Jesse Sizemore—a former star on the high-school football team—had recently been laid to rest. "It was the biggest and the saddest funeral we've ever had in these parts," said one of his cousins. A neighbor said Sizemore's parents "aren't getting over it. And I don't think they ever will. He was their youngest boy."

---

* Set in Peru in 1714, *The Bridge of San Luis Rey* tells the story of a Franciscan missionary who witnesses the collapse of a rope bridge that sends five people plummeting to their deaths in a ravine far below. In a quest to understand why God chose to end the lives of the five individuals who perished, the missionary spends the next several years investigating the backgrounds and lives of the victims. The novel won the 1928 Pulitzer Prize for fiction.

## CHAPTER EIGHT

# *"We are all on the plane."*

O N DECEMBER 2, Gibbons, Vigil, and Weadick filed a petition asking that the court "permit doctors, psychiatrists, and specialists to examine and treat the defendant as his personal physicians and psychiatrists as may be required, and to assist counsel."

In a separate motion, the attorneys sought dismissal of the case on three separate grounds:

1. That the information does not state facts sufficient upon which a conviction can be had.

2. That the court does not have jurisdiction in this cause of action.

3. That there is improper venue, and for that reason the cause is improperly before this court.

Explaining the first claim to reporters, Gibbons asserted that Bert Keating had made a critical mistake by having Pat Patterson sign the affidavit supporting the charging document: according to Gibbons, because the United Air Lines president did not "know anything about the facts surrounding the perpetration of the offense," he had no basis for giving a jurat.*

Anticipating the first real battle in the case, the newspapers and television stations assigned numerous cameramen to cover the December 9 hearing on the defense team's motions.

They needn't have bothered.

For twenty years, a national controversy had been brewing concerning whether to allow photographs to be taken during court proceedings. The debate—the outcome of which would ultimately be greatly influenced by the trial of John Gilbert Graham—had begun two decades earlier in a small courthouse in the town of Flemington, New Jersey.

---

*A statement attesting to personal knowledge of the facts alleged.

After a nationally publicized manhunt lasting almost three years, a German immigrant named Bruno Richard Hauptmann was captured and charged with kidnapping and murdering the infant son of Colonel Charles Lindbergh, the revered aviation pioneer. In January 1935, Hauptmann was put on trial in a circus-like atmosphere so prejudicial to the rights of the defendant that novelist Edna Ferber declared it made her "want to resign as a member of the human race."

More than 500 spectators and reporters had jammed into a courtroom designed to hold just 260 people. Judge Thomas W. Trenchard lost all control over the mob of peanut-eating spectators, repeatedly allowing laughter from the gallery to interrupt the testimony of witnesses. Newspapers published at the time described the trial as a "sideshow," a "jamboree," and a "freak show." Outside the courthouse, thousands of people gathered to listen to the prosecutors' inflammatory public statements and purchase souvenir miniature ladders resembling the one the kidnappers had used to gain access to the Lindbergh baby's nursery. Hauptmann was found guilty based on circumstantial evidence of questionable strength; in 1936, he was executed in the electric chair.

In the wake of the Hauptmann trial, blame for the unseemliness of the proceedings was unfairly directed at the courtroom photographers. Exaggerated reports began circulating indicating that dozens of obstreperous cameramen had wandered freely throughout the courtroom, brazenly taking photographs while the trial was in progress and discharging flashbulbs in the faces of witnesses. In fact, only 4 of the 130 photographers who were in attendance had been allowed into the courtroom each day, and during the entire five-week trial, there had only been two instances in which the cameramen had violated Judge Trenchard's order not to take photographs while the court was in session (and both of those transgressions had been committed surreptitiously).

Nevertheless, based on the overstated accounts of the disruptive photographers, in 1937 the American Bar Association passed Judicial Canon 35, a complete ban on courtroom photography designed to prevent the "improper publicizing of court proceedings." The rule was soon adopted, or followed in spirit, by all forty-eight states. Although a few trial judges continued to allow courtroom photography, no state explicitly condoned the practice.

In 1952, the American Bar Association amended Canon 35 to add a prohibition against television cameras:

Proceedings in court should be conducted with fitting dignity and decorum. The taking of photographs in the courtroom, during sessions of the court or recesses between sessions, and the broadcasting or televising of court proceedings are calculated to detract from the essential dignity of the proceedings, distract the witness in giving his testimony, degrade the court, and create misconceptions with respect thereto in the mind of the public and should not be permitted.

In 1954, a year after the Colorado Supreme Court had adopted the amended version of Canon 35 as a nonbinding recommendation, a *Denver Post* photographer smuggled a camera into the murder trial of LeRoy Leick and took several photographs to "prove that candid camera techniques make it possible to take news photos of a trial without upsetting the decorum of the court." The judges of the Denver District Court were outraged by the stunt, and they soon implemented their own rule forbidding all courtroom photography. However, the Colorado Supreme Court struck down the Denver ban, concluding it "constituted an invasion of freedom of the press."

The suspension of the Denver District Court rule left the question of courtroom photography to the discretion of individual trial judges. As a result, Judges Noland and Keating had both allowed television and still cameras to record the proceedings at John Gilbert Graham's first two court appearances. The photographers had not interfered with the hearings, and Judge Noland had even made a point of thanking the cameramen for following his "instructions and suggestions, and for their part in keeping order during the courtroom proceedings." However, Colorado Supreme Court Justice E. V. Holland saw the television footage and persuaded his colleagues that the case was becoming a "spectacle." On Thursday, September 8, he called Judge Keating with instructions not to allow any further courtroom photography.

When the deputies brought John Gilbert Graham into the crowded courtroom on Friday, December 9, there was a third prosecutor seated next to Bert Keating and Greg Mueller. Thin, gray-haired, and dapperly dressed, sixty-three-year-old Max D. Melville looked, according to one reporter, "somewhat British." He was not. A native of Durango who had acquired his sartorial habits while attending Yale Law School, Melville was known as "Mr. Law" for his scholarship. Two of his books—*Criminal Law in Colorado* and *Criminal Evidence*—were relied on by judges and attorneys throughout the

Left to right: John Gibbons, Gloria Graham, and Helen Hablutzel outside the courtroom. (*Rocky Mountain News,* Bill Peery, Courtesy of Denver Public Library, Western History Collection, Call # RMN 2608)

state, and Melville used the works as texts for the criminal law classes he taught at the University of Denver Law School, the Westminster Law School, and the Denver Police Academy. In addition to his keen intellect, Melville was endowed with a "prodigious and photographic memory." He "could not only cite book and page where a case could be found, but could also relate the place on the page where the principle of law appeared." Although Melville was a staunch Republican, he was so talented that Bert Keating disregarded party affiliations and appointed him Assistant District Attorney, the most senior unelected position in the office.

Responding to Vigil's arguments, Melville had no difficulty persuading Judge Keating that venue was proper in both Denver County—the place where the bomb allegedly had been constructed and secreted aboard the plane—and Weld County, the place where the victims had died. Relying on similar reasoning, Melville convinced the judge that there was no merit to Vigil's argument that the federal court had exclusive jurisdiction over the offense. Turning to Gibbons's claim that Patterson's signature rendered the charging document defective, Melville dismissed the idea as "an absurd contention," arguing that "no person except Graham can testify to his personal knowledge that a bomb was placed on the plane." Judge Keating agreed and scrawled the word "denied" across the top of the defense motion.

The assistant district attorney also objected to the defense lawyers' request for the appointment of psychiatrists to treat Graham before he entered his plea. "There are plenty of physicians to examine him at the county jail if he is ill," Melville stated, warning that any type of treatment would give rise to a doctor-patient privilege that would prevent the prosecutors from calling the physicians to testify at trial. Melville maintained that Graham was "no different than anyone else, except for the wholesale slaughter he committed." At the prosecutor's suggestion, and over the loud objections of the defense attorneys, Judge Keating proceeded directly to arraignment. After reading the one-page information to Graham, the judge directed him to enter his plea.

"I'm certainly not guilty," Graham stated, "and not guilty by reason of insanity at the time of the alleged offense, and since."

Judge Keating accepted the alternative pleas, directed that a separate trial be held on the issue of Graham's sanity before the trial to determine his guilt or innocence, and ordered Graham to the Colorado Psychopathic Hospital for a thirty-day examination, the maximum period allowed by statute.

Each year, the judges of the Denver District Court rotated their division assignments, swapping their dockets according to a set of longstanding procedures designed to promote fairness to both the judges and the litigants. It was a dry administrative matter that rarely received any attention. However, in December 1955 the process became an undignified competition to preside over the Graham case.

Of the nine judges on the Denver District Court, six were Democrats and three were Republicans.* Because the Democrats held the majority and controlled the assignment of divisions, it was clear the Graham case would not be assigned to one of the Republican judges.

---

* In 1966, the voters of Colorado amended the state constitution and did away with partisan judicial elections. Under the current system, a bipartisan nominating commission recommends three candidates for each judicial vacancy, the governor selects an appointee, and the judge then participates in periodic elections limited to the question of whether he or she should be retained in office.

According to custom, the two judges with the least amount of seniority were to be assigned to the court's criminal divisions when the rotation went into effect in January 1956. The two judges slated to move to the criminal courts were both newcomers to the bench: Judge Joseph M. McDonald, a Democrat who had been elected in November 1954, and Judge H. Joe Rawlinson, a member of the same party who had been appointed in 1955 to fill a vacancy created by the death of a judge. Normally, Judge McDonald—as the slightly

Prosecutors Max Melville, Greg Mueller, and Bert Keating. (*Denver Post*, reproduced by Colorado Historical Society)

more senior judge—would have been entitled to choose whichever criminal division he preferred. However, Judge Rawlinson had been lobbying for the assignment to Division Eight—the division overseeing Graham's case—because he thought the publicity from handling the Graham case would increase his odds of retaining his seat on the court in the special election that was to be held in November 1956.

Rawlinson's bid for the Graham trial was considered a long shot because the district captains of the Denver Democratic Party had not endorsed his appointment to the bench, and the Democratic judges of the District Court were not inclined to thwart the party bosses by bestowing a plum assignment on a disfavored candidate. But Rawlinson was not the only judge who wanted to use the Graham case to improve his prospects at the polls. Judges Albert T. Frantz and Edward C. Day—both Democrats with seniority to McDonald and Rawlinson—had already announced their plans to run for the Colorado Supreme Court in the 1956 election. Frantz and Day had also made it known that they wanted to handle the Graham case, and there was public speculation that the two judges might "lock horns" over the issue in "an embarrassing intra-party battle."

In addition to these political concerns, the more senior Democratic judges were worried that adherence to the regular rotation schedule could subject the entire court to criticism or ridicule. Although McDonald and Rawlinson had both served as judges on the Municipal Court, the only criminal cases they had handled were misdemeanors. Neither man had ever presided over a single felony trial, and the other judges had serious reservations about assigning a novice to conduct the most important criminal trial in state history.

On Friday, December 9, the six Democratic judges met behind closed doors to discuss the matter. According to an account of the meeting that was later leaked to *Denver Post* reporter Zeke Scher, when seated around a table face-to-face, none of the judges was willing to admit that the airplane bombing case should be treated differently than any other matter. Nor were any of the judges willing to question the capabilities of any of their colleagues. By default, the judges voted unanimously to rotate divisions according to the established procedure: Judge Joseph M. McDonald would take over the Graham case from Judge Keating in January.

That same day, the media organizations that had been shut out of the Graham proceedings decided to take their case to the public. Harold E. Fellows, the president of the National Association of Radio and Television Broadcasters, circulated a copy of the telegram he had sent to the Colorado Supreme Court:

> Broadcasters, along with other media, have been fighting for access to public proceedings not for selfish reasons, but because we believe the people have a right to see and hear their government in operation. No one will deny that each of us as citizens has the right to attend a trial and witness the proceedings, as long as space permits. What about that portion of the public that is not able to be physically present but wants to know what is going on?

Hugh B. Terry, the president of Denver station KLZ-TV, recorded an editorial lambasting the court's decision, a scolding he broadcast for three consecutive nights during the evening news. Reading from a prepared statement, Terry appealed to the seven justices of the state's high court:

> Justice Holland said it was the feeling of the court that the Graham case had been given bad publicity, and it was being made into a spectacle. May

we respectfully ask if it is a function of the court to determine what is good or bad publicity, and how much or what type of reports of a hearing can be made to the public? On Friday, we were fully prepared to bring our audience pictures and voices of those involved in the case. Then came the blackout of visual recording—a barrier erected in the path of the free flow of information and the right of the people to know in the fullest degree what goes on in the courtrooms of the state.

As Fellows and Terry were launching their campaign against the ban of courtroom photography, some members of the public were beginning to question the excessive and inflammatory coverage of the case. In a letter to the *Denver Post,* one Boulder resident predicted that it would be impossible for Graham to get a fair trial:

> With the newspapers serving as prosecuting attorney, judge, and jury, Graham has already been tried and sentenced for the crime of murdering forty-four persons aboard the United Air Lines plane. . . . Only illiterate hermits—people who don't read the papers, listen to the radio, or watch television—could make up an impartial jury for the Graham case. . . . I am not asserting that Graham is innocent, but I do believe that his guilt or innocence should be determined by a court of law, not by newspapers sitting in judgment. Trial by newspaper may be good for circulation, but it is also a flagrant infringement on the rights of the individual.

Similarly, a writer from Englewood castigated the *Rocky Mountain News'* columnists for their one-sided coverage of the case: "Believe me, I have no time for murderers, for insurance, or for any other reason. Neither do I have time for newspaper columnists who assume a man's guilty before he is tried. . . . It took time to ferret out the cause of this disaster. It will take time to prosecute the perpetration of this ruinous crime."

Another writer took a broader view, linking the Graham case to the ongoing nuclear arms race:

> If it can be said there is any good to be found in the November 1 airplane tragedy, it is that most people are horrified by it. It is strange that we are not equally horrified at the many statements emanating from the Pentagon on our preparations for war.

This same sentiment was expressed somewhat more eloquently in *The Saturday Review* by Norman Cousins, the distinguished peace activist. In an essay titled "The World of John Gilbert Graham," Cousins used the bombing of Flight 629 as a platform for his Cold War criticisms:

We are all on the plane. The hold of the plane is already packed with explosives and detonators. A madman at the head of a nation can touch off the first big blast and the others will go off automatically.

· · ·

John Gilbert Graham is a monster, but he is also a miniaturist. He has given us diamond-size and diamond-sharp an image of the world in which we live. He has spelled out on the head of a pin the predicament of our species.

· · ·

If the world is not to belong to the John Gilbert Grahams sometime soon the central problem will have to be seen for what it is. The central problem is to tame the nation and to keep human life from becoming extraneous.

## CHAPTER NINE

# *"You couldn't put your arms around her."*

THE TREMENDOUS AMOUNT of publicity surrounding the Graham case was causing unusual problems for John Waters, the twenty-eight-year-old manager of the Sherman Plaza Garage. Waters—who bore a startling resemblance to John Gilbert Graham—first realized his looks were going to cause him difficulties on the day after the accused plane bomber made his heavily photographed trip from the FBI's office to the federal court-house. "I was riding the bus," Waters said, "and a man reading a newspaper suddenly stared at me, hurriedly thumbed to the picture of Graham, and then stared first at me, and then at the picture. It was most embarrassing."

Waters's friends kidded him about "assuming an alias" and "escaping from jail," and customers at the garage routinely commented on the many striking similarities, especially his facial features and short dark hair. One morning, Waters went into a café near the garage for breakfast. "When I walked in," he said, the waitress looked "really shook." He later found out why. "Apparently, she had been telling customers about Graham eating breakfast there occasionally."

Waters was tiring of the constant stares, but he was receiving little sympathy on the home front. "My wife and kids think it's funny," he said, adding that they were particularly amused when a used car dealer tried to hire him to work as a John Gilbert Graham look-alike for a sales promotion in which he would have been paraded "around the car lot in handcuffs."

On Saturday morning, ten heavily armed sheriff's deputies transported Graham from the Denver County Jail to the Colorado Psychopathic Hospital at the University of Colorado Medical Center campus. Located to the east of Colorado Boulevard on Eighth Avenue, the Psychopathic Hospital had been founded in 1925 as a "hospital and laboratory" for "the active treatment of patients who are mentally ill." Two years later, the doctors were given the additional responsibility of examining the sanity of accused criminals.*

For three decades, the hospital had remained largely unchanged. However, two weeks before Graham arrived for his evaluation, construction workers put the finishing touches on South-3, a new ward on the third floor with seclusion cells for "disturbed" men. Thus, Graham was the first person to occupy Room 307, a nine-foot by eleven-foot windowless chamber at the end of the corridor.

With concrete walls covered in ceramic tile, the cell had the look of an oversized bathroom. The only furnishings were a bed, a table and chair, a toilet, and a wash basin. The water controls for the sink and toilet were located in the hallway, on the other side of a solid iron door separating Graham from the two-man teams of deputies working eight-hour shifts to provide around-the-clock security. The single recessed light in the ceiling was protected by shatterproof glass, as was the small window above the six-inch slot for delivery of food trays. The only reading material was a stack of old magazines that had been left on the table to help Graham pass the time between his appointments.

During his month at the hospital, Graham was to be examined by two sets of psychiatrists. Dr. James Galvin, the medical director of the hospital, and his assistant, Dr. John Macdonald, would make their report directly to the court. Other psychiatrists appointed by the court to assist the defense team would submit their reports to Vigil, Gibbons, and Weadick. All of the psychiatrists were charged with answering a single question: was Graham insane at the time he committed the crime? The assessment had the potential to determine Graham's fate. If the two state psychiatrists concluded that he was insane, the sanity trial would be a mere formality and Graham would be committed to the Colorado State Hospital in Pueblo until he was "restored to reason." He would never stand trial for murder. However, if the state psychiatrists concluded that he was sane, their opinions would be tested at a sanity trial where a jury would be called upon to consider the conflicting opinions of the defense psychiatrists (in the event they disagreed with the state's psychiatrists) or any other evidence indicative of insanity. If the jury found that

---

* In 1967, the facility was renamed the Colorado Psychiatric Hospital in order "to conform to modern professional usage."

Graham was insane, he would be committed; if not, he would be tried for murder in a separate trial.

The psychiatrists' assessment of Graham's sanity would not be made according to a medical definition; the question was a legal inquiry. The 1955 insanity statute, which set forth a test substantially similar to the test that is in effect today, provided as follows:

> A person who is so diseased in mind at the time of the act as to be incapable of distinguishing right from wrong with respect to that act, or being able so to distinguish, has suffered such an impairment of mind by disease as to destroy the will power and render him incapable of choosing the right and refraining from doing the wrong, is not accountable; and this is true howsoever such insanity may be manifested, whether by irresistible impulse or otherwise. But care should be taken not to confuse such mental disease with moral obliquity, mental depravity, or passion growing out of anger, revenge, hatred or other motives, and kindred evil conditions, for when the act is induced by any of these causes the person is accountable to the law.

To answer this question, the psychiatrists would rely primarily on interviews with their subject. However, they would also review the records of Graham's medical history, his criminal offenses, his service in the Coast Guard, his performance in school, and his time at Clayton College.

The records from the orphanage were particularly revealing. When originally admitted to Clayton College in September 1938, Graham was "rather mischievous, but he was not considered a bad boy." His bed-wetting, which "had occurred almost every night" during the time he had lived with his grandmother, "stopped almost immediately." However, after Daisie wed Earl King in 1941, Graham's behavior began to deteriorate once he realized his mother—though wealthy by virtue of the marriage—had no intention of retrieving him from the orphanage. A 1941 report described the changes in his personality: "Jack is very unhappy and depressed at times, has trouble getting along with other children and adults. Careless with other people's possessions. Clamors for undue attention, rebellious when not given. Feels [his] mother does not love him because he was put in an institution."

On several occasions Jack Graham had run away from Clayton College to be with his mother. However, each time he was returned to the institution. In 1942, Daisie King made arrangements to have her ten-year-old son come to the ranch to celebrate Christmas. Jack—who evidently thought he "would not have to return to the Clayton College and could live permanently with his mother"—had "been looking forward to this for weeks in advance" according to his teachers, who said they had "never seen him so excited." When at last he arrived at the ranch, his mother and stepfather surprised him with a Christmas gift—a pony. However, after the holiday Jack learned that the pony would be staying at the ranch, while he would be going back to Clayton College in Denver.

A 1943 behavior report described the devastating impact of this incident of maternal rejection: "Jack cannot understand why he can't be with his mother

A family photograph of Daisie E. King (date unknown).

who showers him with attention during vacations. Adjustment very hard to make. Very disappointed over having to return to Clayton College." A few months later, when the mother of one his classmates caught him inside her home stealing money, the officials of Clayton College, feeling "Jack's place [is] with his remarried mother," discharged him "under dishonorable conditions."

During the time he lived with his mother and stepfather, Jack had an above average scholastic record at the Toponas Elementary School near Yampa. However, after completing one year at the Sterling High School, he dropped out in May 1947 to work on the King ranch. Things quickly took a turn for the worse.

One evening that summer, Daisie King telephoned the Routt County sheriff in a panic. "Send help," she pleaded. "Jack has a gun and he is going to kill Earl." When Deputy Lester Holden arrived at the ranch, he discovered that Jack had locked his mother out of the house. Looking through an open window, Holden could see that Jack had a revolver, and he could hear the youth muttering that he was going "to do something" about the fact that Earl

King had not been treating him "right." The deputy persuaded Jack to surrender the gun, and Daisie persuaded the deputy not to make an official report.

Soon after this incident, Jack Graham left the King ranch and headed for Alaska to live with his sister. But he made it only as far as Seattle, where he took a job working as a longshoreman. In April 1948, the sixteen-year-old youth enlisted in the Coast Guard with the assistance of Daisie, who "aided him in his deception that he was eighteen years of age."

Graham's time in the Coast Guard was of great interest to the psychiatrists at the Colorado Psychopathic Hospital. However, because the Coast Guard records had not yet been delivered to Denver, little was known about this period of Graham's life. In one of his meetings with Drs. Galvin and Macdonald, Graham—clad in hospital dungarees, a blue and white striped bathrobe, and a pair of black shoes—stated that he had received psychiatric treatment after going A.W.O.L. for forty-three days. Describing the events that led to the hospitalization, Graham said that "it seems that I gave the Commodore the wrong answer, because as soon as he and his hat came back to earth, I was sent back to New York and they asked me to stay in a Marine Hospital." Graham also "claimed that he was given five or six electric shock treatments while at the hospital, and he was able to give a convincing description of electro-shock therapy."

Graham was "polite, friendly, and courteous in his manner" when speaking with the psychiatrists. He preferred to talk about "impersonal topics," though he was quite candid when discussing his relationship with his wife. Describing Gloria as the "first girl" he had ever "really cared for," Graham's professions of devotion disclosed an unhealthy need for control: "To me, it's the only thing that matters, it's hard to describe. Some people take their wives for granted. I couldn't. If I came home and she wasn't there, I had to find out right away where she was. I wanted to put her up on a shelf and not let anyone else touch her or see her."

On at least one occasion, Graham's need for control had erupted in violence. During her November 19 interview with FBI agents, Helen Hablutzel had "recalled that, during the summer of 1955, Graham awoke from sleeping and found Gloria gone. He located his wife playing cards with his sister and mother and, for no apparent reason, became enraged and cuffed and backhanded her several times. During this occurrence, Daisie King had become extremely frightened, apparently afraid he might also hit her." In this same interview, Helen—who said she thought her brother was "not mentally sound"—had revealed that he had once "knocked her down and kneed her in the chest so severely that her ribs were injured"; on another occasion, he had "threatened to hit her with a hammer" before she "escaped by locking herself in a room."

Inevitably, the psychiatrists began asking Graham about his relationship with his mother. When they did, they noticed that Graham "became somewhat reserved" and was "forthcoming only in response to very specific inquiry."

"We loved one another," he said, "but she wasn't a person you could call 'Mom.' She wanted you to call her by her Christian name. You couldn't put your arms around her. You couldn't show affection like that to her. I always depended on her a lot. If she got mad at you, she'd stay mad for fifteen years."

Based on these conversations with Graham, as well as their interviews with other members of the family, Drs. Galvin and Macdonald formed a composite impression of Daisie King:

> She was very generous in providing toys and money for her children, but spent very little time with them. She appeared to have been quick tempered, somewhat domineering, and not an affectionate mother. . . . Her gifts were accompanied by demands, and whenever she caused particular feelings of anger, she would effectively prevent their expression and arouse a sense of guilt by some generous monetary gift. At the same time, she would play the role of the martyr. According to a relative, she was once found unconscious after a suicide attempt with drugs.

Although Judge Keating had ordered a complete news blackout on Graham's activities and mental examinations at the Colorado Psychopathic Hospital, Zeke Scher managed to coax some information out of the deputies who were working at the hospital as guards. According to the deputies, Graham appeared "happier" after arriving at the hospital, telling them "the bed here is a lot better than the one in the jail." Graham also enjoyed the frequent visits from his wife, sister, minister, and attorneys, and he regularly engaged the deputies in conversation by speaking through the small slot in the heavy metal door. The *Rocky Mountain News* reporters also extracted a few details about the conditions of Graham's confinement, regaling readers with reports of his meals, including a "Sunday dinner of roast beef, mashed potatoes, gravy, string beans, lettuce salad, and vanilla ice cream"—a meal eaten entirely with a spoon, the one dull utensil Graham was allowed to use.

In addition to his daily interviews with the psychiatrists, Graham was subjected to a battery of tests. The doctors ordered X-rays of his skull to determine whether he had any brain injuries (he did not) and an electroencephalograph to see whether any abnormalities were visible in the tracings of his brain wave patterns (none were observed). Using less sophisticated tests, the doctors measured his reflexes (which were normal) and his intelligence quotient (115, in the middle of the "high average" range).

After several days, the psychiatrists rewarded Graham for his cooperativeness by granting him limited access to the common areas. Observing Graham's interactions with the other residents, the doctors noted that he "showed good judgment in handling of situations in the ward, carried on lively conversations with others, and entered with zest into recreational activities."

While the psychiatrists were conducting their examinations, Charles Vigil and Bert Keating participated in a public debate concerning the value of psychiatric testimony in criminal trials. Appearing at the Broadmoor Hotel in Colorado Springs as members of a panel discussion for *Sounding Board*—a public affairs radio program on the Mutual Broadcasting System—Vigil and Keating aired their opposing viewpoints. The district attorney argued that "psychiatry is not an exact science—it's merely the opinion of one person, and it should be judged as such." Vigil disagreed, countering that psychiatrists' opinions were entitled to the same degree of deference routinely shown to "all doctors." During the question-and-answer period at the end of the program, Vigil chided Keating for his zeal, observing that "every district attorney sees himself as a potential governor of the state, and that's why they are always out for convictions."

On Tuesday, December 21, Charles Vigil and Bert Keating clashed again, this time in front of Judge Keating. The hearing—convened on short notice to address two motions from the defense team—had not been publicly announced beforehand. As a result, there were only half a dozen spectators present when the deputies escorted Graham into the courtroom. Although the photographers were excluded from the courtroom in accordance with Justice Holland's directive, they had reason to hope that situation might change in the future, because during the time Graham had been under observation at the Colorado Psychopathic Hospital, the Colorado Supreme Court had announced that it would hold a public hearing at the end of January at which "anyone interested in sustaining or amending Canon 35 will be heard."

The first matter before Judge Keating was the defense lawyers' petition to grant the defense psychiatrists access to "all laboratory and medical facilities at Colorado General Hospital, including examinations and reports on file at the hospital concerning the defendant."

Bert Keating pointed out the imprecise wording of the request by feigning incomprehension. "I don't understand this," he told Judge Keating. "Do they want all the facilities at the hospital, including the ambulances?"

"No," John Gibbons snapped, "we just want the report from the military hospital where the defendant was treated for four and one-half months for a mental condition. All the psychiatrists are holding up their diagnoses awaiting that report." Judge Keating approved the request.

The second motion filed by the three defense lawyers was a challenge to the rotation procedure by which Judge Keating was to be replaced by Judge McDonald in January, a move Charles Vigil characterized as "an illegal and involuntary change of venue." "We are cognizant of the Denver court rules," he said, "but we don't say they are proper. If this case were to go on for a long period of time, there could be several judges handling the case. The defendant is entitled to have the same judge hear all matters in the case." Relying on Judge Keating's earlier refusal to transfer the case to Weld County, Vigil argued that the ruling effectively constituted a determination that "no other judge" could preside over the case. It was a weak argument, but Judge Keating agreed to take the motion under advisement and announce his ruling after Christmas.

On Christmas Eve, Bert Keating received Graham's medical records from the Coast Guard. "I shall have copies of this report made and distributed among all the psychiatrists appointed by the court to examine Graham," he told reporters, noting that the records refuted Gibbons's assertion that Graham had suffered a "mental condition" involving frequent "blackouts." "There was no evidence he was ever insane," the district attorney emphasized. "Nothing was wrong with him except he was a brat who refused to follow the orders of his superiors."

Keating's summary of the records, though gratuitously sarcastic, was fairly accurate. The report made no mention of the shock treatments Graham claimed to have received. It did, however, include Graham's own explanation for his behavior:

> I just took a notion I'd get out of the service by going A.W.O.L. I was fed up with saying "Yes, sir" and "No, sir," and getting punished for things that didn't seem important. I had $200, and went to New York, Chicago, Georgia, and Washington, D.C. I was hitch-hiking. I had a lot of fun drinking, dancing, going to parties. I don't feel sorry about it, but I'm not happy about it; it's just one of those things, but I don't want a bad conduct discharge. If I stay in the Coast Guard and don't get leave, I'll go over the hill again to see my mother.

The report also set forth the Coast Guard's discharge assessment:

> This man is an exceedingly immature individual who has exhibited poor judgment and who tends to act on impulses. He is a dependent person, with strong ties to his mother. He tolerates frustrations, even those in the normal course of work, very poorly. Other evidence of his poor judgment and impulsive behavior are to be seen in his sleeping on watch, stealing food while on watch, and returning to work drunk.

> At this time [Graham] wishes to leave the service and return home. However, as might be anticipated, his plans are very vague and don't exhibit careful thinking. He has some tentative ideas of becoming an airplane pilot.

The week before Christmas, Helen Hablutzel had called United Air Lines to book a flight home from Denver. Although United had resumed its full schedule after the flight engineers ended their strike on December 15 (a settlement announced without any mention of the dueling recriminations that had been made in the first days of November), there still was only one evening flight from Denver to Seattle that would allow her to make her connection for the flight to Anchorage. With no other options from which to choose, Daisie King's daughter departed from Denver aboard United Air Lines Flight 629.

Upon returning home, Helen learned that two crates had arrived while she was away—large boxes filled with gifts from the Denver Dry Goods Company that Daisie had shipped to Alaska the day before she boarded the doomed flight. Most of the gifts were items of clothing, sad reminders of the Christmas that might have been. To Helen's dismay, none of her four children was willing to wear the new clothes because "Grandma Daisie wasn't there to give them the presents."

In Denver, Gloria tried to make the most of the holiday. Speaking with reporters, she expressed optimism. "I hope he will be home with us before next Christmas," she said as she walked into the Colorado Psychopathic Hospital. Because the hospital did not allow visitors to bring glass items inside, Gloria was unable to deliver the one Christmas gift she had for her husband: a framed photograph of Suzanne, the couple's ten-month-old red-haired daughter.

Graham did receive one gift from his aunt, Mrs. Helen Smith. It was a copy of *As a Man Thinketh,* James Allen's thin volume of meditations on the power of thought. That afternoon, an article in the *Denver Post* about Graham's "One Yule Gift" quoted the passage of the book deemed most significant to the accused plane bomber's predicament:

> *Mind is the master—power that molds and makes,*
> *And man is mind, and evermore he takes,*
> *The tool of thought, and shaping what he wills,*
> *Brings forth a thousand joys, a thousand ills. . . .*

In the same edition of the *Post*, Zeke Scher delivered a Christmas present to the prosecution. In a piece captioned "Defense-Hired Alienist* Declares Graham Sane," Scher revealed that Dr. Jack P. Hilton—a psychiatrist who had previously indicated that he was too busy to accept an appointment as one of the examining doctors for the defense—had been privately retained by John Gibbons to determine Graham's sanity. The fact that Hilton had met with Graham had not been previously revealed, and the disclosure of his opinion was a surprising development that, according to Gibbons, meant the doctor's report would "never be used in court." The defense attorney also was quoted as saying that the privileged document should be destroyed. The article did not reveal how it was that the highly confidential report had come into the hands of the resourceful reporter.[†]

Two weeks later, Scher obtained another confidential psychiatric report and splashed the opinions of Drs. Robert Cohen and Leo Tepley across the front page of the *Post*. Like Dr. Hilton, both of the psychiatrists appointed by the court to assist the defense team had determined that Graham was sane on November 1, as well as when he signed the confession on November 14. Scher's article detailed Graham's meetings with Cohen and Tepley, in which he had consistently denied any involvement in the bombing. According to the psychiatrists, Graham had insisted that the confession was

---

* The term "alienist," which has since fallen into disuse, refers to a specialist in the legal aspects of psychiatry.
† In an interview with the author, Scher revealed that he obtained Dr. Hilton's report from John Gibbons.

"suggested by an FBI agent" and "completely untrue." Pointing to passages of the signed confession, Graham had told the doctors that he "wouldn't have phrased something that way." Disputing another section of the confession, in which he had purportedly stated that he had kept the dynamite in the trunk of his car for several days, Graham joked that anyone who would do such a thing "would have to be insane." Once again, the article did not offer any hint concerning the source of the report.

Judge Keating—who thought he had entered his last ruling in the Graham case a week earlier when he denied the defense motion challenging the rotation of judges (a denial that had been accompanied by an expression of gratitude to the defense attorneys for "honoring" him with the request to remain on the case)—was angry about the premature publication of the psychiatric report prepared by Drs. Cohen and Tepley. "I issued a court order December 12 giving express orders to all the principals in the case not to release information relative to the trial until it had reached the court," he said. "The order has obviously been disregarded."

On Sunday afternoon, Judge Keating announced that he would convene a hearing the next day to identify the source of the leak. While offering assurances that the special proceeding would not be a "kangaroo court," he also promised that he would "do everything in my power" to make sure Graham received a fair trial. "If my investigation discloses any contemptuous action," he threatened, "I'll dispose of it as a contempt of court [and] somebody will go to jail."

On the afternoon of Monday, January 9, the two psychiatrists appeared in court to testify about the breach. Dr. Cohen informed the judge that he had not discussed the sanity evaluation with anyone other than Gibbons, and Gibbons testified that he "had not divulged the report to anyone." When Dr. Tepley was placed under oath, he also testified that he had not said "anything about the report to anyone."

Zeke Scher—the man at the center of the storm—took the stand and verified that the testimony of the other three witnesses was accurate. Although Judge Keating was distressed by the "irregularities," he adjourned the hearing without asking Scher to disclose the source of his information.*

---

* In an interview with the author, Scher explained how he obtained the report. On the afternoon of Friday, January 6, Scher went to Dr. Tepley's office to ask the psychiatrist about the results of the sanity evaluation. After informing Scher that he would be submitting the confidential report to the court over the weekend, Dr. Tepley deposited a copy of the evaluation in a wastebasket directly in front of the reporter.

On Thursday, Judge McDonald took the bench for the first hearing in his first felony case. He was only thirty-eight years old, but the black robe added several years to his appearance, and his jowliness added a few more. The father of four, Judge McDonald had graduated from the University of Pennsylvania Law School in 1941 and enlisted in the Air Force immediately after the attack on Pearl Harbor. When the war ended, he had returned from the South Pacific and settled in Denver, where his wife had been living with relatives during his absence. In 1951, after a few years in private practice, he was appointed to the Municipal Court by Mayor Quigg Newton. In little time, McDonald became known as one of the most competent and hardworking judges on the lower court bench.

Judge McDonald's first official act in the Graham case was the unsealing of the evaluation prepared by Drs. Galvin and Macdonald—the one report that had not been leaked to Zeke Scher prior to the hearing. The results were not surprising: the two state psychiatrists had concluded that Graham was sane. What was unexpected was the defense attorneys' announcement that, in spite of the unanimous opinions of the psychiatrists, their client would persist in his plea of not guilty by reason of insanity. Hearing of the gambit, the spectators in the overflow crowd studied the accused mass murderer looking for some sign of derangement, but Graham—dressed in a gray suit, a light-colored shirt, and a dark tie—listened impassively as the opposing teams of attorneys negotiated the calendaring of his trial.

Chief Deputy Greg Mueller pushed for an early trial date, urging the judge to start the sanity phase of the proceeding in just ten days, on January 23. Vigil and Gibbons balked at the proposed date and pleaded with the judge to be considerate of the fact that the case was disrupting their private law practices. After much haggling, Judge McDonald set the sanity trial for March 5.

The expeditious trial setting was welcomed by many of the victims' relatives, but it came too late for Martin Bommelyn. Two days earlier—and only six weeks after eating dinner with his son John at Stapleton Airfield—the grief-stricken father had passed away. "He had been sick," said one of his surviving sons, "but the loss of my brother, I feel, hastened his death."

## CHAPTER TEN

# "The tension has been released."

Justice O. Otto Moore disliked his first name so much he used an initial to conceal it for half of his life. Neither his classmates at the University of Denver—which he attended on a football scholarship—nor his colleagues in the Denver District Attorney's Office—where he made a name for himself in the 1920s prosecuting bootleggers and Klansmen—ever knew what the "O" stood for. However, in 1948 he was forced to reveal his given first name—Ostis—when he was elected as a justice of the Colorado Supreme Court.

Justice Moore agreed with Justice Holland that the Graham trial should not be televised. Nevertheless, when Hugh Terry of KLZ-TV had editorialized against the courtroom photography ban, it was Justice Moore who had approached his colleagues and urged them to grant the news organizations their day in court. The other justices agreed on one condition: Moore would have to serve as a special master and oversee the proceeding.*

The announcement of the Denver hearing on Judicial Canon 35 generated nationwide interest, and numerous media organizations assigned representatives to attend it. The Scripps-Howard Newspapers Corporation, the American Newspapers Publishers Association, the American Society of Newspaper Editors, the National Association of Radio and Television Broadcasters, the International News Service, and the National Press Photographers Association all asked to be heard. On the other side of the issue, the American Bar Association was the lone defender of Canon 35.

On the morning of Monday, January 30, 1956, Justice Moore convened the hearing in the Supreme Court courtroom, a cavernous chamber on the north side of the State Capitol Building with a massive wooden bench and

---

* Unbeknownst to Justice Moore, Terry had deliberately targeted him by broadcasting the editorials during the 10:00 P.M. news. Terry knew that Justice Moore—whose son-in-law was the station's evening weatherman—was a faithful viewer of the late news program.

an ornate one-ton chandelier hung from a carved plaster ceiling.* Speaking in a booming voice that required no microphone, Justice Moore began by reading into the record the results of a poll he had conducted of Colorado's district court judges: of the twenty-nine who had responded, eighteen favored a change in Canon 35, while eleven wanted to leave it unaltered.

One of the survey respondents—Judge Noland, the substitute judge who had allowed cameras to record Graham's first appearance in state court—asserted that a repeal of the photography ban would engender greater respect for the judicial branch of government:

> I am not in favor of bringing into our courtrooms, in the words of an Eastern court decision, "the distractions and disturbances of the marketplace." That is a catchy and high-sounding phrase, but I don't adhere to the argument that we are limited to the choice of a closed courtroom or a marketplace fiasco. . . . To most people outside our legal ranks, the courtroom is a mysterious place where sits a black-robed, austere judge, surrounded by attorneys talking in un-understandable lingo, the "slickest" of whom always wins the case. [The courtroom] is strictly off limits for the man who has no business there, and he doesn't want to have anything to do with the place. If you don't believe this, talk to the clerk in the grocery store, the laborer over at the factory, the farmer. His ideas on courts have been gained mostly from paperback books, sensational written versions of trials, or the movies. I believe that a survey would show that the great majority of American people have never witnessed a trial, perhaps never entered a courtroom. . . . I want our citizens to know and realize what a truly sound [court system we have], and if we can't bring these people to the courtroom, I would like to take the courtroom to them.

Charles T. Mahoney, a veteran Denver trial attorney, took another approach. Mahoney urged Justice Moore to view Judicial Canon 35 as an usurpation of authority by the American Bar Association, deriding the organization as a "minority group of lawyers" with a "feeling of superiority" who were trying to "straight jacket" the courts by acting as "commissar rule-makers for the rest of the lawyers." Nostalgically recollecting the days before the photography ban, Mahoney said he missed the "the old flashbulbs and the heavily veiled woman in black who was always slipping in the back door."

Over the course of the next several days, Justice Moore heard from a variety of witnesses. Joseph Costa, the board chairman of the National Press Photographers Association, testified that the public was entitled to

---

* In 1977, the Colorado Supreme Court moved across the street to a building located on Fourteenth Avenue. The abandoned courtroom is now used as a legislative hearing room by the Colorado General Assembly.

"objective visual reporting" and complained that "the photographer has become the whipping boy for all the grievances that anybody has against newspapers generally." To demonstrate that flashbulbs were no longer needed due to the development of high-speed shutter systems, Costa used a thirty-five-millimeter camera concealed in his jacket to stealthily snap three photographs of Justice Moore. Costa developed the photographs over the lunch hour and presented them to Justice Moore that afternoon.

Building on this presentation and Costa's testimony, Fred Mazzula, the Denver attorney who was representing the National Press Photographers Association, brought in an artist to make sketches of the proceedings. Mazzula pointed out that the artist—who was balancing a bulky drawing pad on his lap and periodically using binoculars to observe the facial expressions of the participants—was far more distracting than the cameramen who were discreetly taking photographs using telephoto lenses. Mazzula also sought to make a distinction between his clients and the television cameramen. Fearing the two groups might be lumped together, Mazzula argued that the handheld cameras used by photographers were less obtrusive than the "cumbersome technical equipment" necessary to produce a television broadcast.

Justice O. Otto Moore. (Courtesy of Denver Public Library, Western History Collection, Call #WH 1174)

The television and radio stations realized they faced an uphill battle to persuade Justice Moore that they could record court proceedings without interfering. In anticipation of the special hearing, the stations had banded together and formed the Denver Area Radio and Television Association, an ad hoc consortium assembled for the specific purpose of mounting a

Above: Photographer Gordon Yoder uses a newsreel camera to film Justice Moore. (Photograph courtesy of National Press Photographers Association)

Left: Joe Costa, of the National Press Photographers Association, removes his jacket to reveal a hidden thirty-five-millimeter camera at the request of attorney Fred Mazzulla. (Photograph courtesy of National Press Photographers Association)

united front against Judicial Canon 35. As its first official act, the association hired Richard M. Schmidt Jr., a Denver attorney specializing in media issues who had previously worked as a radio broadcaster.

When it was Schmidt's turn to make a presentation to Justice Moore, he began by presenting testimony from witnesses who had participated in televised trials. There had been only two such broadcasts. In 1953, additional lighting had been installed in a courtroom in Oklahoma City to allow a local television station to film a murder trial, portions of which had been shown on the evening newscast. Two years later, a television camera mounted on a tripod had been placed in a balcony above the jury in order to produce a live broadcast of a murder trial in Waco, Texas. Although the witnesses who had been involved in those experiments testified that the television cameras had not interfered with the proceedings, Schmidt knew it would take more than anecdotal evidence to change Justice Moore's mind.

After the hearing adjourned for the day, Schmidt brought a team of engineers from the local television stations into the courtroom. With the permission of the Clerk of Court—but without the knowledge of Justice Moore—the engineers replaced the door to the cloakroom with a similar door they had constructed that had a small glass window in its center. After hanging the door, the engineers wheeled in a television camera mounted on a large metal tripod and concealed it in the cloak room. Before leaving, they placed a television set on the center of the bench next to Justice Moore's black leather chair.

The next morning, Schmidt's first witness was Joe Harold, the manager of Denver station KBTV. After eliciting a description of the rapid developments being made in television and radio technology, Schmidt asked Harold whether it would be possible to discreetly produce a live audio "broadcast of the hearing we are conducting here today."

"We are," said Harold, opening his jacket to reveal a small wireless microphone attached to his inner breast pocket. As Harold demonstrated how the signal was transmitted using a wire antenna running down the leg of his trousers, Justice Moore leaned forward in his seat, clearly fascinated by the miniature device.

Schmidt then addressed Justice Moore directly. "Your Honor, would you please turn on that television set?"

Moore turned the knob and watched the flickering black and white pixels assemble into an image. Staring at the screen in disbelief, Moore carefully examined his own startled expression. Keeping one eye on the television, he looked from side to side in search of the hidden camera. He finally gave up and asked Schmidt to show him where it was.

At the end of the six-day hearing, Justice Moore informed the participants that he would make a written report to the other justices. Although Moore did not disclose what his recommendation would be, the American Bar Association lawyers defending the photography prohibition were not optimistic.

At the same time the media organizations were trying to get cameras into Colorado's courtrooms, *Rocky Mountain News* photographer Morey Engle was trying to figure out a way to sneak his bulky "sound on film" movie camera equipment into the Denver County Jail. The surreptitiousness was necessary because Engle did not want the managers of the local television stations to learn he had outfoxed them by obtaining what they all wanted: permission to film a full-length interview with Jack and Gloria Graham.

A "shooter" who had been chasing hard-to-get images his entire life, Morey Engle had begun his freelance photography career as a Denver teenager by listening to a homemade police monitor and pedaling his Schwinn bicycle to accident scenes. After hiring on as a staff photographer for the *Rocky Mountain News* in 1946, he soon discovered that his job security depended on his tenacity and ingenuity. At a time when city desk editors often dispensed assignments with an accompanying threat—"get the picture, or you're fired"—Morey Engle always managed to get the shot. If there was a fire, he would take his heavy Graflex 4x5 Speed Graphic camera and climb the ladder behind the firefighters. If there was a flood, he would pilot a small plane over the inundated area, tilting the Speed Graphic out the side window with one hand while steering the aircraft with the other. And if there was a murder, he would gain access to the crime scene by any means necessary, at times holding a silver dollar in front of his wallet and flashing it quickly to make it look like a detective's badge as he drove past a police barricade.

But in this case, the permission to film an interview with the Grahams had come to Engle through less adventuresome means: he had become friends with Gloria while at her home photographing her for the *Rocky Mountain News*. After clearing the idea with Graham's attorneys, Engle made the necessary arrangements to film the interview in Warden Dolliver's office.

The interview would be conducted by Gene Amole, a well-known Denver radio broadcaster who had recently founded KDEN, a jazz and news station with a studio and signal tower on top of Ruby Hill, not far from the Grahams' home. Although Amole and Engle had collaborated on several projects, including *Stop, Look, and Listen,* an independent television program featuring human-interest stories, the two had never done anything like the Graham interview before. Both men hoped the endeavor would produce a piece of film they could sell to a national outlet for thousands of dollars. It was, in Amole's words, "enterprise journalism."

The interview was scheduled for a Sunday, a day when the reporters and photographers who covered the crime beat were rarely present at the jail. To conceal the purpose of their visit, Engle and Amole rented an old car and removed the backseat to make room for the camera equipment.

They then drove to the jail's sallyport on the west side of the building, an entrance normally reserved for food deliveries, where they were met by a group of prisoner trustees who helped unload the sixteen-millimeter Auricon camera, tripod, lights, and metal canisters of film.

With Warden Dolliver and John Gibbons looking on from behind the camera, Gene Amole sat next to Graham, extended a handheld microphone, and asked about his relationship with Daisie.

"I loved my mother very much," said Graham, speaking with convincing sincerity. "To me, she meant a lot. It's very hard for me to say exactly how I feel. . . . She's left so much of herself behind even though she was killed in the accident. She's helped so many people and everything."

"In other words," suggested Amole, "you still feel very much a part of your mother, don't you, Jack?"

"Very much."

When Amole asked about the confession, Graham protested his innocence: "I know I didn't do it. I was trying to prove to them I didn't do it. At the time, they just wouldn't let me. This is the consequence of it."

"Why did you sign the statement? Was it because they said they were going to come get your wife?"

"That's right. They said she lied to them. We now know that they filled in some of the paper after she signed it, but at that time I thought she had signed it. I wasn't about to let them touch her in any way, shape, or form. I would have signed anything to keep them from touching her."

"What are your thoughts as you await your trial?"

"I know I'll be found innocent."

After Amole had finished his questioning, Engle filmed a segment showing the Grahams talking to each other. Gloria—looking considerably younger without her glasses and without the twenty pounds she had shed since November—asked her husband about the conditions of his confinement.

"It's real good as far as being in jail is concerned," Graham said, "but I'll sure be glad when I'm home with you and the kids. That's what I miss the most."

"Well, we miss you too, dear," Gloria said lovingly, "very much."

"It won't be very long," Graham assured his wife. "I know as soon as this trial is over, why I'll be able to come home."

A few days after filming the interview, Morey Engle traveled to Manhattan with the footage and showed it to a vice president of NBC. The executive liked what he saw, and he wrote out a check for the full asking price—ten thousand dollars. However, before giving Engle the payment, the executive insisted that the corporation's attorneys would have to view the film and sign off on the purchase.

It did not take the NBC lawyers long to deliver their verdict: the interview should not be broadcast because the sympathetic portrayal of Graham might complicate the jury selection and generate public backlash against the television network. Upon hearing the attorneys' advice, the executive told Engle he was withdrawing his offer. To emphasize the finality of the decision, he tore the check into small pieces.*

On the evening of February 10, just over two weeks after visiting her husband at the jail on his twenty-fourth birthday, Gloria drove to her parents' house for another birthday celebration, a small party for one-year-old Suzanne.

At the same time Gloria and her family were gathering in Lakewood, several miles to the east Deputy Sheriff James Martin was retrieving Jack Graham's dinner tray. "That's not much to eat," said the guard, noticing that the only thing missing was a cherry turnover. Graham did not reply.

A few minutes later, Graham lay down on his bunk and Martin settled into the wooden chair outside the cell. Looking through the flat steel bars, Martin could see only Graham's legs.

Martin, who had "become conscious of Graham's normal breathing" from his many nights posted outside the cell, heard Graham's inhalations "suddenly speed up like a scared rabbit." Springing from his chair for a better view, Martin could see Graham "in a half upright position with one hand on his stomach and the other hanging by his side." Martin called out to him in a panic, "Jack!"

Graham did not respond.

Martin ran to the main corridor of the jail and yelled for assistance. Deputy Warden Dave Kelbach and Captain Jack Pinneo heard Martin's cries and hurried to the cell block. The three men entered the cell together and immediately spotted a makeshift garrote wound tightly around Graham's throat. Martin ripped away the two black silk socks fastened to a cardboard toilet-paper tube and began administering mouth-to-mouth resuscitation. Kelbach sprinted back down the hallway to fetch Warden Dolliver.

---

* Although Engle tried to sell the film to the other networks, he encountered similar resistance. As a result, the interview was not aired until 1995, when segments were shown for the first time in *Murder at Mid-Air*, a documentary.

By the time Graham regained consciousness, Warden Dolliver, Safety Manager Edward Geer, and two police detectives had all squeezed into the small cell. Fifteen minutes later, a physician, Dr. Burton Forbes, arrived and administered oxygen. Suddenly, Graham began thrashing violently and making "sounds like an animal." The guards pinned him down as Dr. Forbes injected a hefty dose of Seconal. As soon as Graham was sedated, Warden Dolliver and the deputies put him in a straitjacket and strapped him to a mattress on the floor.

Dr. Forbes examined the garrote and the bruises to Graham's neck. Forbes was convinced the suicide attempt with the crude device "could have been successful. The ingenious way he twisted the device would have kept the knot against his neck, shutting off the blood and air, even when he passed into unconsciousness."

An hour later, Gloria raced to the jail with John Gibbons. Warden Dolliver refused to let them inside. "I expect he'll be a security problem all night," he said. Gloria could not fathom the situation. Recollecting her visit the previous Sunday, she described her husband as being "as cheerful as he could be under the circumstances. He didn't seem any different than before. I didn't think he would ever do anything like this. I have no idea why he did it."

Gibbons, who had last seen Graham two days before, was similarly perplexed. "We discussed the trial for about an hour. He seemed marvelous then. There is no logical reason why he should do this." Although Gibbons claimed he did not understand Graham's motive, he clearly understood the potential benefit of the attempt. "He might have gone stark, raving insane," said the lawyer. "And you can't try a man if he is insane."*

At 10:30 A.M. the next morning, Gibbons was allowed to see his client with Dr. Hilton, the psychiatrist whose report deeming Graham sane had been disclosed on Christmas. Gibbons later described the meeting: "He did not even recognize me. He was babbling and incoherent, and he refuses water and food. It's possible his brain was damaged as a result of his suicide attempt—maybe it was damaged by lack of oxygen." Dr. Hilton concluded that it was "obvious Graham is disturbed mentally. He is not responsive to anyone. Our first problem will be to get him quiet and then we can see what mental condition he is suffering from. Artificial feeding will probably be necessary for a while. A cell is no place to keep a man in this condition."

---

* In contemporary terminology, a criminal defendant's inability to comprehend the workings of the trial proceeding is referred to as "incompetency" —a condition that acts as a constitutional bar to prosecution for so long as it exists.

Judge McDonald agreed with the latter part of Dr. Hilton's assessment. Shortly before noon, he issued an emergency order recommitting Graham to the Colorado Psychopathic Hospital for another psychiatric examination.

At 12:45 P.M., Graham—still trussed in a straitjacket—was strapped to a gurney and wheeled out of the jail. Gloria watched from a distance, crying as two attendants loaded her husband into the back of an ambulance and drove away with a police car following close behind.

To prevent the high-profile prisoner from making another attempt at taking his own life, Warden Dolliver assigned several extra deputies to the hospital to keep a constant watch over the occupant of Room 307. In anticipation of Graham's eventual return to the jail, Dolliver instructed the deputies that Graham would no longer be allowed to wear socks, that toilet paper would be given to him without the cardboard roll, and that the light in his cell would remain on at all times. The warden brought in workers with acetylene torches and had them remove the upper bunk from the isolation cell so that Graham could not hurl himself to the floor. Dolliver also had the workers cut peepholes in the three enclosed sides of the cell so that the additional guards who would be assigned to each shift would be able to see Graham from all angles.

Although Dolliver was determined to keep Graham alive long enough to have a jury decide his fate, others questioned the wisdom of protecting Graham from himself. Not long after the accounts of James Martin's lifesaving resuscitation appeared in the newspapers, anonymous hecklers started calling the deputy's home. There were so many calls that Martin had to have his telephone disconnected because the harassment was upsetting his pregnant wife.

As the members of the public debated the wisdom of interfering with the suicide attempt, the lawyers involved in the case put forth competing theories concerning the significance of the incident. District Attorney Bert Keating thought the "act resulted from emotional upset or consciousness of guilt," while Gibbons opined that Graham "blew a cork as a result of the constant scrutiny. I've never seen an accused man kept under such constant surveillance. He had nobody to talk to but his guard. I don't think his try at suicide has anything to do with his guilt or innocence."

After visiting with Graham at the Colorado Psychopathic Hospital, Gibbons described the encounter: "I asked him if he remembered trying to commit suicide. He just had a blank look. He looked at me and said 'no,' he didn't remember anything about it. He isn't the same person I knew last week. The man is gone." Gibbons told reporters that he and Charles Vigil would insist the March 5 sanity trial proceed as scheduled, "even if Graham is violent and has to be drugged or put in a straight jacket for the trial."

Gloria also went to the hospital. Although she had been granted a full hour to visit, she left after only ten minutes, explaining that the man she saw "just wasn't my Jack." She did not view the suicide attempt as a sign of guilt. "I know he didn't do it," she said. "I am praying for the time we can be together as a family again."

Drs. Galvin and Macdonald began a second series of interviews to deter-mine whether Graham had the mental capacity to be put on trial. They carefully documented their observations:

> He walked very slowly and stared straight ahead with a vacant expression on his face. When interviewed, he started over breathing, turned his head from side to side, and rolled his eyes in all directions. He would not even look at his doctor when asked to do so, and at first did not reply to ques-tions. Later, he responded in a monotone and claimed that people were against him, and were trying to poison him. He said he did not know why he was in jail and, when informed that he was in a hospital and that he had been charged with the murder of his mother, he replied: "Is it for parking my truck on the railroad tracks?" Shortly afterward, he asked whether his mother could visit him. He claimed that he had seen his stepfather. Al-though he said he could not recall his wife's name, he remembered the names of his doctors, attorney, and probation officer. When asked the names of his children, he gave his wife's name.

The two psychiatrists concluded that Graham's "patchy amnesia, inter-mittent disorientation, and absurd as well as correct answers to simple arithmetic problems" were indicative of "simulated insanity." In layman's terms, Graham was faking it.

The doctors intensified their questioning. On February 15, Graham finally abandoned his affected symptoms and admitted that his nonsensical statements were part of a ruse. Through tears, he confessed to the bomb-ing, telling the doctors he had originally intended to blow up the drive-in and had decided to put the explosives on the airplane only after Daisie re-fused to stay in Colorado for Thanksgiving:

> I tried to tell her how I felt about it. She just said she wouldn't stay, she wouldn't give me any reason at all, no reason why she didn't want to stay. I thought it was the last time she was going to run off and leave me.

I wanted to have her to myself for once. Since I was a little kid, she'd leave me with these people, those people. I wanted to get close to her, every time I'd get close to her she'd brush me off like I was a piece of furniture, as if I didn't mean anything more to her than nothing. If she gave me money, I was supposed to realize that was enough. I just wanted to do things with her, to sit down and talk to her—just like everybody else's mother would do.

I just had to stop her from going—yet it seemed I had to be free from her, too. She held something over me that I couldn't get out from under. When the plane left the ground, a load came off my shoulders, I watched her go off for the last time. I felt happier than I ever felt before in my life. I was afraid to do anything without asking her, and yet I wanted to go ahead on my own without asking her. Down deep, I think she resented me, little things she would do to aggravate me. It's such a relief to tell somebody what I did. It was such a terrible thing I couldn't bear to tell anybody. I deserve to be taken out and shot. I can't find an excuse for something like that.

Graham also told the psychiatrists that he had attempted suicide in the past, thus revealing his motivation for parking his truck on the train tracks. Yet, when discussing the other victims, he was unremorseful:

I just felt if it killed somebody, that was tough. It seemed the odds were big enough, there was more fun that way. I just didn't think about the other people on the plane. I don't think it has hit me yet. I guess I thought I could keep it all inside me and forget about it. I finally decided I couldn't live with myself. I don't feel sorry for anyone on that plane or their relatives. If someone said there were forty-four dead ducks on that plane it wouldn't make a difference to me. I guess it's not the right thing to say.

Galvin and Macdonald were convinced that Graham's problems had begun at the orphanage. They theorized that the "teachers were, for him, a shadowy father figure. He viewed them as unjustly demanding, implacable, and unreasonably punitive. The authority figures were merged together into 'society' so that his poorly directed anger and indignation against them justified, for him, his antisocial behavior."

The psychiatrists also prepared a "dynamic formulation" of Graham's relationship to Daisie, concluding that her constant "pattern of rejection, punctuated by periods of indulgence" had caused serious damage:

The consequence was that this young man had an extremely intense ambivalent relationship with his mother. He continued to hope for real and lasting affection from her, but his experience made him view her as rejecting, frustrating, and a great cause for anger. In his ambivalent relationship, he repressed and suppressed much of his hostile feeling and when he spoke of his mother it was usually in loving terms.

With his warm, accepting wife, he had not only adult and mature satisfactions, but also important infantile satisfactions which permitted a partial mastery of the conflict with his mother. With both wife and mother, he had great separation anxiety. His helplessness when threatened by this separation anxiety added to his hostility against his mother. In the year before the tragedy, he was miserably unhappy with his mother.

After his marriage, his sociopathic patterns seemed to become less. There were some social aberrations, but he did work steadily, was successful in his university examinations, and spent much time with his family. The experience arising out of his marriage of increased drive satisfaction on both adult and pregenital levels had slightly changed his anger and rebellious attitude toward society.

The period of relative social adjustment was ended by his mother's return into his life. The recapitulation of the infantile situation with her engendered so much strong emotion that his substitute gratifications paled in significance. He became more and more hostile, he began to have increasing fantasies of violence, and at the end of the year he acted these fantasies out. He at once destroyed his tormentor and, in a counterphobic way, dealt with his fear of separation from her.

Because Judge McDonald had issued an order imposing a complete news blackout, the two psychiatrists kept the details of their report confidential. The only information disclosed to the public was contained in Dr. James Galvin's February 16 letter to Judge McDonald: "It is my opinion that [Graham] has not suffered any damage to his brain. It is further my opinion that he does not suffer from any psychiatric condition which would impair his sanity."

Three days later, Graham was returned to the jail. He was in high spirits during the fifteen-minute trip through downtown Denver, joking with the deputies and commenting on the new 1956 model cars he spotted along the way. When they arrived at the main entrance on Kalamath Street, Graham greeted Warden Dolliver warmly and struck a smiling pose for the many photographers who had gathered to chronicle his return.

On Tuesday, February 21, Graham sat for another interview with Zeke Scher. Laying the groundwork for the change in defense strategy that was about to occur, Graham dismissed his confession to the FBI as the product of "Gestapo-type questioning" and adamantly reasserted his innocence: "Of course I still deny I'm guilty. I didn't do it. I will take the witness stand and prove to the

jury that I am innocent." He insisted that Lyman Brown was mistaken and suggested that the dynamite seller "get his glasses checked." When Scher asked
about the suicide attempt, Graham attributed it to the stress of incarceration:

> I guess I had to have a release from the pressure, more or less. I just
> couldn't stand being locked up. The tension built up to a point where I
> couldn't stand it. I've been treated more than fair here, but just the fact
> of being locked up for that length of time got on my nerves. I don't even
> remember doing it. I'm sure if I had been able to think about what I was
> going to do, I would have thrown the socks out of the cell. The only thing
> I can remember is waking up at the hospital. I consider the whole move
> not very bright. It was very stupid. I know the average person will think I
> did it because I'm guilty. But it's not what the person on the street says,
> it's the jury that counts.

Turning to speak to Warden Dolliver, Graham apologized for his earlier
actions. "I'm sorry I caused you all the trouble I did. You won't have to worry
about it happening again. I feel fine now. The tension has been released."

On Friday, the three defense attorneys filed with the court a document the
prosecutors had been anticipating for weeks. Captioned as a "Petition of
Defendant to Withdraw Pleas," the document, signed by Graham, asked
Judge McDonald to enter an order "striking and vacating my pleas of insanity heretofore entered." Although Bert Keating and Greg Mueller were not
surprised by Graham's request to abandon his claim of insanity, the prosecutors were taken aback by the accompanying demand that the trial to determine his guilt or innocence proceed on March 5, the date originally
scheduled for the sanity trial.

At a hearing on the motion, Bert Keating objected to maintaining the
original trial date, arguing that he needed more than nine days to secure
the attendance of the 150 witnesses whom he had endorsed to testify.
Charles Vigil asked Judge McDonald to honor Graham's constitutional
right to a speedy trial, reminding the judge that "the district attorney
previously was very anxious to get to trial."

Judge McDonald recognized the defense move as a last-ditch attempt to
force the prosecutors to proceed with an incomplete case. Striking a com-
promise between the two teams of quarreling lawyers, McDonald set the
trial for Monday, April 16, concluding that an additional six weeks was "not
an unreasonable delay."

Graham arrives for a court hearing at the Denver City and County Building on February 24, 1956, with Sergeant George Hayes *(front left, hand on revolver)*, Lieutenant Robert Stratton *(rear left)*, Captain Logan Ketchum *(holding Graham by chain)*, and Undersheriff Charles Rudd *(front right)*. (Courtesy of Denver Public Library, Western History Collection, Morey Engle Collection)

On Monday, February 27, Colorado became the first state to officially sanction courtroom photography and televised trials. In a written report unanimously adopted by the other justices, Justice O. Otto Moore set forth his findings:

Gloria Graham sits with her husband outside the courtroom on February 24, 1956, after the hearing at which Graham withdrew his insanity plea. (Courtesy of Denver Public Library, Western History Collection, Morey Engle Collection)

For six days I listened to evidence and witnessed demonstrations which proved conclusively that the assumption of facts as stated in the canon is wholly without support in reality. At least one hundred photographs were taken at various stages of the hearing which were printed and introduced as exhibits. All of them were taken without the least disturbance or interference with the proceedings, and, with one or two exceptions, without any knowledge on my part that a photograph was being taken. A newsreel camera operated for half an hour without knowledge on my part that the operation was going on. Radio microphones were not discovered by me until my attention was specifically directed to their location.

Several hours were devoted to the techniques involved in modern production of live telecasts and for one whole day the events taking place in the courtroom were produced on a closed circuit telecast and shown as they happened on the television set in the courtroom. Cameras used in

photo and television demonstrations were of different kinds. In still photography and newsreel activity they were not noticeable and were operated in such manner that I was unaware that they were functioning. The
television cameras shown were of several kinds, varying from the large,
already outmoded one which is mounted on a movable tripod, to the
small one which is 4" x 5" x 7" in size. All equipment used, whether
large or small, is capable of installation outside the courtroom with only
the lens appearing on the exterior wall, through an otherwise concealed
door or window, or from a booth in the rear of the courtroom. Only the
regular lighting at all times functioning in the courtroom was used, and
any courtroom with adequate sunlight for ordinary court proceedings
would require no additional lighting.

   There was nothing connected with the telecast which was obtrusive. The
dignity or decorum of the court was not in the least disturbed. Many persons entered and retired from the courtroom without being aware that a live
telecast was in progress. Others who took seats which were so located that
they could see the television screen which was reproducing the hearing were
obviously surprised when they observed it a brief time after being seated.

Moore acknowledged that "many well-meaning persons, including
some leaders of the bench and bar, are of the firm conviction that some, or
all, of the prohibitions contained in Canon 35 should be continued and en-
forced without variation," and he admitted that prior to the hearing, he
"leaned definitely toward that view in so far as television and radio were
concerned." He then proceeded to set up, and knock down, all of the arguments supporting the ban against courtroom photography.

   To the objection that "coverage of court proceedings going beyond the
inaccurate word pictures painted with the pen of the courtroom press reporter would be merely to satisfy 'idle curiosity' for entertainment purposes," Moore pointed out that:

   Generally only idle people pursuing "idle curiosity" have time to visit courtrooms in person. What harm could result from portraying by photo, film,
   radio and screen to the business, professional and rural leadership of a community, as well as to the average citizen regularly employed, the true picture
   of the administration of justice? Has anyone been heard to complain that the
   employment of photographs, radio and television upon the solemn occasion
   of the last presidential inauguration or the coronation of Elizabeth II was to
   satisfy an "idle curiosity"? Do we hear complaints that the employment of
   these modern devices of thought transmission in the pulpits of our great
   churches destroys the dignity of the service; that they degrade the pulpit or
   create misconceptions in the mind of the public? The answers are obvious.

That which is carried out with dignity will not become undignified because more people may be permitted to see and hear.

In a thinly veiled reference to the anticipated courtroom antics of John "Chesty" Gibbons, Moore rejected the argument that the presence of cameras would lead to grandstanding:

It is contended, usually orally and in smothered words or whispers, that some trial judges, and lawyers who are hungry for publicity, will conclude that they are actors, and by some psychological motivation "play to the galleries" and so conduct themselves as to satisfy their own vanity, or otherwise exploit themselves. Any judge or lawyer who so demeans himself before a camera does not change his inherent characteristics for that particular occasion. A "showoff" or a "strutter" will be just that whether a camera is present or not. They are readily identified by any person of ordinary intelligence and are ultimately adequately and justly disposed of by the people. If a larger segment of society is permitted to witness such offensive conduct the offender will be properly judged by the people sooner than might otherwise be possible. Actual experience, however, has led to the majority view that participants in legal proceedings are far more careful in their conduct and indulge in less bickering in those cases where cameras are permitted to operate under court supervision.

Equipment employed in broadcasting, either by radio or television, is such that if any participant evidenced an intention to offend in this matter all the judge would have to do would be to press a button and the offensive conduct would be inaudible and invisible to any person except those in the courtroom. The capable trial judges of this state can keep full control of any such situation which might arise. It is perfectly obvious that the solution of the problem does not lie in arbitrarily forbidding the photographing or broadcasting of court proceedings. A constitutional right of all citizens cannot be denied because a very few persons may conceivably make fools of themselves before a larger audience than that which might otherwise be subjected to their offensive conduct.

In the final section of the report, Moore set out the Colorado Supreme Court's order replacing the prohibition of Judicial Canon 35 with a new rule granting the state's trial judges full discretion to permit all types of media access.

Immediately after the report was released, Judge McDonald was deluged with media requests to photograph and broadcast the Graham trial. McDonald indicated that he was inclined to allow such coverage, but he said he would need time to consider the logistical difficulties of accommodating so many members of the press in his small courtroom.

On Thursday, March 1—the same day an incomplete account of Graham's confession to Drs. Galvin and Macdonald appeared in the *Rocky Mountain News*—Graham filed a request that had the potential to free up twelve additional seats in the courtroom for photographers:

> I have been advised by counsel as to my constitutional right to have a jury try the case, but I desire to have the case heard by the court without a jury and hereby expressly waive my right to a trial by jury. I feel that I can obtain a fair and proper trial before the Honorable Joseph M. McDonald.

At a hearing on the motion, John Gibbons argued that it would be impossible to find impartial jurors in Denver. "I have talked to many and diverse people," he said, "and not one person would give me an ear and listen to the facts." Pointing at Graham, he asked, "Where could this defendant get a fair trial? Only from Your Honor."

Bert Keating opposed the request. "We would be glad to join in this attempted waiver," he told Judge McDonald, "except that the laws of Colorado do not permit it." He was right. On two previous occasions, the Colorado Supreme Court had held that, pursuant to statute, a defendant "may not waive the right to trial by jury" in a first-degree murder case. Although the district attorney did not dispute the defense lawyer's assessment of the prevailing public sentiments, he pointed out that there was another remedy available: "If, as Gibbons says, every person in Denver has guaranteed him an unfair trial for Graham, he can seek a change of venue as provided by law."

As expected, Judge McDonald denied the motion and ruled that the case would be decided by a jury. The deputies handcuffed Graham and returned him to the jail.

When it was built in 1890, the Denver County Jail was designed to house three hundred prisoners. By the late 1940s, the population in the sandstone-block structure had swelled to two and a half times that number. With the increase in prisoners had come a proportional increase in problems. There had been several riots and nine attempts at mass escape. To quell the unrest, several of the guards had resorted to brutality—abuses that, when they came to light during a grand jury investigation, ultimately led to the dismissal of Warden Dolliver's predecessor.

Since taking over the facility, Dolliver had experienced "a lot of headaches" due to the overcrowding. But all of that was about to end. On February 27, law enforcement officials from throughout the Rocky Mountain region had attended a ribbon-cutting ceremony to celebrate the opening of Denver's new jail. Located on the eastern edge of the city at the intersection of Smith Road and Havana Street, the modern facility had the capacity to hold up to one thousand inmates. For a week after the grand opening, guards escorted hundreds of members of the public on tours of the empty buildings and the small farm where prisoner trustees would grow vegetables for the kitchen. At the end of the week, the guards began making final preparations for the new occupants.

To decrease the possibility of inmates escaping during the transfer between the two jails, Warden Dolliver kept the exact date of the prisoner relocation secret, withholding the information even from the deputies who worked in the cell blocks. Finally, on the evening of Saturday, March 10, Dolliver called in every available man.

The warden had carefully planned all aspects of the operation. The 304 prisoners who were charged with felonies would make the trip in eight Colorado Motorway buses; the remaining 383 inmates who were being held for misdemeanors would make the trip in a variety of city vehicles. More than sixty armed deputies and police officers would provide security, and not a single prisoner from the general population would be removed from the old jail until the two most infamous inmates were relocated to their new adjoining cells.

At 8:30 P.M., the deputies led Graham out of the jail. He looked tired, blinking into the flashbulbs and television camera lights as the deputies ushered him into a waiting patrol car. Five minutes later, the deputies brought out LeRoy Leick—who had been convicted a second time and resentenced to death—and placed him in another police cruiser. The officers then slowly drove away from the jail, carefully navigating their way across ten miles of ice-covered streets.

When they arrived at the new jail, the guards escorted Graham through the gates and locked him in an eight-foot by eight-foot cell in the maximum security wing. He soon fell sound asleep. The next morning, Graham arose and looked out his west-facing window to see what he could see.

He had an unobstructed view of the airplanes taking off and landing at Stapleton Airfield.

## CHAPTER ELEVEN

# "They won't look at me."

I T TOOK HELEN HABLUTZEL two full weeks to drive back to Denver
from her home in Spenard, Alaska—a journey of 3,300 miles. She
would have made the trip to be at her brother's trial even if she had not
been subpoenaed to testify. "I taught Jack to walk," she said, "and I want to
be near Gloria and their two children. I'm praying that everything turns
out all right. I feel so terribly sorry for Jack and his family."

When she arrived at her sister-in-law's house, Helen unpacked her suitcases in the basement bedroom previously occupied by Daisie. Because Helen
was unsure how long she would be staying in Colorado, she had brought a tape
recorder with her to make audio journals to mail home to her children, all of
whom insisted "Uncle Jack didn't do anything wrong with the plane."

This disbelief in Graham's guilt was a sentiment shared by many of the
adults who had come to know him during the time he lived in Spenard.
"Everybody in Alaska liked Jack and was impressed with his hard work,"
said Helen. "They all sent their sympathy and regards to him."

The week leading up to the trial was a period of intense preparation for the
prosecution team. Bert Keating and Greg Mueller conducted daily practice
sessions and set up a small office down the hall from the courtroom in
which to store exhibits, legal treatises, statute books, and the voluminous
FBI reports. "We have spent more time in preparation of this case than any
since I took office eight years ago," said Keating. "We are still wrapping up
loose ends and will probably still be doing odds and ends on the case when
the trial begins next week."

The three defense attorneys were equally busy, but it was not clear what
theory the trio planned to rely on at trial. "We will have a number of surprises

in store," said Gibbons. "And that is as far as we can state at this time. There will
be a surprise defense." Charles Vigil—who had recently announced that he
would likely run for Congress once the trial was over—was no more forthcoming: "We are going to trial seeking justice. Graham has said he wants to
take the stand, but he may elect not to when the time comes. He will be
guided by our views. This is a complex case and anything could happen."

One thing that definitely was not going to happen was a live television
broadcast. On April 1, Judge McDonald had exercised the discretion given
to him by the Colorado Supreme Court and ruled that he would allow film
and audio recording only if the television and radio stations agreed to
delay their broadcasts until the end of each day.*

Judge McDonald appointed the manager of KLZ-TV to coordinate the
television and radio coverage through a pool system, cautioning the broadcaster that "it must be remembered at the outset that the concern of everyone involved in every trial is that all parties should be offered a fair trial.
One portion of a fair trial imports an orderly procedure, and anyone
whose conduct interferes with such orderly procedure will be forbidden
the privilege of the courtroom." To minimize the possibility of any such interference, Judge McDonald authorized the construction of a wooden
booth in the back corner of the courtroom to conceal the single "sound on
film" movie camera that would be shared by the television stations.

Judge McDonald also imposed restrictions on the still photographers,
ordering that no more than four cameramen would be allowed in the
courtroom at any given time and directing them not to use additional lighting, flashbulbs, or any camera larger that a RolleiFlex.†

The requests for access to the courtroom by print media far exceeded
the number of available seats. Rather than sift through the applications
himself, Judge McDonald delegated the task to Zeke Scher of the *Denver
Post* and Ed Oschmann of the *Rocky Mountain News,* charging the two local
reporters with the task of fairly allocating the few spaces to the national
newspapers, magazines, and wire services.

Scher and Oschmann assigned a front row seat to James Kilgallen, a legendary newspaperman who had made his reputation covering a string of sen-

---

* Judge McDonald explained that he was mandating this delay so that he would have the ability to prevent the
  broadcast of anything he deemed unfairly prejudicial—a simpler method of censorship than the button
  mechanism Justice Moore had described in his report.
† The Rolleiflex, a German twin-lens reflex camera, was used by many newspaper photographers in the 1950s.
  The rectangular camera measures approximately 10" x 4" x 4" when the top-mounted focusing hood is
  unfolded.

sational criminal cases, including the Bruno Hauptmann trial. Kilgallen was coming to Denver—the city where he had married his wife, a former singer in the Tabor Grand Opera House—to cover the Graham trial for the International News Service, the syndicated press agency of the Hearst newspaper chain.

The Hearst newspapers had devoted extensive resources to the case ever since the day of Graham's arrest. In January, Erle Stanley Gardner—the famous author of the popular Perry Mason mystery series—had written an article titled "The Case of the Exploding Airliner" for the *American Weekly,* the Hearst Sunday supplement. In the article, which was accompanied by an artist's sensationalistic rendition of a low-flying airplane blowing apart above a farmer who was looking up at the falling bodies, Gardner predicted that the Graham trial "might well write one of the most dramatic chapters of courtroom history."

Exactly how long that chapter would be was the subject of considerable speculation. John Gibbons, Charles Vigil, and Paul Weadick predicted that it might take as long as twenty-eight days to pick a jury and present the evidence. The prosecutors' estimate was thirty-nine days. Based on these projections, Judge McDonald announced that he would hold court six days a week to minimize the amount of time the jurors would be sequestered.

In 1956, Colorado law required that jurors in capital cases be sequestered "during all recesses from the time the jury is selected until discharged by the court."* To comply with this mandate, the Denver District Court maintained a dormitory on the second floor of a municipal building located at Fifteenth Street and Cleveland Place, directly across from the City and County Building. Initially, the dormitory housed only men. However, after the Colorado Constitution was amended in 1944 to permit women to serve as jurors, the dormitory was divided into separate sections. In the week before the Graham trial, the rooms were readied for the dozen jurors and one alternate who would spend their evenings there without access to newspapers, magazines, television, or mail.

Graham's right to have the jury sequestered—unlike his right to a jury trial—was one he had the ability to waive. However, John Gibbons made it clear that this was not going to occur, hinting that he might even ask to have the prosecution's 184 witnesses "locked up like the jurors." Upon hearing

---

* In 1984, this requirement was eliminated and Colorado judges were given discretion to decide when to sequester a jury. In 1998, the rule was amended a second time to limit sequestration to "extraordinary cases."

of this proposal, Bert Keating scoffed at it as being so "ridiculous" it did not "even call for a response." Eventually, Gibbons acknowledged the absence of any precedent for the request and abandoned the idea.

He did not, however, abandon his objection to the televising of the trial. In a last-minute motion asking Judge McDonald to reconsider his decision, Gibbons alleged that the presence of a television camera would be a distraction. On Thursday, April 1 2, the deputies transported Graham to court for a hearing on the issue.

Graham looked pale and nervous, and it was apparent he had lost a great deal of weight since being moved to a jail cell in which he constantly heard the droning sound of the propeller-driven planes coming and going from Stapleton Airfield. When he took the witness stand to verify that he objected to "any live or 'canned' television during the trial," his voice was so soft that both Gibbons and Judge McDonald had to ask him to speak louder.

Bert Keating took no position on the request, and he did not ask Graham any questions. Judge McDonald had only one question, and he directed it at John Gibbons.

"Does the defense object to still photography?"

Gibbons conceded that he did not.

"I can see no difference," said McDonald. He denied the motion but indicated that he would honor the objection of any witness, including Graham, who asked that his or her trial testimony not be broadcast.

Judge McDonald made it clear that he planned to run the trial according to a strict schedule, telling the attorneys he did not want "ten minutes of shuffling around after I take the bench." The proceedings would begin each day at 9:30 and adjourn each evening at 5:00. There would be fifteen-minute recesses at 10:45 and 3:30 and a two-hour lunch break at noon.

Security would be tight. Four officers from the Sheriff's Department would take Graham to and from the jail and sit near him in the courtroom to prevent an escape. In addition, three plainclothes detectives from the Denver Police Department would be seated in the gallery to thwart any attempt on Graham's life. Two uniformed officers would be stationed in the back of the courtroom, and two more uniformed officers would stand guard in the hallway to search the spectators for weapons. To publicize the precautions and discourage any would-be vigilantes, six of the officers posed with their revolvers for a *Denver Post* photographer.

On Saturday, the jail barber trimmed Graham's crew cut to neaten his appearance for the jurors. Later that day, Gloria made her final pretrial visit, emerging afterward to tell reporters her husband was "anxious to get it over with—and not afraid." For the rest of the weekend, the guards helped Graham pass the time by competing with him at Scrabble—the word game that had become a national obsession since its introduction two years before.

On Monday morning, Graham stepped from the elevator onto the fourth floor of the City and County Building surrounded by five plainclothes officers, who escorted him toward the courtroom. They walked alongside a two-hundred-foot rope partition that had been positioned in the center of the hallway to contain the crowd. Graham looked straight ahead, ignoring the now-familiar blasts of light from the photographers' flashbulbs.

Once they were inside the prisoner waiting room, the deputies removed Graham's handcuffs. They then led him into the courtroom and seated him at the defense table with his three attorneys.

While waiting for the judge to appear, Graham read through the list of prospective jurors looking for names of people he recognized. Six hundred Denver residents had been summoned for jury service—a new record. Gathering such a large number of jurors was a difficult task due to the odd laws concerning jury service that existed in 1956. Persons under the age of twenty-one, convicted felons, and "professional gamblers" were not allowed to serve. In addition, there were exemptions for railroad conductors, state and county officers, newspaper reporters and editors, judges, clerks of court, justices of the peace, attorneys, telephone and telegraph managers, registered pharmacists, persons over the age of sixty, National Guardsmen, volunteer firemen, postal employees, and Seventh-day Adventists.

Because six hundred Denver citizens would not all fit in the small courtroom, Judge McDonald had ordered the bailiff to bring the prospective jurors up from the assembly room in groups of seventy-five. By the time Graham entered the courtroom, the first batch of potential jurors was already in the gallery, as were Gloria Graham and Helen Hablutzel, the plainclothes detectives, and the handful of spectators who had arrived early enough to secure the few remaining spaces. The gaggle of reporters and cameramen sat in a separate section directly across from the empty jury box.

The bailiff rapped his gavel and called the courtroom to order. Judge McDonald entered through a door leading from his chambers and stepped briskly to the bench. The clerk of court, Diane Carroll—a law student and the daughter of former Congressman John A. Carroll—announced the case: "Denver District Court number 42604, the People of the State of Colorado versus John Gilbert Graham."

Bert Keating and Charles Vigil both stood.

"The People are ready, Your Honor."

"The defense is ready, Your Honor."

At Vigil's request, Judge McDonald briefly returned to his chambers to hear a defense challenge to the composition of the jury panel. Vigil's motion—which sought to disqualify the jurors on the ground that they were not residents of the county where the crime had occurred—was merely a reformulation of the venue claim he had made in December. Judge McDonald recognized it as such, denied it, and returned to the bench.

At 10:20, Diane Carroll reached into a wooden box and pulled out a slip of paper with the summons number of the first prospective juror. After the first person called was seated in the box, the clerk repeated the process twelve more times.

Judge McDonald made his introductory remarks and then called on Bert Keating to question the prospective jurors. Although the judge had allotted to each side fifteen peremptory challenges that could be exercised to remove prospective jurors for any reason, neither the prosecution nor the defense would use those challenges until they had first made their objections "for cause" to remove those persons who were biased.*

Standing at the podium dressed in a black suit, white shirt, and light gray print tie, Keating began his inquiries. Several prospective jurors admitted that they had been exposed to so much pretrial publicity that they could not set aside their preconceived views and reach a verdict based solely on the evidence presented at trial. Many others admitted that they were morally opposed to the death penalty.† As Judge McDonald dismissed each of these prospective jurors for cause, Diane Carroll drew another slip of paper and called a replacement.

The prospective jurors all knew it would be a lengthy trial, and some of their claims of partiality were transparent excuses to avoid serving. "I'm afraid I couldn't be fair," said one woman. "My family flies a lot."

---

* The prosecutors also were allowed to make challenges for cause to prospective jurors who said they were incapable of imposing the death penalty.

† Public sentiment concerning the death penalty was sharply divided in Colorado during the 1950s. In 1955, a bill abolishing capital punishment had come within one vote of passage in the Colorado House of Representatives.

Keating attempted to address this problem by asking another potential juror a question that suggested the trial might not last as long as had been reported in the newspapers: "If we don't call all 184 witnesses, and I can just about promise you we will not—you won't think we're trying to conceal anything and hold it against us, will you?" The juror said he would not.

During the midday break, reporters for the national wire services rushed to file their stories using the teletype machines and telephones that had been installed in a city office down the hall from the courtroom. Graham spent the lunch recess in the prisoner waiting room. The deputies refused to identify the restaurant from which they had obtained his food, fearing that "somebody might try to put something in his lunch if we made it public." Pursuant to the orders of Warden Dolliver—who had become concerned that the media reports of Graham's dramatic weight loss might lead to accusations of malnourishment—the deputies made a detailed record of every meal Graham was served and each item of food that he ate.

An hour after the proceeding reconvened, Bert Keating completed his questioning, gathered up his papers from the podium, and announced that "the prosecution passes the panel for cause."

Charles Vigil then questioned the prospective jurors for the remainder of the afternoon. Through his inquiries, he implicitly acknowledged the strength of the prosecution's evidence. Rather than ask the jurors about their ability to acquit, Vigil asked about their willingness to consider the lesser offenses of second-degree murder and voluntary manslaughter.

At the end of the first day, Judge McDonald informed the thirteen potential jurors that they would be spending the night at the city dormitory. The jurors obediently followed the bailiffs from the courtroom.

The next morning, John Gibbons complained that the presence of the two uniformed police officers in the courtroom was giving the jurors "the impression that Jack Graham is a dangerous man." Charles Vigil agreed. "I can't see any reason for any great number of officers," he said. "I don't think there should be any great display in this trial different from other trials." Hearing no objection from the prosecutors, Judge McDonald granted the request and ordered the uniformed officers to leave.

When Vigil resumed his examination, he shifted the focus of his questioning and asked the prospective jurors whether they would think Graham was guilty if he exercised his constitutional right not to testify. Those who said they would harbor such a suspicion were excused.

At 10:00 A.M., one of the bailiffs walked to the defense table and whispered in the ear of Paul Weadick, the junior attorney who had a nonspeaking role on the defense team. Weadick smiled and rushed to the hallway. Ducking into a phone booth, he called Saint Joseph's Hospital and spoke with his wife, who told him that she and the twin boys she had delivered an hour before were all doing fine. As Weadick hurried back to the courtroom, a reporter asked him what names he had chosen. "Darned if I know," said Weadick. "I'll have to see 'em first."

On Wednesday, April 18, the prosecution and defense began exercising their first peremptory challenges. Each time a seat was vacated, the lawyers were allowed to make challenges for cause to the prospective juror called as a replacement. One woman, a seemingly ideal juror, surprised everyone in the courtroom by telling Bert Keating she had not heard a thing about the airplane bombing. However, she was subsequently dismissed when she said she did not believe in capital punishment.

James Motley was another prospective juror who initially appeared to be a good candidate for service. When asked by Bert Keating whether he had "formed any opinion as to the guilt or innocence of the defendant," the Lowry Air Force Base clerk said he had not.

"So you can serve here as a fair and impartial juror, is that correct?"

"Well, I wouldn't say that."

"Why? Do you have some problem concerning your employment or personal life?"

"I have a physical disability."

"I see, and are you under a doctor's care?"

"No, not exactly."

"Do you feel your physical condition would prevent you from serving fairly and impartially and from giving your undivided attention to the trial?"

"I do."

"Is it a physical condition you have had for some time?"

"Yes."

"Is it of a serious nature?"

"Well, I wouldn't know what you would say is serious. I'll tell you what it is. I can't sit still."

Once the laughter had died down, Judge McDonald excused the antsy man.

A short time later, the bailiff handed the judge a note from Mrs. Mary Margaret Rose, one of the original thirteen juror candidates who had already been passed for cause by both sides:

> I thought I could be a fair juror and wanted to be honest in doing my civic duty as a juror. I was sincere in this, but the longer I look at the defendant the more I realize I could not consent to the death penalty, if necessary. He is too near the age of my own boys. I am sorry.

Bert Keating used one of his peremptory challenges to excuse her.

On Wednesday afternoon, Nick Ursini—a butcher who had been accepted by both sides—told the bailiff he was experiencing severe stomach pains. At Judge McDonald's request, a doctor was summoned from Denver General Hospital to meet with Ursini in the jury deliberation room. After conducting his exam, the physician told Judge McDonald that the prospective juror should be excused because he was suffering from "acute anxiety," a condition that would only increase as the "emotional tension" of the trial became more intense. The judge followed the doctor's recommendation, and Ursini walked unsteadily from the courtroom.

A half hour later, Mrs. Margaret Roecker, another juror who had been accepted by both sides, stood up in the jury box and called out to the judge, "Your Honor, Your Honor. I would like to be excused. I did not realize we would be locked up at all times." Judge McDonald was exasperated. Holding his head in his hands, he asked her to sit down. After discussing the issue with the lawyers in his chambers, McDonald asked Mrs. Roecker to explain why sequestration would be a hardship for her. The mother of three children told the judge she needed to be home in the evenings because her husband worked the night shift at the General Iron Works. McDonald let her go.

When John Gibbons took over the questioning of the prospective jurors, his emphasis was noticeably different from Vigil's. Wearing a suit that one *Rocky Mountain News* columnist said made him look as "natty as a gambler going to his best friend's funeral," Gibbons asked several jurors questions that suggested United Air Lines had a financial interest in showing the wreck had been caused by sabotage rather than by a mechanical defect.

Bert Keating resumed his examination with a question designed to undermine Gibbons's implication: "Just because a witness works for United Air Lines, you won't think he has any interest or prejudice, will you? After all, United isn't a party to this case—it's the People versus John Gilbert Graham." Greg Mueller followed up with a similar inquiry: "This business counsel for the defense is talking about—an interest in the case. You know, don't you, that anything like that has to be brought out by evidence?" The prospective jurors said they would not presume bias.

By the end of the day, each side had used four peremptory challenges. The prosecutors had dismissed only women; the defense attorneys had dismissed only men. Bert Keating candidly admitted his strategy. "I have nothing against women," he said. "But they are supposed to be more sentimental and softer than men."*

Gloria Graham had not been able to attend the trial on Wednesday. Her son Allen was suffering from a sore throat and fever, and she did not want to leave him with Helene West, the neighbor who had been looking after the children during the trial. Gloria was not feeling well either. "The roof of my mouth has broken out in sores," she said, "as it does when I'm nervous. . . . This is a nightmare I keep thinking I'll wake from."

Using an old washing machine that had once belonged to Daisie, she laundered a fresh shirt and underclothes for her husband to wear to court the next day. She was concerned about how he appeared to the jurors. "His suit is too large. . . . He seems very calm, but if you know him very well, you can tell he's nervous." In addition to the emotional upheaval, Gloria was experiencing financial difficulties. At one time, there had been enough money for small luxuries. "Jack liked me to look nice, and he liked clothes too. He always dressed well. After Jack was jailed, I sold our 1955 pickup truck. We've been living on that money, but it's getting short." To make ends meet, she had started selling Tupperware kitchen containers at parties hosted in the homes of her many friends. "I don't need any pity," she said. "I like [the Tupperware business], and I need the money."

On Thursday, Bert Keating questioned Mrs. Madeline McClure, a prospective juror called into the box to replace a juror who had been excused on a peremptory challenge. Mrs. McClure did not stay long. Her husband, a super-

---

* In 1994, the United States Supreme Court ruled that attorneys cannot exercise peremptory challenges on the basis of gender.

intendent with Sinclair Oil and Gas Company, had once hired Brad Bynum, the geologist who had perished on Flight 629 along with his pregnant wife.

By the end of the day, the attorneys had questioned a total of 130 prospective jurors, eclipsing the old record, which had been set at the trial of LeRoy Leick. And they were not even half done. After the attorneys exercised their peremptory challenges, only five jurors remained in the box.

The Friday morning session was not productive. All eighteen of the prospective jurors called into the box were dismissed for cause. Some refused to afford Graham the presumption of innocence, others were opposed to the death penalty, and a few convinced Judge McDonald that jury service would be a hardship.

One juror who successfully pleaded hardship was Jack Blatherwick, an insurance adjuster who had served as a juror in the 1938 murder trial of Joe Coates—the "bad boy of Larimer Street." Blatherwick and eleven other jurors had sentenced Coates to the gas chamber for fatally shooting a Denver police detective who had tried to arrest Coates for abusing a prostitute. In response to Greg Mueller's questions, Blatherwick said he "couldn't do it again." As Mueller made his challenge for cause, Gibbons leapt to his feet, obligingly announcing that the defense had "no resistance to the challenge."*

When it was Gibbons's turn to examine the newest prospective jurors, he asked whether they would be able to disregard a confession if they concluded it was not voluntary. This was a new line of inquiry, and it provided Bert Keating and Greg Mueller with a possible explanation of why, earlier that day, the defense had surprised them by subpoenaing the four psychiatrists who had examined Graham and declared him sane. There was also another possibility. Under the Colorado Supreme Court's recent decision reversing LeRoy Leick's first conviction, a defendant charged with first-degree murder was now entitled to present psychiatric testimony to show he lacked the capacity to deliberate and form the requisite intent.

The next morning, readers of the *Rocky Mountain News* were given a unique perspective on the previous day's court proceedings—a diary Graham had written at the request of one of the newspaper's columnists:

---

* Coincidentally, the chief prosecutor for the Coates trial, former Congressman John A. Carroll, was in the courtroom as a spectator on the same day his daughter Diane called Jack Blatherwick into the jury box.

It is Friday, April 20. I come out of a deep sleep hearing the guard dragging his keys across the cell bars. I ask him the time. He says 5 A.M. This is another day. When will this end? The trial has been going since Monday. Monday, Tuesday, Wednesday, Thursday, Friday—five days. It seems an eternity.

I roll out of the sack. The guards take me to the shower. It feels cold this morning. I brush my teeth and then shave. They watch me while I shave. I'll wear the gray stripe suit with the white shirt and the blue tie. The tie was a Christmas present from Gloria, my wife.

Breakfast. I'm not hungry. I nibble on a roll. Then I eat some cereal and milk. No coffee. I hate coffee. Then guard Bill Rose locks me up. How about a game of chess? We play. I like chess. It is relaxing. We have a standoff because the six [deputies] show up.

Outside it is beautiful. It is 8:30 and the birds are singing and a big plane is taking off from nearby Stapleton Airfield. It feels wonderful in the open air. That courtroom will be hot and smelly by midafternoon.

Five of us get in one car and the detectives ride behind. We drive slowly through town and into the garage behind the City and County Building. Then we are in the sheriff's office and I see my attorneys. John Gibbons, whose pretty wife is with him, Charles Vigil, and Paul Weadick.

We go into court at 9:30. The cuffs come off. I rub my wrists. Gloria isn't around. Gibbons says she is coming at noon.

The jury comes in. The faces are familiar. They won't look at me. I wonder which of them is lying when they say they will sit in this case with an open mind. That's all I want. I want someone to listen to the facts and then I want them to be honest. I know I am innocent, and I want them to listen and be honest so we can prove it.

I fidget. I can't sit still in that chair. Too bad I can't be excused like that juror who couldn't sit still. . . .

There are five women and eight men up there. Makes no difference which sex. Just let them be honest and listen. Pray that they do. This isn't like playing games with kids. This may mean my [life.]

Recess. Noon. Lunch. The guards buy my food at a restaurant. It is good. Better than at the jail. . . . Back to the trial. Will it never end? Let's get going. Recess. Adjourn. Drive home with the six [deputies]. Back in the cell. There is some peace here. The planes make noise.

Dinner. Celery soup. Cottage cheese. Baked fish. Baked macaroni and cheese. Potatoes. No coffee. They bring tea. I like tea. I don't smoke. Never have. There is prune pie. I pick [at it.]

No chess tonight. I want my Bible. I like the Psalms and the Proverbs. I got no fixed religion, I guess. Methodist. I was married in Lakewood Methodist Church. When was the last time I went to church? November 1? No, it was the day I was arrested. Sunday, November 13. That's the last time.

It is 7:45. I am tired. My eyes hurt. No chess? That's guard Jim Detavio. No chess. Bible tonight. The proverbs:

> *"A false witness shall not be unpunished, and he that speaketh lies shall not escape. The desire of a man is his kindness: and a poor man is better than a liar."*

> *"There are many devices in a man's heart; nevertheless, the counsel of the Lord, that shall stand. He that wasteth his father and chaseth away his mother is a son that causeth shame and bringeth reproach."*

> *"Cease my son, to hear the instruction that causeth to err from the words of knowledge. An ungodly witness scorneth judgment: and the mouth of the wicked devoureth iniquity."*

> *"Judgments are prepared for scorners, and stripes for the backs of fools."*

It is almost 8:00 P.M. I am sleepy.

> *"For they sleep not, except they have done mischief; and their sleep is taken away, unless they cause some to fall."*

I sleep.

On Saturday, two of the potential jurors called into the box said they knew Graham. Gloria Hansen, a typist at the General Adjustment Bureau, had met Graham when he worked at the insurance firm as a "mail boy." She also had been involved in processing the insurance settlement for the gas explosion at the Crown-A drive-in. Judge McDonald excused her.

W. R. Ancell, general chairman for the Brotherhood of Maintenance of Way Employees, a railroad union, said he had known Graham when Graham attended school in Yampa. He also had known Daisie King when she belonged to the Order of the Eastern Star, an organization affiliated with the Masons. Judge McDonald excused Ancell because the prospective juror admitted that his knowledge of the defendant and the victim would "substantially influence" his opinion.

At 11:35 A.M., Diane Carroll asked for "the defense's tenth peremptory challenge." After huddling with John Gibbons and Paul Weadick, Charles Vigil announced, "Jack Graham accepts the jury." But Bert Keating did not, and he used his eleventh peremptory challenge to remove yet another woman.

The prospective juror summoned to fill the vacant seat was G. Donald Bell, a driver for the Railway Express Company. Like Jack Blatherwick, Bell had served as a juror in a highly publicized murder case—the 1946 trial of Frederick Smith, a Grand Junction police officer sentenced to life imprisonment for the "Ship Tavern shooting," a drunken killing committed in the bar of the Brown Palace Hotel.* After Judge McDonald granted Bell's request to be excused, the former juror expressed his relief: "When you begin deliberating about sending a man to the gas chamber, it's something to think about. Once was enough."

At the end of the Saturday session, the attorneys had questioned a total of 216 jurors. The defense had used ten peremptory challenges, all of them against men. The prosecution had used a dozen of its challenges, all but two of them against women. Although Judge McDonald was frustrated by the pace of the jury selection, he was pleased that the experiment with court-room photography was such a success. "There is not a bit of disruption," he said. "There has been no distraction at all that I am aware of." Bert Keating agreed. "It's working fine," he said. "Prospective jurors never know when a camera is on them. There's been nothing to interfere with the orderly procedure of the trial." Charles Vigil concurred, saying he had seen in the newspaper photographs of himself that had been taken without his knowledge. Even John Gibbons admitted it was going well. "This is amazing," he exclaimed. "I was the one who feared picture taking would upset the courtroom. I don't even know when it is going on."

On Sunday, the thirteen sequestered jurors went on an outing arranged by Judge McDonald. It was a welcome diversion, particularly for the four jurors who had been in custody since the first day. Under the supervision of the two bailiffs, the seven men and six women boarded a chartered bus that took them

---

* In another coincidence, the first officer to arrive at the scene of the shooting in the Ship Tavern was George Boyles, one of the uniformed policemen guarding the door during the Graham trial.

Clerk Diane Carroll (back to camera) administering the oath to the jurors. Front row, from left to right: Mrs. Elva Prouty, Fred Anderson, Lester B. Donnelly, Mrs. Mary M. James, Floyd H. Franzen, and Mrs. Hildred L. Brinkman. Back row: Francis T. McCullough, Ralph W. Bonar, Laprelle T. Smith (partially obscured), Mrs. Marjorie R. Cowen (partially obscured), Mrs. Esther F. Locke, Lyle A. Parsons, and Mrs. Lillian F. Baker (alternate). (Courtesy of Denver Public Library, Western History Collection, Dick Davis Collection)

to dinner at the Mount Vernon Country Club in Golden. Afterward, the driver made a detour through the Idaho Springs area for a bit of sightseeing.

On Monday, following the midmorning recess, Bert Keating quizzed Mrs. Lillian F. Baker, a self-described "housewife" whose husband worked as a messenger for the Santa Fe Railroad. Mrs. Baker said she had a "small opinion" about the case that she could set aside. Keating told Judge McDonald he was satisfied: "The prosecution accepts the jury."*

Seven men and five women would decide Jack Graham's fate: Fred Anderson, a plumber for Johnson & Davis Company; Ralph W. Bonar, the assistant to the president of a film company; Mrs. Hildred L. Brinkman, a clerk-typist for the Colorado Game and Fish Department; Mrs. Marjorie R. Cowen, a real estate "saleslady" and Denver native; Lester B. Donnelly, a repairman for the Mountain States Telephone & Telegraph Company; Floyd H. Franzen, a lithographer for the Standard Reproduction Com-

---

* Because Mrs. Baker was the thirteenth juror to be accepted by the parties, Judge McDonald designated her as the alternate.

pany; Mrs. Mary M. James, a bookkeeper for the U.S. Transfer and Storage Company; Mrs. Esther F. Locke, a clerk-typist at the Air Force Finance Center; Francis T. McCullough, a civil engineer for the United States Department of the Interior who had served as a pilot in World War II; Lyle A. Parsons, a real estate salesman who had recently sold a house to one of the district attorney's investigators; Mrs. Elva Prouty, president of the Colorado Federation of Garden Clubs, who as a beauty pageant contestant in the late 1920s had once held the titles of Miss Denver, Miss Colorado, and the Queen of Pulchritude; and Laprelle T. Smith, a truck driver with a son close in age to Graham.

After thanking and excusing the prospective jurors in the gallery who had not been selected, Judge McDonald recessed until 2:30 P.M., allotting an extra half hour before opening statements so that George Young—the court stenographer who had been making a handwritten record of every word spoken—would have time to label the prosecution's 150 exhibits.*

---

* In 1955, Colorado law allowed for the transcription of court proceedings by written shorthand or by stenographic machine. However, earlier in the week, the owner of a company seeking to obtain certification of an alternative recording mechanism known as the "Stenomask" had brought one of his machines into the courtroom in hopes that its use at the Graham trial might serve as an advantageous marketing opportunity (the "Stenomask" generated an audio recording of the operator of the device repeating each word spoken during the court proceedings into a mask attached to the operator's face). When Judge McDonald noticed the unauthorized recording device, he ordered it removed.

CHAPTER TWELVE

# "Graham—the liar."

"THE STATE WILL SHOW that Mrs. King fell approximately 5,800 feet to earth, and that the impact caused her death," Keating told the jurors. He then proceeded to carefully summarize the evidence in a lengthy opening statement. He described Graham's plan as a "diabolic scheme of destruction and death" that had been carried out "coldly, carefully and deliberately," and he assured the jurors he would convince them "there is only one possible penalty, and that is death."

When Keating was finished, Charles Vigil announced that he would defer his opening statement until the prosecution had rested its case, explaining that he expected "various things will develop in the evidence."

During the brief recess that followed, Judge McDonald allowed each side to pick one advisory witness who could sit at the counsel table throughout the trial. Bert Keating and Greg Mueller selected Roy Moore, the FBI assistant special agent-in-charge who had supervised the investigation. The defense team chose Dr. John Macdonald, the psychiatrist from the Colorado Psychopathic Hospital who had examined Graham and declared him sane.

The first witness called to testify was not cooperative. When Keating showed Helen Hablutzel a photograph of Daisie King, Helen equivocated: "I guess it's a picture of my mother. It's a very poor one. It could be almost anyone." When Keating asked her to identify a sample of Daisie's handwriting, she did so reluctantly: "I'm no handwriting expert, but it resembles her handwriting." When Keating handed her several items written by her brother, she hedged: "Those are his signatures, but I don't recognize the handwriting." Keating was frustrated by this bumpy start of his case, and he asked Judge McDonald for permission to treat the witness as hostile. However, before the judge could rule on the request, John Gibbons stipulated to the authenticity of the documents, thus clearing the way for admission of the handwriting samples that would later be compared with the handwriting on the flight insurance policies.

Keating next called Daniel Lynch, the assistant to the vice president of flight operations for United Air Lines, who testified that the Mainliner flight from New York to Seattle had stopped in Chicago before arriving in Denver slightly behind schedule. When John Gibbons began his cross-examination, his first question demonstrated how little he had prepared; he could not even remember the flight number. His subsequent inquiries, particularly those having to do with a nonexistent fuel-line problem he suggested had been repaired in Chicago, only reinforced this perception.

The first witness to provide incriminating testimony was Jack Legg, a passenger agent at United Air Lines who had been working at the ticket counter on the evening of November 1, 1955. Legg testified that Daisie King had arrived at the counter at 6:10 P.M. accompanied by Jack and Gloria Graham:

> After weighing the baggage, I found out that she was in excess of the allowable amount [of 66 pounds], and I told her how much the charge would be, and she seemed rather reluctant or hesitant as to whether to pay the amount. . . . I made a suggestion that there might be something she could leave here in Denver and have it shipped to her. . . . Mrs. King asked [Gloria Graham] what she thought about whether anything should be left here that might possibly be shipped to her later; and [Mrs. Graham] then called Mr. Graham [over] and they asked him . . . what he thought . . . and Mr. Graham said to Mrs. King, "You'll need all of your things there."

The next witness, Hugh Chance, the pilot who had flown Flight 629 to Denver, testified that the only mechanical problem with the aircraft was a malfunctioning propeller deicer on one of the engines. During cross-examination, Charles Vigil asked Chance to confirm that the plane was transporting a shipment of cordite, an explosive substance containing nitroglycerin. Chance said he had no such knowledge.

On Tuesday morning, Judge McDonald informed the lawyers that he had received a phone call the previous evening from the wife of Lester Donnelly, one of the jurors, who had reported that a man identifying himself as "Mr. Kennedy" had come to her home the week before asking about her husband. Mrs. Donnelly had not thought anything of it at the time, but she had become concerned when she stopped by the courtroom to watch part of the trial and spotted the same man talking with one of Graham's attorneys.

When confronted with this information, Gibbons admitted that he had hired a private investigator named R. J. "Little Mac" McDonald to look into the backgrounds of the jurors. "As far as I am concerned, the guy didn't do anything wrong," Gibbons protested, adding that such investigations were routinely conducted "in every murder trial I've ever heard of."

At a hastily convened hearing on the issue, McDonald testified that Gibbons had hired him to "find out how the wives [of the prospective jurors] feel about the case." Judge McDonald was incensed, and he did not believe the investigator's claim that he had not used a false name when interviewing Mrs. Donnelly. "I don't appreciate the methods you've used," the judge said, angrily informing McDonald that he was directing Bert Keating to take the matter before a grand jury to determine whether "what you've done is illegal."

When the trial resumed later in the morning, the prosecutors called half a dozen United Air Lines baggage handlers to describe how they had loaded all of the luggage and cargo originating from Denver into the number four cargo pit, the rear lower storage compartment of the DC-6B. Through cross-examination of one of these witnesses, Gibbons tried to show that the men would have detected a bomb: "If you were picking up a bag, and if in that bag there was a timer that was making a sound similar to a timer—[an] alarm clock, but a bit louder—do you think you could hear that?" The baggage handler said he would not be able to hear such a soft sound while working on a busy tarmac.

Using a procession of witnesses, Keating and Mueller moved along the timeline toward the fateful moment the bomb had exploded. A United Air Lines flight dispatcher testified that the pilot, Lee Hall, had checked the weather and filed his flight plan before walking out to the aircraft to conduct his preflight inspection. Merrill Yaney, who had been working in the air traffic control tower, recalled clearing the plane for takeoff. Yaney testified that he and his partner soon "noticed two very bright lights north and slightly northwest of Denver. It appeared to be parachute flares. . . . And, as the lower flare of the two extinguished, we saw a brilliant flash in the sky to the north, and it illuminated the base of the clouds."

Another witness with an unusual vantage point was James Stevenson, a United Air Lines pilot who had been flying a plane at nine thousand feet above sea level directly behind Flight 629:

> We saw a bright light to the west of us two thousand feet higher than
> we were, approximately. And after about thirty seconds, we saw
> another bright light in the approximate same line northwest of us

at approximately the same altitude. And while watching those, we noticed an explosion, or a bright flare, and on the ground a tremendous explosion.

Stevenson recalled that conditions were "slightly choppy" but otherwise good, with "very sharp" visibility permitting him to see the lights of Fort Collins.

The day concluded with testimony from half a dozen witnesses who lived near the area where the wreckage had fallen. The men and women called to the stand painted a vivid portrait of the explosion, describing its house-shaking force and the giant ball of fire filling the night sky east of Longmont.

Late that afternoon, Charles Vigil filed a suppression motion in federal district court, where the case charging Graham with interfering with a national defense utility was still pending. The motion, supported by an affidavit from Graham, alleged that the searches of Graham's house and cars were unlawful and asked the federal court to prohibit FBI agents from testifying in state court about the evidence they had found. The motion also sought suppression of Graham's confession on the ground that the FBI agents had waited an unreasonable amount of time before taking him to court for an advisement of his rights.

Gibbons thought Vigil's suppression motion was a waste of time. "We haven't seen eye-to-eye on this case in the four and a half months we've had it," he complained.

On Wednesday morning, a representative of the Douglas Corporation identified a 1/18-scale model of a DC-6B mounted, as if in flight, on a metal pole rising from a circular floor stand. Built by the aircraft manufacturer at a cost of $2,500, the model had a six-foot wingspan and interior details that could be viewed by removing the side panels to expose the passenger compartment and cargo storage pits. At Bert Keating's request, Judge McDonald directed the jurors to "come out of the box and look at the exhibit, file by it without touching it or commenting upon it." One by one, the jurors carefully examined the model, paying particular attention to the lower rear cargo pit.

The next exhibits admitted into evidence were not replicas. William Mentzer, the general manager of engineering for United Air Lines, identified each item as Keating showed it to him: a seat cushion, a piece of carpet from the aft section of the plane, a container for storing food in the

Trial exhibits: The 1/18 scale model of a DC-6B; several pieces of the damaged aircraft; an Eveready "Hot Shot" battery; a hand-wound electric timer; and two sticks of dynamite. (Courtesy of Denver Public Library, Western History Collection, Dick Davis Collection)

small galley, an armrest, and many other pieces of debris recognizable to those jurors who had flown in an airplane.

When Mentzer finished testifying, Jack Meyer took the stand and described how he and the other members of the United Air Lines recovery team had worked through the night gathering the many bodies scattered near the parts of the plane. The defense attorneys did not ask any questions, apparently realizing that probing for further testimony about the horrific crash site would be counterproductive.

At noon, Judge McDonald informed the jurors that they would not be needed again until late that afternoon. He did not tell them that the delay was necessary because Graham was scheduled to appear in federal court for the hearing on Vigil's suppression motion. With little else to do to pass the time in the dormitory, the male jurors spent the afternoon playing cards, checkers, and dominoes. The women took turns mending their clothes using a sewing machine delivered by the bailiff.

At 1:30 P.M., in the august courtroom of Federal District Judge William Lee Knous,* Charles Vigil faced off against Donald Kelley, the man who had succeeded him as United States attorney for Colorado. There were no photographers due to the federal prohibition against cameras in the courtroom.

The first witness, Roy Moore, testified that Graham had signed forms giving the agents permission to search his house and cars. Moore also described the circumstances surrounding Graham's confession:

> He began at 12:07, and it took him about fifteen minutes to complete his oral admission. I then directed the agents and the boy to move into the office of the special agent-in-charge, where I had called a stenographer from her home to take the statement and record it, and type it up. . . . Jack seemed to have difficulty in forming this confession in his own words, and we inferred that he would prefer that we lead the thing, which we did, and Mr. Bush and Mr. Wagoner then would dictate a sentence or a paragraph to the stenographer. They would then turn to Jack and say, "Is that right?" And he would agree. That is the way we proceeded until the statement was finished. . . . The girl retired from the room to type the statement. . . . In the interval immediately after the statement was taken I called in [a physician] to examine the young man and to inquire from him whether he had been mistreated either mentally or physically—to which he replied in the negative.
>
> After he was photographed [and] fingerprinted and his property inventoried, I asked him if he preferred now going to the city jail, which was his prerogative after he was under arrest, or whether he would desire to remain in the office the remainder of the night. He stated he would prefer to remain in our office the remainder of the night rather than going to the city jail, and I asked him to execute a statement to that

---

* William Lee Knous, a former mayor of Montrose who had also served as a state legislator and as a justice on the Colorado Supreme Court, was the governor of Colorado from 1947 until the time of his appointment as a federal judge in 1950.

effect, which he did. I had the boys bring a leather couch from the ladies' room into the office of the special agent-in-charge, and he retired for the night and slept until nine in the morning, when I came in and offered him breakfast.

The only other witness, Gloria Graham, testified that she had signed several forms giving the FBI agents permission to search the house and cars. "I figured as long as [Jack had] signed one it was all right," she said. "We had nothing to hide."

Judge Knous rejected Vigil's claim that the Grahams' consent to the searches was the result of "intimidation and duress." Knous also rejected Vigil's claim that the agents had violated a federal rule of procedure by waiting until the morning before taking Graham before a commissioner, though he left open the possibility that "if constitutional questions would arise with respect to the admissibility of the confession, they can be reviewed in [state] court." As soon as the one-hour hearing adjourned, the deputies whisked Graham back to the fourth-floor courtroom in the City and County Building, where he spent the remainder of the afternoon chewing gum while listening to witnesses testify about transporting the parts of the shattered plane from the crash site to the warehouse in northeast Denver.

The Thursday morning session began without any indication of the impending disruption. When Charles Vigil objected to the testimony of C. E. Bennett, United's chief of aircraft maintenance, he made his objection respectfully, arguing that testimony about bodies other than Daisie King's was "wholly prejudicial" and designed to "inflame the jury." Although Judge McDonald overruled the objection, Vigil did not display any frustration as Bennett described the difficult task of retrieving the remains of the dead:

> All the bodies were wrapped that we were able to find except what were left in the fuselage, which we were unable to get to on account of the darkness and insufficient equipment to spread the fuselage apart and get in there and get the bodies out, because these bodies in the fuselage were very badly mutilated, and it was an impossible job to do before daylight.

After Bennett was excused, Keating and Mueller wheeled two carts into the courtroom loaded with parts of the plane. As Keating sifted through the parts looking for an exhibit, Charles Vigil charged toward the

Bert Keating and Greg Mueller carrying a box of aircraft parts. (*Denver Post*, David Mathias,
Courtesy of Colorado Historical Society, Fred Mazzulla Collection, #10032920)

cart, his face flushed with anger. The defense lawyer grabbed a piece of the
plane and hurled it to the floor. Like almost everyone else in the courtroom, Judge McDonald stared in disbelief. Some, including Graham,
laughed at the outburst. Vigil—seemingly egged on by the laughter—continued tossing pieces of metal onto the floor until Judge McDonald hammered his gavel and admonished the attorney for his behavior.

Once order was restored, three United Air Lines employees who had
assisted with the reassembly of the fuselage identified the parts of the aircraft. A fourth witness, Carl Christenson, the United Air Lines director of
safety, testified that he had organized a search at the outskirts of the crash
site on November 6, five days after the disaster. He and dozens of other
men had spaced themselves "at arm's length and then very carefully
walk[ed] slowly back and forth" across the sugar beet fields, farther away
from where the main sections of the aircraft had fallen. As he was looking
down at the furrowed ground, Christenson spotted "a piece of metal, a
small box, and a piece of dark material that appear[ed] to be of a carbon nature. . . . a broken section of a rod." When shown the piece of metal by
Keating, the director of safety recognized it immediately. "It was lying with
the shiny side up. . . . I remember it very well, because on the other side is
a red paint stripe and the letters, in blue, 'OT'."

That afternoon, Dr. Earl Miller, the physician who had dined with Daisie the night before she died, testified that he had been called to the Greeley Armory three days later to identify her corpse. The body, tagged as number thirty-eight, "was exposed down to the waistline. Because of my long familiarity with her face, hair, and body proportions, there was no question whatsoever in my mind about the identity of the body."

In cross-examination, Gibbons asked Dr. Miller how long he had known Graham. Miller said he had first met Graham when Graham was "ten months old and just toddling around chairs and furniture. I was called to treat him for a cold." Since that time, he had "been in his home hundreds of times." In an attempt to undermine Bert Keating's opening statement emphasizing the significance of the piece of yellow wire FBI agents had recovered from Jack Graham's house, Gibbons directed the doctor's attention to the deer-hunting trip he had taken with Graham on the King ranch the week before Daisie was killed, asking the witness whether "anything unusual" had occurred. Miller replied:

> There was a little incident. Jack and I separated. We were alone up there in the morning on the range, and I wasn't too familiar with the terrain. I'd never been in that section of the country, so I hunted more or less within the vicinity of the jeep. Jack, knowing the terrain, took off across a valley onto another ridge where he had shot deer in preceding years. And a little later in the morning, I wasn't too far from the jeep, I heard the motor start, so I figured Jack was back to the jeep and it was time for me to get back to it.
>
> When I went back, why, the hood of the jeep was raised, and I said, "Are you having trouble?" And he said, "Well, I got a buck over there, and when I dressed it out I left my coat over there. I didn't realize I left the keys to the jeep in my coat until I got back here and tried to start it." So I said, "Well, how did you manage to start the jeep?" And he said, "I found a piece of wire in the . . . back of the jeep, and I short-circuited the ignition and got it going." And that's what he used to go back to where his coat and the buck were. . . . After we'd driven around about a mile and a half over rough terrain to get back to where Jack's coat was, when we loaded the buck, why, he took the wire off . . . the motor and put it in his pocket.

It is unclear whether Gibbons's decision to elicit this testimony was the result of foolishness, deviousness, or unpreparedness. However, it is clear that the blunder cost him a great deal of credibility with the jurors. During redirect examination, it took Bert Keating less than a minute to establish that the piece of wire Dr. Miller had seen was not covered with yellow plastic insulation like the strand the FBI agents had found in Graham's shirt pocket.*

After excusing Dr. Miller, Judge McDonald announced the lunch recess. The timing was fortuitous. It is doubtful any of the jurors would have had much of an appetite if the midday break had come after the testimony of the prosecution's next two witnesses.

H. Ross Adamson, the Weld County coroner, provided a detailed description of body number thirty-eight:

> The injuries were to the lower extremities. . . . [T]he legs were mangled. The abdomen and chest cavities were open. There was a crushed skull, more on the top than on the back of the head, and [as for] the upper extremities, the arms were broken [with] multiple fractures.

Dr. George J. Kidera, medical director for United Air Lines and a member of the Aero Medical Association, a group of physicians specializing in medicine relating to aviation, provided his opinion as to the cause of Daisie's death:

> Any one of these injuries could have been responsible for her death: the skull injury, as described with the brain leaking out; the opening into the chest cavity with the vital chest structures being pushed forward through that hole; the abdominal injury with portions of the intestines pushed out and torn away; or the severe mangling of the legs. Any of these four, in my opinion, could have been the cause of death. I would say, though, that death was instantaneous due to the head injury.

The final witness of the day was Roy Mischke, one of the FBI agents who had interviewed Graham before he was a suspect. Through Mischke, the prosecutors demonstrated that Graham knew his inheritance under Earl King's will and his ownership interest in the Crown-A drive-in both were conditioned upon Daisie's death.

On Friday morning, Dr. William J. Magee, an FBI chemist, testified that he had examined approximately one hundred parts from the airplane. "I identified the . . . foreign materials present on the airplane parts as sodium carbonate, minor traces of sodium nitrate, and still smaller quantities of

---

* It is unclear why Keating did not ask Dr. Miller about Graham's statement during this same hunting trip in which he had jokingly suggested the doctor could get some "action" by firing a shot into a shack where dynamite was stored.

Above: Dr. J. William Magee, an FBI chemist, identifies a piece of the aircraft for Bert Keating, watched by jurors (from left to right) Lester B. Donnelly, Mrs. Marjorie R. Cowen, Floyd H. Franzen, and Lyle A. Parsons. (*Denver Post*, David Mathias, Courtesy of Colorado Historical Society, Fred Mazzula Collection, #10032919)

Below: Two sticks of dynamite introduced as exhibits. (Courtesy of Denver Public Library, Western History Collection, Dick Davis Collection)

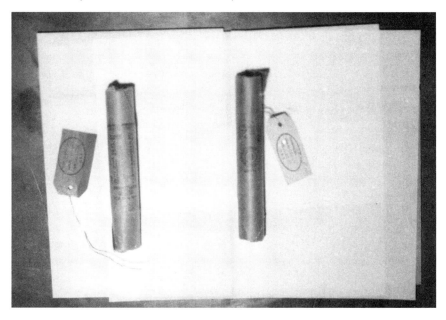

sulphur-bearing compounds. . . . In my opinion, the residues on these parts which I examined originated from exploding dynamite." After having Magee show the jury several of the parts he had tested, Bert Keating handed the chemist two sticks of dynamite.

Magee examined the exhibits and turned to Judge McDonald. "I would like to just say one word of caution."

A wave of nervous laughter rippled through the gallery.

Holding up one of the sticks, Magee pointed out that it "has been opened, and the contents are now spilling out, and some people are ex-tremely susceptible to nitroglycerin. I mean, if it gets on your skin it kicks up the heartbeat quite considerably. It's just not a good idea for the mate-rial to be dribbled around all over the courtroom."

"It's not explosive, is that right?" the judge asked.

"Oh, yes, it very definitely is explosive," replied Magee, a response that prompted a few spectators to stand and walk from the courtroom.

McDonald asked what it would take to detonate the dynamite.

"It would have to be initiated by one of several means," said the chemist. As he was about to elaborate, Max Melville interrupted, jokingly calling out a warning to Charles Vigil that "it shouldn't be thrown on the floor."

During cross-examination, Dr. Magee testified that there were dozens of brands of dynamite on the market. Although he admitted he could not definitively state what type had been used to blow up Flight 629, he testi-fied that the combination of trace elements in the "the residue . . . could have resulted from the explosion of DuPont dynamite."

Building on Magee's testimony, the prosecutors called Lyman Brown to testify that he had sold twenty-five sticks of DuPont dynamite to Graham on a Saturday evening in late October. Anticipating a defense attack on Brown's recollection, and mindful of the fact that Graham had an alibi for the night of October 29, Greg Mueller asked the Kremmling merchant to explain how it was that he had determined the sale had occurred on the evening of October 22. Brown said he was quite sure of the date:

> The fifteenth of October was the day hunting season opened. We were very busy. In fact, most of my clerks and myself didn't go home to sup-per. The next Saturday was the twenty-second, and it was rather quiet. My clerks, most of them, went to supper at that time. The next Saturday night would be the twenty-ninth, and at that time a very peculiar event took place. My friend and partner, the late James Eskridge, was killed in an airplane accident. He was my partner in uranium prospecting. And at

six o'clock, or shortly thereafter, I received word that he had died in an airplane crash. Immediately thereafter I went home, and was home for at least two hours.

In cross-examination, Gibbons attempted to establish that Brown might have erroneously identified Graham as the purchaser because Brown had known Graham when Graham attended the Kremmling high school during 1946 and 1947. Gibbons also attacked the absence of any documentary proof, asking Brown whether he had a receipt from the "cash register showing the sale of this dynamite." Brown admitted that he did not, and he conceded that he had originally told *Denver Post* reporters the sale had occurred on October 29.

That afternoon, Judge McDonald again directed the jurors back to the dormitory, apologetically informing them he had to deal with yet another matter outside of their presence. After the jurors were gone, the judge called upon the lawyers to address the voluntariness and admissibility of Graham's confession, the issue that would determine whether the jury would be given the option of imposing the death penalty.

Roy Moore took the stand again to rebut the defense lawyers' claim that the confession was coerced. Graham watched the agent uneasily, fiddling with the cuffs of his trousers and shifting in his chair. Repeating his earlier testimony, Moore explained that he had advised Graham of his rights before interrogating him as a suspect and confronting him with Gloria's admission of lying about her knowledge of the Christmas gift. Moore denied directly threatening to charge Gloria with giving a false statement, though he admitted he had told Graham he had the ability to do so.

Dr. Robert Harrington, the physician who had been called to the FBI office to examine Graham, testified that he had arrived at 1:42 A.M. "[Graham] assured me that everybody had treated him perfectly all right . . . and then I did a complete history and physical on him and found that he had no unusual marks or abrasions or anything upon his body at that time."

James Wagoner and Donald Sebesta, the two agents who had spent the afternoon of November 13 with Graham and taken him to lunch before returning to the FBI office for additional questioning, both testified that the confession was not the result of any threats or promises.

When it was the defense team's turn to present evidence, Gibbons called Graham to the stand. Graham leaned back in the leather witness chair, licked his lips nervously, and spoke to Judge McDonald. "I'd like to ask that the television and radio be turned off at this time." McDonald granted the request, to the

Special Agent Donald Sebesta testifies. (Photograph courtesy of Federal Bureau of Investigation, Denver Field Office)

great disappointment of the television cameraman and Gene Amole, whose radio station was broadcasting two hours of trial testimony each evening.

Gibbons asked his client why he had confessed to a crime he had not committed. "They said they would arrest my wife for lying to a federal officer," Graham replied. "Because of what they had told me about my wife, me being scared of what they would do to her, I made a statement to them." Continuing, Graham claimed that he had not dictated the statement to the agents, and he accused them of having refused to let him use the telephone.

Once Gibbons was finished with Graham, Bert Keating conducted a cross-examination. He had two objectives in mind: convincing Judge McDonald that Graham lacked any credibility, and demonstrating to Graham that he would be exposed as a liar if he elected to testify in front of the jury. At first Graham seemed unflappable, confidently testifying that he had signed the consent-to-search forms because he did not have anything to hide. However, as the prosecutor moved closer and peppered him with questions, the color began to drain from Graham's face. "Do you mean to tell this court," Keating asked disdainfully, "that you assumed the responsi-

Bert Keating cross-examines Graham, with court reporter George Young and Judge Joseph McDonald in the background. (*Rocky Mountain News,* Courtesy of Denver Public Library, Western History Collection, Dick Davis Collection)

bility for forty-four deaths because something was said about your wife going to jail?

"That's right," Graham shot back, an answer that caused such a commotion in the audience that Judge McDonald threatened to clear the courtroom.

Returning to the podium, Gibbons attempted to rehabilitate Graham's credibility, asking, "Why else did you sign it?"

"Because I knew it wasn't the truth and we could prove it," Graham replied.

In a second round of cross-examination, Keating issued a challenge. "When do you propose to prove that this isn't a true statement?

"When we put on our testimony," Graham replied, leaving everyone in the courtroom with the impression that he intended to tell the jury his version of events.

At 6:00 P.M., after hearing additional testimony from other FBI agents who had participated in the interrogation, Judge McDonald made his ruling: "The court is fully convinced that this is a voluntary statement of the defendant. Accordingly, [it] will be admitted into evidence."

No one was more pleased by the judge's decision than Roy Moore. Earlier that day, the agent had predicted that if the confession was not admitted, J. Edgar Hoover would assign him to "a dogsled somewhere north of Nome."

On Saturday morning, FBI agent James Wagoner told the jury of the lengthy interrogation, describing how Graham had abandoned his original story about purchasing the X-acto tool set from the mysterious stranger when the agents confronted him with his many contradictory statements and the incriminating evidence discovered in the search of his house. Beginning with Graham's statement that it had "all started about six months ago" when Daisie King was "raising hell about the drive-in," Wagoner testified that Graham had confessed first to disconnecting the gas line at the drive-in and to deliberately stalling his truck on the train tracks. The FBI agent then detailed Graham's confession to the bombing, including the story of "Karl," the German explosives expert Graham claimed he had met in a Larimer Street bar.*

Wagoner said that Graham had disavowed any financial motive. "He told us after some time that approximately four or five years ago he had wanted to take his own life. He said that he believed that if he caused the plane to crash that he would be found out and that his life would be ended. He told us that if he had not been found out he was going to tell someone in order that his life would be ended." Based on Wagoner's testimony, Keating obtained Judge McDonald's permission to read the signed confession to the jury:

> I, John Gilbert Graham, make the following voluntary statement to James R. Wagoner, Paul E. Bush and Brendan P. Walsh, who have identified themselves to me as special agents of the Federal Bureau of Investigation, United States Department of Justice. I realize that I do not have to make any statement and that any statement that I do make can be used against me in a court of law. I have been advised I have a right to consult a lawyer at any time. No threats, promises or moneys have been offered to me to make this statement. I make this statement because I desire that the truth be known concerning this matter.

---

* During his testimony outside the presence of the jury the day before, Graham had mentioned that the wall of the room where he was interrogated in the FBI office had "a picture that had people that were apprehended during the war, I believe, by the Federal Bureau of Investigation for sabotage—showed their pictures, and had a small memorandum underneath." Unbeknownst to the prosecutors, while Graham was at the Colorado Psychopathic Hospital, he had revealed that this photograph—which depicted the eight Nazi saboteurs who had been arrested by the FBI after they landed at Amagansett, New York, and Ponte Vedra Beach, Florida, in 1942—had inspired him to create "Karl," his fictional German co-conspirator

My name is John Gilbert Graham and I was born on January 23, 1932, in Denver, Colorado. I received a high school certificate from the University of Denver Extension Division in 1950 and have completed one year of college at the University of Denver.

I am the son of the late Mrs. Daisie E. King, who was killed in the wreck of a United Air Lines plane on November 1, 1955, while en route from Denver, Colorado, to Anchorage, Alaska.

On about October 18 or 19 I placed in the trunk of my 1951 Plymouth sedan twenty-five sticks of dynamite, 40–60 percent, a timing device, and an Eveready six-volt dry cell "Hot Shot" battery and two dynamite caps with about eight feet of wire attached to the caps. All of this was placed in a cardboard box about eighteen inches long and about eight inches wide and about six or eight inches deep. I covered this carton containing the above items with a blanket and left it in the trunk of my car until the afternoon of November 1, 1955. It was the day my mother, Mrs. Daisie E. King, was due to leave Denver on her proposed trip to Anchorage on United Airline Flight 629 scheduled to leave at 6:30 P.M.

On the afternoon of November 1, 1955, at about 5:15 P.M., my wife, Gloria Graham, and my mother, Mrs. Daisie E. King, with our son, Allen Graham, age twenty months, left our residence at 2650 West Mississippi in my mother's 1955 Chevrolet en route to the Denver Motor Hotel, 1420 Stout Street, for the purpose of placing my mother's car in storage until she returned from Alaska. I told my mother and my wife that I would place my mother's luggage in my automobile and meet them at the Denver Motor Hotel, from where we would all continue to the Denver Municipal Airport so that my mother could board the United Air Lines plane en route to Alaska.

As soon as my mother, wife and son had left our residence, I went out to my car, which was parked in the driveway in front of my house, and there in the trunk of my car I placed the twenty-five sticks of dynamite in a paper sack around the two dynamite caps. To each dynamite cap was attached two strands of wire approximately eight feet in length. I then wrapped about three or four feet of binding cord around the sack of dynamite to hold the dynamite sticks in place around the caps, leaving the wires which were attached to the dynamite caps extending out of the paper sack. I then connected one of the wires from one of the caps to one of the battery poles, having run this wire through the timing device. I connected the other wire of this same cap directly to the other battery pole. I then connected the second cap in the same manner. The purpose of the two caps was in case one of the caps failed to function and ignite the dynamite. I then set the timer to detonate the dynamite in one and

one-half hours, because that was the maximum time on the timer. At this
time, an hour and one-half, I knew that the circuit between the caps and
the battery, which was broken by the timer, would be closed by the timer
mechanism and detonate the caps, which would detonate the dynamite.

I then took this sack of dynamite with the battery and timer attached and
placed it in my mother's large Samsonite suitcase, which she had previously
packed to take with her on her trip to Alaska. I placed this suitcase in the
trunk of my car, together with another smaller suitcase and a briefcase,
which my mother had packed to take with her on her trip. I then drove to a
surplus store on Alameda [Avenue] near Federal [Boulevard] in Denver,
where I purchased two olive-colored web straps. I then drove to the Denver
Motor Hotel, where I picked up my mother, wife and son.

We then drove in my car to the Denver . . . airport. I let my mother, wife
and son out of the car at the entrance to the main building at the airport. I
then parked my car at one of the parking meters about a half block from the
main entrance to the airport terminal. I then took the two web straps
which I had purchased and fastened them around the large suitcase in which
I had placed the dynamite. I then took this suitcase, together with the one
small suitcase and briefcase belonging to my mother, to the United Air
Lines ticket counter in the main airport terminal building, where I turned
all the luggage over to my mother. My wife and I then waited at a point
about thirty feet from the United Air Lines counter while my mother
checked her luggage onto United Air Lines Flight 629.

After my mother had finished checking her luggage, my wife and I went
with her to the passengers' gate, where my wife and I told my mother
goodbye and watched her board the plane with the other passengers. My
wife and I then watched the United Air Lines plane taxi down the runway,
after which we, with our small son, went into the coffee shop at the airport
and had dinner. We were in the coffee shop for approximately one hour and
as we were leaving I heard the cashier of the coffee shop make the statement that there had been a wreck of an airplane about forty miles out of
Denver. Later on that evening, after my wife and I had returned to our
home, we heard over the radio—and later verified by United Air Lines personnel—that there had been an explosion on United Air Lines plane 629
that evening near Longmont, Colorado, and that all the passengers aboard
had been killed.

I have read the above statement consisting of this page and four others
and it is all true. I have initialed the pages.

(signed)

John Gilbert Graham

After Keating finished reading the confession, Judge McDonald gave the jurors the afternoon off so that he could tour the Denver warehouse containing the reconstructed sections of the aircraft. He was accompanied by the prosecutors, who wanted the jurors to view the wreckage, and by the defense attorneys, who, surprisingly, had not previously visited the warehouse and had not yet decided whether to object to the prosecutors' request for a jury viewing. William Bentson, the superintendent of flight engineers for United Air Lines, guided the group through the debris for an hour. Upon seeing the rows of battered seats and the many other reminders of the dead passengers, Gibbons and Vigil voiced their objection to the idea of bringing the jurors to the warehouse, arguing that such a field trip was unnecessary because the jurors could be shown photographs of the reconstructed fuselage. Keating did not press the issue, withdrawing his request in order to avoid giving Graham potential grounds for an appeal.

Despite the fact that portions of the proceedings were being broadcast on television, the demand for seats in the courtroom was so great that the Denver University law students attending the trial brought bagged lunches to avoid losing their places during the midday break. Other seats were reserved for people connected to the case, such as United Air Lines president Pat Patterson, who was present for Keating's opening statement, and the wives of the FBI agents, who came to watch their husbands testify. Yet, other than Helen Hablutzel and Gloria Graham, not a single relative of a victim had been spotted in the spectators' gallery during the first week of the trial. "I can't see that anything would be gained by going to the trial," said Sally Ann Scofield's mother. "For us, it's over and done with. We wouldn't consider going." William Bommelyn, who had lost his brother, felt similarly. "I would feel very upset if I saw that man," he said.

However, when the trial resumed on Monday morning, a thin woman wearing a light blue hat entered the courtroom and sat in the area reserved for relatives of the victims. The elegantly dressed woman displayed no sign of her grief. Sitting patiently, Sally Hall of Seattle waited to hear the prosecutors build their case against the man charged with putting a bomb aboard the plane that had been piloted by her husband.

Judge McDonald (left) inspects the reconstructed cargo pit with John Gibbons (reconstructed upper section of the fuselage in background). (*Denver Post,* April 29, 1956, David Mathias, Courtesy of Colorado Historical Society, Fred Mazzulla Collection, #10032921)

Bert Keating picked up where he had left off on Saturday, calling FBI agent James Wagoner back to the stand to identify the four sketches of the bomb components Graham had drawn after he confessed. Charles Vigil did not score many points in cross-examination, though he did get Wagoner to admit that the FBI agents, while claiming not to believe Graham's claim that he had been aided by an accomplice, had spent a great deal of time searching for "Karl."

Agent Donald Sebesta's testimony was much the same as Wagoner's. During cross-examination, Gibbons attempted to draw out a few sympathetic facts by asking the agent what he knew about Graham's decision to leave home as a teenager. Sebesta testified that Graham had told him he ran away because of problems stemming from his stepfather's drinking. Sebesta also testified about Graham's time in the Coast Guard and his subsequent work at Elmendorf Air Force Base while living with his sister in Alaska. Although Bert Keating could have objected to this evidence as being beyond the scope of his direct examination, he voiced no such complaint. Instead, on redirect examination, the district attorney asked Sebesta what he knew about Graham's activities during 1951, the one year that Gibbons had skipped over when asking about Graham's work history. The question prompted a loud outcry from the defense table. After the bailiff removed the jury, Keating argued that Gibbons had opened the door to the otherwise inadmissible evidence of Graham's forgery and bootlegging convictions. In a rare victory for the defense, Judge McDonald ruled that the jury would not hear about Graham's prior convictions.

But they would continue to hear about his confession. Again, and again, and again. By the end of the day, so many FBI agents had testified concerning the confession that the jurors likely could have recited the text of the document from memory.

On Tuesday morning, the deputies were especially careful when escorting Graham into the courtroom. The day before, they had neglected to remove the shackles before the jurors entered the courtroom, an oversight that had nearly resulted in a mistrial. At a special hearing concerning the incident, Charles Vigil had argued that the restraints suggested Graham was dangerous, basing his claim on a 1946 decision of the Colorado Supreme Court that reversed the murder conviction of a defendant who had been put on trial while wearing county jail coveralls. Although Judge McDonald ultimately concluded that it was unlikely any of the jurors had seen the chains because Graham had been surrounded by deputies, he issued a stern warning not to let it happen again.

When the trial resumed, the manager of the Illinois Powder Company, a Denver explosives store located near Graham's house, identified a blasting cap from his store. The blasting cap, which had been deactivated before it was brought into the courtroom, was attached to two yellow wires.

Dr. Magee of the FBI then returned to the stand and testified that the yellow wire on the blasting cap was identical to that found in Graham's house. Magee also testified that the small scrap of metal with the letters "OT" found at the crash site had come from the word "SHOT" on an Eveready "Hot Shot" battery, and that the battery had been located close to the source of the blast. After waiting a full minute for the bells in the tower of the City and County Building to toll—a clamorous sound that had been interrupting the testimony at regular intervals throughout the trial—Keating handed the battery fragment to the jury along with a magnifying glass with which to examine it.

William Mentzer was also called back as a witness to explain how he and Jack Parshall, the Civil Aeronautics Board investigator, had organized the reassembly of the wreckage. Using the scale model of the DC-6B and photographs from the warehouse to illustrate his testimony, Mentzer told the jury he was certain the plane had been "destroyed in the air as a result of an explosion . . . in the lower rear cargo compartment . . . commonly known as pit four." During cross-examination, Vigil tried to get Mentzer to confirm that the explosion was similar to one at the Chicago airport caused by a mechanic who had accidentally ignited vapors leaking from a fuel tank. Mentzer disagreed, explaining that the Chicago blast was "quite different in that it simply opened the plane up rather than breaking it into very small pieces, as was the case in this explosion." Vigil shifted his focus and asked whether the pressurized cabin mechanism on a DC-6B had "ever gone out of control in any way." Mentzer conceded that there had been malfunctions, but "not in the overpressurization sense, inasmuch as there are three separate means of preventing excessive pressure." Vigil then tried a different approach, suggesting that the deployment of the flares indicated that the crew was aware of a mechanical problem. However, Mentzer testified that the simultaneous release of the flares was more consistent with an explosion because "the normal practice is to release one flare at a fairly high altitude to get an overall view of the terrain, and then after a likely spot is picked out, to release the second flare much closer to the ground." Vigil was about to give up when he asked Mentzer whether he had participated in the investigation of the crash on Medicine Bow Peak that had occurred the month before the Flight 629 disaster. Mentzer said that he had.

"And what caused that?"

"I don't know."

Having at last elicited a concession, Vigil returned to his seat.

The prosecutors thought that evidence of the Medicine Bow Peak crash was relevant, too, but for an entirely different reason: to show that Graham had planned for Flight 629 to go down in the same area.

Late Tuesday afternoon, after subjecting the jury to the tedious testimony of an FBI handwriting examiner who identified Graham as the person who had filled out the information on the $37,500 flight insurance policy naming himself as the beneficiary, Greg Mueller called Charles T.

Wifler to the stand. Wifler, the credit manager for Murphy-Mahoney Chevrolet, testified that he had spoken with Graham on November 11 when Graham retrieved the truck that had been damaged by the train:

> The reason for the conversation was in regard to the payment of the fifty-dollar [insurance deductible for the repairs]. Mr. Graham told me that he was unable to pay the fifty dollars because his . . . joint bank account[s] . . . were tied up by the FBI as the result of an investigation, . . . that if he could have the half-ton pickup, if we would release that, that he would probably be able to get the money and pay the fifty-dollar deductible.

When talking about Daisie, Graham had told Wifler that "it was very difficult for him to realize she was gone." He had also shared his theory about how his mother might have been killed:

> Mr. Graham explained that, in his opinion, . . . after the airline had taken the luggage and put it on . . . carts, . . . it would be relatively easy for anyone familiar with the airport to exchange luggage by entering . . . over a small fence whereby you could replace one piece of luggage with another. He indicated that he felt . . . to explode the plane it would take about two gallons of nitroglycerin . . . [and that] a timing device would need to be used.
>
> He mentioned that . . . the United crash could have been caused possibly by the same individual that had caused a recent . . . crash in Texas where the tail section and pieces of the airplane were distributed or blown over quite an area. That it looked to him like it could have been the same type of explosion.[*]
>
> He mentioned that the plane was . . . late in departing Stapleton Airfield, and that if it had departed on time it would very likely have been somewhere in the area that a previous airliner of United Air Lines had crashed.

The final witness of the day was Damon Ward, the owner of Ward Electric, a Denver supply company located on Tenth Street. Ward told the jurors that he had first met Graham in early October, when Graham asked him for a job. "He said he wanted to get further work in the electrical line and that he would be willing to start at a nominal wage in order to get further experience." Soon after he was hired, Graham told Ward that he wanted to buy a timing device. "He claimed what he had to have could not

---

[*] On November 8, 1955, a B-47 Stratojet—one of the planes used by the Strategic Air Command for carrying atomic bombs—exploded above Marlin, Texas. Three years later, after several other accidents involving B-47s, the Air Force grounded the entire fleet for structural repairs.

have an outside source of energy to supply the motivation for it," Ward recalled. "It had to have something that was spring-loaded that would supply
its own power, something that he could set for a predetermined time . . .
not to exceed two hours." Ward told Graham that he did not have anything
meeting those specifications. The next day, Graham called to say he would
not be coming to work because he had been called for jury duty.

   Ward never heard from him again.

On Wednesday morning, Joseph Grande of Ryall Electric testified that on
October 17—the same day Graham told Damon Ward he had been summoned for jury duty—a man named "Jack" from the Colorado-Texas
Pump Company had come in and ordered a hand-wound electric timer. After identifying Graham as the purchaser of the timer, Grande told the jurors about the erroneous order of the "on" timer, the expedited order of
the "off" timer, and Graham's eventual decision to exchange the latter device for the former. In response to a question by Charles Vigil, Grande
stated that the maximum setting on the timer was sixty minutes. Upon
redirect examination, Bert Keating had Grande explain how it could be
modified to run for an additional ten minutes—a sufficient amount of time
if Graham had activated the device in the parking lot at Stapleton Airfield.

It had been a week and a half since Helen Hablutzel had first testified against her
brother. The passing of time had not made her any less reluctant a witness.
When recalled to the stand on Wednesday morning, she appeared to be on the
verge of tears. Dressed in a brown pullover sweater and a plaid skirt, she fid-
geted with a medallion around her neck and gestured nervously as she side-
stepped Keating's questions about the items she had found in Daisie's basement
bedroom shortly after the crash. Undeterred by her evasiveness, Keating confronted Helen with a statement she had made to the FBI and forced her to confirm that she had opened a dresser drawer and discovered in it items that Daisie
had intended to bring with her on her trip: several packages of nylons, a robe, a
pair of deerskin gloves, an antique powder horn, and a set of "stocking tops"—
Angora wool anklets that Daisie had made as a Christmas present for her grand-

daughter. As Keating continued extracting the incriminating testimony, Graham twisted sideways in his chair and turned his back on his sister. Keating ignored the display and asked Helen what Graham had said to her when she had inquired about the unpacked items.

"He said, 'She had so much stuff that . . . the suitcase was just too full. She just left them.'"

Keating pressed on, forcing Helen to admit she had told the FBI that her brother had said their mother had packed "damn near forty pounds" of ammunition, and that he had laughingly envisioned the "shotgun shells going off in the plane every which way, and the pilots and passengers and [Daisie] jumping around."

"You stated to him that you saw very little humor in this joke, isn't that correct?" asked Keating.

"Probably. I don't think it's very funny now."

The prosecutors completed their case at 3:05 P.M. "The People rest," Keating announced, his voice imbued with confidence in the testimony of the 78 witnesses and 174 exhibits he and Greg Mueller had presented. Upon hearing the district attorney's declaration, Judge McDonald released the jurors for the afternoon and told them they would not have to return until 1:00 P.M. the following day.

After the jurors left for the dormitory, Charles Vigil made a motion for dismissal, resurrecting his tired claim that the case should have been tried in Weld County. In an even weaker argument, Vigil asserted that the prosecutors had failed to prove the cause of Daisie King's death because there had not been an autopsy. Max "Mr. Law" Melville—who until this point in the trial had been playing a behind-the-scenes role advising Keating and Mueller on points of law—responded on behalf of the prosecution. "The woman's body had been ripped open and her head split," he exclaimed. "That establishes the cause of death well enough." Judge McDonald agreed, ruling that "the state has made a prima facie case."

When the trial resumed, Charles Vigil made his opening statement, telling the jury that the prosecutors had failed to prove beyond a reasonable doubt that Graham purchased the dynamite from Lyman Brown. He spoke for only a minute and a half.

John Gibbons called the first defense witness: Mrs. Helene West, the Grahams' neighbor who had been caring for the Graham children while Gloria attended the trial. Mrs. West thought the Grahams were "very nice people," and she had a clear memory of Jack Graham's whereabouts on October 22, the day Lyman Brown thought he had sold Graham the dynamite. "He was cleaning the house before Gloria came home [from a trip to Missouri with Daisie]. He was waxing the floors . . . and he came over to borrow part of my waxer." Helene West had loaned Graham the machine and invited him to join her and her husband for dinner. That evening, after eating at 5:30, "Jack finished feeding the baby for me, and he stayed and played with the children a little while, and we talked, and I'd say it was around 7:00 [when he left]."

She also remembered the events of November 1, the night she had agreed to look after Suzie Graham while Jack and Gloria took Daisie to the airport. At approximately 5:00 P.M., Graham had come to her door with his infant daughter, some diapers, and a bottle. After putting the baby to sleep, Helene West had waited for the Grahams to return:

> I sat and watched television and sewed for a while. One of the programs I
> was watching was interrupted by a news bulletin of this plane crash, and
> they didn't know too many details about it. . . . I was alarmed at the time it
> might be Daisie King's [flight]. . . . Shortly after eight, they came home, and
> by then I was rather wrought up about it, and I ran across the street, and
> Jack and Gloria were getting out of the car, and I was half crying.

She was still at the house when Graham called United Air Lines. During that time, Gloria told her that Jack had eaten some fish at the airport café "which didn't settle right."

When it was Bert Keating's turn to question Mrs. West, he asked her what else Gloria had told her. Helene West said that, after they learned there had been no survivors, Gloria "had casually mentioned . . . what a shame it was that Daisie wouldn't have her Christmas present now, that Jack had gotten some kind of a drill set for her hobby, which was making shell jewelry, and that he had put it in her suitcase as a surprise [for] when she got up to Spenard."

Gloria's parents, the Elsons, both testified that they had seen Graham when they stopped by his home on the evening of October 22. However, it was evident that the Elsons were not happy about being called as witnesses for the defense. When asked to describe his relationship to the defendant,

Mr. Elson hesitated for a moment before answering. When Gibbons asked the same question of Mrs. Elson, she distanced herself as much as possible, testifying only that "his wife is my daughter." As Mrs. Elson stepped from the stand, Graham looked at her with an apologetic expression. She never saw it, averting her gaze as she walked quickly from the courtroom.

The next witness, Jerome R. Strickland, the attorney who had first represented Graham, told the jury about bumping into Daisie King and the Grahams while at Stapleton Airfield to meet his brother. Strickland testified that he had "noticed nothing unusual" about Graham's demeanor.

Gibbons then called David Ochs, a chemist for Industrial Laboratories, a firm that advised United Air Lines concerning the shipping of chemicals as cargo. Ochs testified that, three days after the disaster, a representative of United Air Lines had called to ask him about Aquapel, a sizing compound that might have been shipped on Flight 629. It was a red herring. In cross-examination, Ochs told Keating that Aquapel was not combustible.

Next, Gibbons put a United Air Lines cargo supervisor on the stand expecting him to testify that an unidentified item of cargo had been shipped on Flight 629. However, the witness testified that he had since determined that the package in question contained a wooden box for storing silverware.

An investigator who worked for Gibbons testified briefly and identified a roll of yellow wire he had purchased, at Gibbons's request, from a nearby electrical supply store. Gibbons then recalled Dr. Magee to the stand and asked the FBI chemist to compare that roll of purchased wire with the wire seized from Graham's house. It was not a successful ploy. Dr. Magee testified that the purchased wire was "obviously not the same color" as the wire the agents had found in Graham's shirt pocket.

At times during the trial, Graham had ignored the proceedings and read a medical textbook, *Mask of Sanity: An Attempt to Clarify Some Issues About the So-called Psychopathic Personality*. This choice of reading material, in conjunction with Gibbons's pretrial comments about a "surprise defense," led most observers to believe that the defense would call Dr. Macdonald to testify. However, after the prosecution rested its case, the psychiatrist had privately informed the defense attorneys that he had not heard anything to alter his opinion that Graham was capable of forming the intent to commit first-degree murder.

During the Thursday afternoon recess that followed the two hours of defense testimony, Gibbons and Vigil tried to persuade Graham that Dr. Macdonald could still be a helpful witness, and that his testimony about Graham's childhood experiences might persuade the jurors not to impose the death penalty. Graham was unconvinced. "Well, I don't see where it would help any. I don't want to go down and sit in prison for fifty years anyway." He also told his attorneys that he had decided not to testify, and he was adamant that they not call Gloria to the stand.

Moving his manacled hands in tandem, Graham signed his name to a document stating that he did not want to present any additional evidence. Judge McDonald made him verify the decision on the record:

"Do you understand the nature of these documents?"

"Yes, sir."

"And this is your wish?"

"Yes, sir."

"This is free and voluntary, and your desire in this matter?"

"That's right."

McDonald accepted Graham's waiver and directed the bailiff to retrieve the jury.

The jurors returned to their seats expecting to listen to more testimony. Instead, they heard Charles Vigil announce, "At this time, if the court please, the defense rests."

On Friday morning, more than two hundred people were waiting for seats to hear the closing arguments. They groaned in collective disappointment when a bailiff stepped into the hallway and announced that the judge and attorneys would be spending the morning working on the jury instructions. Although the trial was not scheduled to resume until 1:00 P.M., many of the spectators stayed put. "We've been here since 7:30 A.M., and we don't want to lose our place now," one elderly woman explained.

At the conference in Judge McDonald's chambers to discuss the jury instructions, Charles Vigil asked that the jurors be told they could consider Graham's "mental derangement" when assessing his intent. He also sought an instruction concerning insanity. Judge McDonald refused both requests, as well as Gibbons's demand that the "not guilty" verdict form be stapled on top of the "guilty" verdict form.

The final set of instructions approved by Judge McDonald advised the jurors that first-degree murder required proof beyond a reasonable doubt of a "deliberate and premeditated killing" committed with "express malice." The jurors were given the option of convicting Graham of the lesser offense of second-degree murder, an intentional killing committed without deliberation and malice. The jurors were told they could infer that malice existed "when no considerable provocation appears, or when the circumstances of the killing show an abandoned and malignant heart." To find "deliberation," they would have to conclude that Graham acted in "a cool state of the blood, in furtherance of a formed design to gratify a feeling of revenge or to accomplish some other unlawful purpose."

The instructions further directed the jurors—if they found Graham guilty of murder in the first degree—to choose between "life at hard labor in the penitentiary or death." Reading from the packet of instructions, Judge McDonald informed them that there were no criteria to guide them in this grave decision. "The selection of the penalty is entirely one of your own discretion. It is not controlled by any test of law or any established pattern of fact."

After Judge McDonald finished reading the instructions, Greg Mueller made his closing argument. Speaking for almost two and a half hours, the chief deputy district attorney meticulously summarized the evidence pointing to Graham as the perpetrator of "this dastardly, horrible mass murder." Mueller emphasized the many times Graham had reaffirmed his murderous intent:

> Under the laws of Colorado and the laws of God, there is a place where a person who has planned a crime can turn back. It has a Latin name. It is the locus poenitentiae, or the place of repentance. It was available to Graham. He could have turned back at any point—when he bought the dynamite, when he rigged the bomb, when he set it in the suitcase, when he gave the suitcase to his mother to check in. The death he decreed for her when he sent her aloft to be hurtled out of the air and have her body ripped open and driven into the ground is the same death this murderer deserves.

As he spoke, Mueller looked directly at Graham. Graham stared right back, seemingly unmoved by the condemnatory rhetoric.

John Gibbons began his closing remarks by telling the jurors he would not be attacking the credibility of the FBI agents. "If you think I'm going to stand here like a muscle head and ridicule the FBI, you're crazy. They're the greatest. Not only in the United States, but in the world." Nevertheless,

Gibbons insisted that the agents had manipulated the substance of Graham's fabricated confession by omitting the outlandish description of an accomplice. "Every time he said something that didn't fit into the jigsaw puzzle the way they wanted it, they said it was a lie. When he sat down and dictated this ridiculous confession, they said he couldn't be telling a lie then. Why? Because he confessed to what they wanted him to confess."

Reading from the signed statement, Gibbons pointed out that the bomb would have detonated at 6:45 P.M. if, as Graham claimed, he had started the ninety-minute timer at 5:15 P.M. "Here you have the uncontradicted testimony of Graham—the liar. According to it, Stapleton Airfield should have been blown to kingdom come. That's it. I don't know what to believe. But I don't believe there was any timer or any bomb in Daisie King's suitcase."

Referring to Graham as an "egomaniac who likes to say the most damnable things," Gibbons asked, "Can you really believe that a little guy—Jack Graham—could destroy a plane worth $1,750,000? I can't. I'm sincere when I say I don't believe he put a bomb in the suitcase. But it's your baby. Remember what will happen. Some bleak night the warden of the state pen will walk down that long narrow corridor and ask Jack Graham if he's ready. He'll lead Jack Graham down those long steps and have him disrobe." As Gibbons started to describe how the gas chamber worked, Bert Keating objected on the ground that there had not been any evidence presented "concerning the method of execution." Judge McDonald sustained the objection and instructed the defense attorney to move on.

Returning to his central theme, Gibbons described Graham as a pathological liar. "If he walked up and told me right now the sun was shining, I'd go out to take a look."

Removing his glasses and waiving them for emphasis, Gibbons reminded the jurors that the evidence indicating the timer could run for only seventy minutes was "uncontradicted, except by Graham—the liar."

After speaking for almost an hour, Gibbons closed by quoting from Rudyard Kipling's "The Ballad of East and West," a poem with no discernible relevance to the case.

When Charles Vigil stepped to the podium to deliver the second half of the closing argument, his hands were shaking and his right eye was twitching. Perhaps it was due to the stress of the lengthy trial and the anonymous telephone calls he had received heckling him for representing a mass murderer. Perhaps his symptoms were caused by the same anger that had led him to toss the plane parts to the floor. Or perhaps it was the fact that Vigil, like the client whose life he was trying to save, had lost his father as a child

John Gibbons delivers his closing argument. (Courtesy of Denver Public Library, Western History Collection, Dick Davis Collection)

and had enlisted in the Coast Guard as a young man. Whatever the cause of Vigil's distress, it was obvious to everyone in the courtroom.

Picking up where Gibbons had left off, Vigil described Graham's lying as "a symptom of his psychopathic personality." He complimented the FBI agents as "experts in the field of investigation" but argued that experts were not infallible. "An expert looking at a pencil my wife sharpened would say she did it with her teeth, but the witness who actually saw her do it would say she did it with a knife." Later, in a poor choice of words that caused tittering in the gallery, Vigil spoke of Graham's temper, saying, "there's no doubt he blows up when the pressure gets too great."

Continuing his colleague's poetry recital with a more pertinent selection, Vigil quoted from Oscar Wilde's "Ballad of Reading Gaol," a prisoner's portrait of a condemned man awaiting execution.

After the dinner recess, Bert Keating addressed the jurors and urged them not to be "misled by the stupid and insulting statements of defense counsel." Pointing to the mangled maintenance log, Keating characterized it as "a voice from the grave [that] tells you that the plane was in good shape until the explosion [of] . . . enough dynamite to blow away a small mountain." He described the FBI agents as "honest, honorable men who have a duty to perform for you and me. They are truthful men. The defense attorneys would have you believe they mesmerized this defendant to have him admit he killed his mother."

Throughout the closing arguments, Helen Hablutzel and Gloria Graham had sat together in the front row. However, when Keating graphically described Daisie King's injuries, Helen stood up and walked out. "The evidence has been overwhelming," she said as she left the City and County Building. "I expect a guilty verdict, but I don't think Jack is really guilty."

Turning to the issue of motive, the district attorney reminded the jury of Daisie's generosity. "Graham operated the drive-in bought for him by his mother. But he wanted more money. He wanted lots of money. He wanted his mother's money. . . . He told his wife he was putting a Christmas gift in his mother's suitcase. It was a gift all right. It was twenty-five sticks of dynamite with two caps to blow her out of this world." He continued:

> Compare the proceedings in this case. Take into consideration the patience and dignity of this court and the three experienced attorneys appointed to protect [Graham's] rights. Compare this system of justice and then come back to November 1. Ask yourself what happened in the trial of Daisie King. This defendant set himself up as the judge, he became the prosecutor, and he said that "I, the jury, decide you must die." He set the place in the sky and then he became the executioner. This woman who bore this man and nursed him to sustain his life died at his hands.
>
> One man alone turned the skies into the death house at 7:03 P.M. on November 1. His mother didn't have any time to appeal for mercy—the only

man she could appeal to was thirty miles away. Her death had been ordained six months before. Only the date of execution remained to be filled in.

At 9:45 P.M., Keating finished with a flourish: "I speak for the dead. If ever a man has deserved the death sentence, that man is John Gilbert Graham."

Before sending the jury to the deliberation room, Judge McDonald thanked and excused the alternate juror, Mrs. Lillian Baker. She was greatly relieved, telling a reporter in the hallway, "I'll be so glad to get home. I hope I never have to go through anything like this again."

At 9:49 P.M., the bailiff escorted the remaining twelve jurors from the courtroom. Zeke Scher sidled up to Graham and asked him what he thought the verdict would be. Graham said he had "no doubt" about the outcome. However, when Sher repeated his request for a prediction, Graham snapped at the reporter: "That's none of your business."

Gloria was not making any predictions either. "We've waited a long time for this. Now that it's here, it isn't very pleasant. It's looked bad from the very beginning. But whatever the verdict, I guess I'll always think he didn't do it."

At 10:58 P.M., the bailiff informed Judge McDonald that the jurors had reached a verdict on their first ballot. As the bells of the clock tower tolled eleven times, the prosecutors and defense attorneys returned to their respective tables. Two minutes later, the sheriff's deputies brought in Graham.

Gloria Graham was too upset to reenter the courtroom. Sitting on a wooden bench in the hallway with her neighbor, Helene West, she smoked one cigarette after another and chewed on her fingernails.

At 11:07 P.M., the jurors somberly filed back into the courtroom. Once everyone was seated, Judge McDonald asked, "Ladies and gentlemen, have you reached a verdict?" Ralph Bonar, the jury foreman, stood up. "We have, Your Honor," he replied. Judge McDonald asked, "Will you please hand your verdict to the bailiff?" Bonar complied, passing the folded sheet of paper to the bailiff, who delivered it to the bench.

The deputies stood behind Graham as Judge McDonald read the verdict in a shaky voice. "We the jury find the defendant, John Gilbert Graham, guilty of murder in the first degree and find that he acted with premeditation and a specific intent to take life as charged in the information herein, and fix the penalty at death." Graham displayed no emotion.*

---

* With one exception, the reporters who were present in the courtroom all stated that Graham received the verdict stoically. However, James L. Kilgallen told readers of the Hearst newspapers that "tears welled in Graham's eyes." It is unclear whether this discrepancy is attributable to Kilgallen's eyesight or to his writing style.

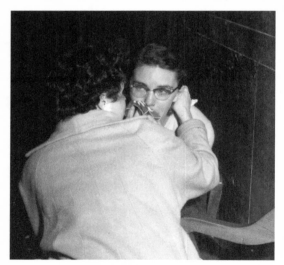

Above: Graham is escorted from
the courtroom by Lieutenant
Robert Stratton *(rear right)*, and
Sergeant George Hayes *(front
right)* after the verdict.
(Courtesy of Denver Public
Library, Western History
Collection, Dick Davis
Collection)

Left: Helene West *(back to
camera)* consoles Gloria Graham
after the verdict.
(Courtesy of Denver Public
Library, Western History
Collection, Dick Davis
Collection)

Gloria was unable to hear the judge read the verdict, but she heard the murmuring of the audience and burst into tears. A moment later, the deputies brought Graham out of the courtroom in handcuffs. Gloria looked up in time to see her husband wink at her as he was led away. "Now I'm all alone!" she gasped.

As Helene West dabbed at Gloria's face with a saturated handkerchief, a dozen reporters burst through the doorway, scrambling to get to the telephones and call in their stories. One of the reporters extended a finger and pulled it across his own throat to signal the result to those in the hallway. Upon seeing the callous gesture, Gloria collapsed into her neighbor's arms.

Soon thereafter, Sally Hall emerged from the courtroom. Walking past the bench, the pilot's widow glanced down at the sobbing widow-to-be. Neither woman said a word.

## Chapter Thirteen

# *"I just want to get gone."*

A T 4 A.M. ON THE MORNING after the jury reached its verdict, two Denver policemen noticed a station wagon filled with luggage parked in front of the Denver City and County Building. The officers peered inside and saw a woman slumped behind the wheel. She was holding a copy of the *Rocky Mountain News* with a one-word headline printed in large, boldface letters: "**DEATH!**"

The officers awoke the woman and asked for her driver's license. When she refused to comply, one of the officers pulled out a summons book and began filling out a "Jane Doe" complaint charging her with public intoxication. "You really got good and drunk, didn't you?" he asked.

"If you just found out your brother had killed your mother," the woman slurred, "you'd get drunk, too."

Upon realizing who the inebriated woman was, the officers offered to overlook the infraction and give her a ride home. "If you take me anywhere," said Helen Hablutzel, "take me to jail." The officers were puzzled, but they did as she asked.

The next morning, after she was released, Helen spoke with reporters and told them she had gone to a coffee shop the previous evening after leaving the courtroom during Bert Keating's "gory" closing argument. By the time she returned, the jury had already delivered its verdict. Although Gloria was still there, she would not comfort her sister-in-law. "I was all alone," said Helen. "I had no one to fall back on. It seemed that Gloria and everyone had turned their backs on me."

Feeling that she was being treated unfairly for her unwilling role as a prosecution witness, Helen drove to the Grahams' house and quickly packed her things. She then returned to the City and County Building, parked her car, and walked to a bar around the corner.

It was about 1:30 A.M. I'd had nothing to eat all day. I had three drinks, but they hit me very hard. When the tavern closed, I walked back to the car, got in, and went to sleep. That's where the officers found me. They asked me if I wanted to go home or go to jail. I took jail. I couldn't have gone back to that house.

Before leaving town, Helen went to the *Denver Post* newsroom to fulfill a promise she had made to Zeke Scher during the trial. Sitting at a desk with a typewriter, she wrote a letter that appeared in the newspaper the following day:

I told you when I had something to say I would tell you. I'd like to tell you now.

What Jack did seems too horrible to be true. But I can't hate him. He's guilty—and I want him to die. I love him. But then, I had a mean dog I cared for a lot. . . .

And what was she like, this woman who dropped out of the skies on November 1? To most she is an interesting story—to me she was my mother. Not too tall, her hair graying these last few years, since Earl, my stepfather, died. . . .

What kind of mother was she? Whatever mistakes she made, she made thinking they were the right things to do. You can ask no more of anyone than that they do the best as they see it.

What kind of a grandmother was she? This was where she tried to make good all the mistakes that she had made with Jack and me. She could buy things and do for them the things that she had never been able to do for Jack and me. A loving grandma, and much missed.

Daisie was temperamental. She was hard to get along with. I wasn't close. All these are true, but there is more, one thing more that cancels it out. I loved Mom. We called her Daisie, not [out of] disrespect—just habit. You love your mother no matter what you call her. You have seen pictures of her. She didn't look like any of them. They are still, and she was seldom still.

She loved her son the best of anything in the world. Me, too. But he was her special pride. She did everything for him she could. Too much maybe.

I loved her. I miss her. This trial has been a time when I was torn between not only loving and hating Jack, but Daisie was there every time we talked. I hope she is relaxed, fishing.

Mom had no figure for Levi's, yet she loved them and we grew to accept this as the happy Daisie who loved the ranch and her fishing. This was the real Daisie. How did she look? Well, she had pretty hands: tanned, and thin, and very expressive. I miss her hands the most of all. Her hands were never still, I seem to see them doing all the things that I loved to see her do. She drove, well and far. Her hands on the wheel were so competent. The hell of it is I see her pretty hands trying to grip the plane—or anything to find a grip. This is the thing that hurts the most.

Daisie was very afraid of heights. A Ferris Wheel at Lakeside [Amusement Park] would frighten her. And when I think of her up there trying to clutch something, the way she used to clutch my arm. Well, as I said, it is hell. . . .

Mom used to be a tomboy when she was a little girl in Buena Vista. I have always regretted that I didn't know her then. She was never a happy person, and she had a very mixed-up life. There was a divorce between her father and mother [at a time] when divorces were not the accepted thing. She grew up all mixed up and easily hurt. Riney, my husband, who loved Mom as well as he did his own mother, said what I think best explains Mom: "She had too big a heart, too close to the surface, too easily hurt." These aren't bad faults, but they can make life miserable.

The kids have the things that Daisie made them. I have the things she gave me, but I don't have a mother any more. I wanted to take her hunting. She loved it so. I wanted to do so many things for her I never got to do. Now she is body number 38, the most talked-about woman around. And she's gone—dead.

It is hard to describe someone so close to you and loved. You remember so many things. When Mom was happy, she had the charm and joy of a little girl and enjoyed everything. When Mom was mad, she had the unreasonable sulk of a hurt child. It would be hard to tell you what she was like. Her moods changed, and a different shade and shape was there. Every time she got mad at someone she did something nice to make it up. How could you get too mad at someone who wanted so desperately to be loved? . . .

How can I not hate him? I don't know. I have only one brother, and we are the only ones each other has. I would expect his loyalty, and I have never had any thought except to give him mine. You stand by your family no matter what the crime they are accused of. This is my creed, and this is the thing that guided my actions. I am more disgusted by the crime than anyone else.

I lost my mother before she could come to me, lost her in the way she would have hated most to go. A death which must have seemed like the drop into hell. A death full of terror, fire, and terrifying sound. Oh, yes, I am well aware of the horror. And the death of the others is more horrible than the death of my mother. There was a reason that my mother died. Someone hated her and wanted her dead. The others there is no excuse for. For them to die, not because someone hated them, just as part of a greedy plan. My God! . . .

How could anyone do that to all the others? How? I love planes. I love to fly. My daughter wants to be a stewardess. My husband worked for the Civil Aeronautics Administration. Our lives . . . revolved around the big planes and their safety. The coming in safely of one of the big planes was a thing which seemed so important. So many lives. How could anyone do something to end all those lives? . . .

I want him to die. There is nothing else. He knows how I feel. Not that death is the worst punishment, but it will keep anyone else from harm. I love him. Don't condemn me. I lost a mother I loved and never under-stood. I'm losing Jack too. . . . I wished I had hate. It is simple. This is not a simple case. I hate the things that he did. There is no excuse for his ac-tions. Don't worry. He is not the calm, unemotional man he seems. There is hell [in] back of those dark eyes. He is suffering. Justly suffering. I know this, and I feel pity for him.

On the same day his sister was putting her thoughts down on paper, Jack Graham wrote a letter of his own:

To the honorable Joseph M. McDonald, judge of the district court, who heard my case:

I don't desire my attorneys to file a motion for a new trial. It is not my intention to appeal my conviction to the Supreme Court of Colorado, or to any federal court.

I accept the verdict of the jury and desire that it be carried out with all convenient speed. This is my wish. I have been advised by my attorneys that under the law the sentence of death requires that it be appealed to the highest [court] of this state. I desire to waive that provision of the law.

(signed)

John Gilbert Graham

After completing his letter, Graham spent the rest of the day sitting on his bunk staring at the wall. The guards tried to engage him in conversa-tion, but he would not speak with them. He refused breakfast and lunch, and he returned his dinner tray after eating only two bites of coleslaw and a spoonful of Jell-O.

The next day, Graham regained his appetite and resumed his Scrabble matches with the guards. When Vigil and Weadick came to meet with him, Graham asked the lawyers not to file an appeal and urged them to withdraw the motion for a new trial they had filed.* The two attorneys were unwilling to comply with their client's demand, explaining that they felt obligated to appeal irrespective of his wishes.

In separate meetings with Gibbons, Graham expressed his frustration. "If that jury believed that crazy confession, there's no use going further. . . . Why wait two or three years and have it wind up the same way? . . . I'm certainly not going to go through that ordeal again. . . . If you file an appeal I'll get up in court and say I don't want it." Although Gibbons was willing to entertain the idea of abandoning the appeal, he wanted Judge McDonald to rule on the request. "It is your own decision," he told Graham, "and you will have to take the stand and explain your position under oath." A hearing on the issue was scheduled for the morning of Tuesday, May 15.

After waiting a respectful period, the reporters approached Gloria and asked for her thoughts about the trial. "Well," she said, "it's over."

But the aftermath was just beginning. She continued to receive harassing phone calls, and a person claiming to be a relative of one of the victims on the plane made a death threat against her neighbor, Helene West. In addition, the Denver city attorney had recently announced plans to sue her to recoup the costs of the trial.† Despite all of this, on Wednesday, May 9, Gloria summoned the strength to make her first trip to the jail since the verdict.

Apparently, the visit lifted Graham's spirits. On Sunday, May 13, the guards at the jail reported that he was "in a jovial frame of mind and cracking jokes." For many, the news that Graham was in such a good mood on this particular day was quite disturbing. It was Mother's Day.

---

* Although the rules of procedure have since been changed, in 1956 an issue could not be raised on appeal unless it had first been presented to the district court in a motion for a new trial.

† Shortly after he was arrested, Graham had transferred his interest in the Crown-A drive-in to his wife. In February 1956, Gloria sold the business and gave $1,000 of the proceeds to John Gibbons to pay for the investigative services of "Little Mac"—a payment that Gibbons did not reveal to Judge McDonald until after the trial. When the judge scolded the court-appointed attorney for failing to disclose the payment sooner, Gibbons claimed that he did not know he was required to, though he admitted he "possibly . . . should have."

At the hearing on the motion for a new trial, Charles Vigil admitted that there was "nothing new" in the document beyond the objections he and Gibbons had made during the trial. Judge McDonald denied the motion.

John Gibbons then called Graham to the stand and asked him to explain why he did not want to pursue an appeal. Graham's response was enigmatic:

> I am personally satisfied with it. . . . I don't see why it should have to be appealed. . . . I don't see why the Supreme Court should have to take any weight off of this court for anything that was ruled upon in this case at all. . . . I feel that this is as far as I want to carry it, that that should be as far as it has to go.

"Let me ask you this," Judge McDonald interjected. "Is this desire of yours prompted in any way by the fact that you feel you didn't have a fair trial here and might not get a fair hearing in the Supreme Court?"

"I don't believe it's all based on that, no."

"Is any of it?"

"I believe I had as fair a trial as could be had under the circumstances."

"You understand, of course, that a review by the Supreme Court is a review of errors of law, not whatever went on factually?"

Graham replied:

> That's right. I mean, I feel that as far as I'm concerned, I'd personally just as soon it went the way it is. I don't see why I have to make a political rally or something out of it. I think it went this far, and I think it should stop right here. Just because it's historically a fact that they appeal them all doesn't necessarily mean you have to do it. I mean, that's my understanding of it.

Judge McDonald was still perplexed. "Does this feeling spring from a consciousness of guilt and the fact that you have to pay the penalty for that?"

"No," answered Graham.

After Graham stepped down from the stand, Charles Vigil asked the judge for guidance on how to proceed. McDonald was unwilling to provide any, noting that—although death sentences had always been appealed in Colorado—there was no statute mandating such an appeal.* McDonald suggested that the attorneys ask the Colorado Supreme Court for instruction, and he reminded them that there was still time for Graham to change

---

* Judge McDonald's statement was slightly inaccurate. In 1934, the State of Colorado executed William Cody Kelly, a Delta farm worker who was unable to finance an appeal of his conviction for a murder he insisted he did not commit.

his mind, because the death penalty statute specified that an execution could not occur until at least ninety days after the date the sentence was imposed.

Judge McDonald's only remaining duty was to pronounce sentence. He did so in a somber voice:

> John Gilbert Graham, it is the judgment and sentence of this court that you be . . . conveyed to the State Penitentiary at Cañon City, Colorado, there to be delivered to the warden . . . to be kept by him in solitary confinement until the week beginning August 26, 1956, and during the week, on a day and at an hour to be selected by the warden, to be executed by the administration of lethal gas, and may God have mercy upon your soul.

At noon, the deputies ushered Graham into the back seat of a blue 1955 Ford, the middle vehicle in the three-car convoy that would take him the 118 miles to Cañon City.

The trip was uneventful. As they drove through Castle Rock on the Valley Highway (now Interstate 25), Graham joked that the officers might get a speeding ticket for exceeding the sixty-mile-per-hour limit. As they approached Colorado Springs, he made admiring comments about a woman in a yellow convertible who honked her horn as she passed. But when the curls of smoke rising up from the Cañon City prison complex became visible against the backdrop of the Sangre de Cristo mountains, Graham fell silent.

At 2:30 P.M., the three police cars pulled into a gated reception area known as the "bullpen." Warden Tinsley was waiting.

Harry C. Tinsley was popular with both the guards and the inmates. A former Buena Vista school teacher, Tinsley had begun his corrections career as a vocational instructor at a prison. In 1951, he had become deputy warden under Roy Best, a controversial figure who was suspended soon thereafter.* In the time since Tinsley had been promoted to warden, there had not been any executions, an interlude for which Tinsley—an opponent of the death penalty—was extremely grateful. However, Tinsley had reconciled himself

---

* In 1951, Governor Dan Thornton filed misconduct charges against Best for using flogging as a form of discipline and for misusing prison funds. The Civil Service Commission found Best guilty of commingling personal affairs with those of the state penitentiary and suspended him from 1952 to 1954. Best died of a heart attack three days before he was to be reinstated.

Graham arrives at the Colorado State Penitentiary at Cañon City with Sergeant George Hayes (white hat). (Courtesy of Denver Public Library, Western History Collection)

to the responsibility when he accepted the position, and he knew he would eventually be called upon to oversee a state-sanctioned killing.

After helping Graham out of the car, the deputies removed the handcuffs and handed Warden Tinsley the court order imposing the death sentence. As the warden examined the paperwork, Graham leaned against the

wall with his hands in his pockets. A couple of reporters who had been allowed into the enclosure approached him looking for a quote, but Graham
gave them a cold shoulder. "I don't want to talk to you," he mumbled.

Warden Tinsley assigned Graham prisoner number 29625, commenting to a reporter that "if four more fish had come in" Graham's gray-striped
shirt would have been emblazoned with the number of the ill-fated flight.
The warden then directed the guards to take Graham to the receiving
building for a shower. Although most incoming inmates were given a hair-
cut, Warden Tinsley concluded that Graham's "hair is short enough now."

The warden let Graham keep the few personal items he had brought
with him: a toothbrush, thirteen dollars to be deposited in his prisoner account for purchases of sundries, a Bible, and his copy of *As a Man Thinketh*,
the book his aunt had given him as a Christmas gift. Tinsley also let Graham
keep the socks he had worn for the trip from Denver.

The warden knew of Graham's February 10 attempt to commit suicide
using the garrote fashioned from a pair of socks and a toilet-paper roll. He
also knew about a second thwarted attempt that had not been disclosed in
the Denver newspapers.* Nevertheless, Warden Tinsley decided to let Graham wear socks "because we feel he cannot damage himself with the close
check we keep on him. We are doing everything feasible, and will make
every effort, to carry out the will of the court."

The surveillance of Graham would be accomplished with far fewer
guards than had been assigned to watch him at the Denver County Jail. As
an occupant of death row, Graham would be housed in one of eight special
cells located on the second floor of Cell House 3, a white concrete building that had been put into use the previous fall. Built at a cost of $369,000,
the maximum-security structure was set off from the rest of the prison by
two walls and a barbed-wire fence. All of the latest penalogical technology
had been installed in the building, including electronic door locks and hidden microphones in the cells that allowed the guards to listen in on the inmates' conversations. Although there was room for 102 men, in the spring
of 1956 only 70 of the prison's 1,500 inmates were housed there.

Thirty minutes after he arrived, Graham stepped into his cell, "1-A-
Left," an eight-foot by ten-foot enclosure with tile-covered walls. Looking

---

* When the deputies delivered Graham to Warden Tinsley, they gave him a letter informing him that "Graham
    stated after his first suicide attempt, 'I will take one more fling at an attempt to commit suicide.' On February
    24, 1956, he undoubtedly had in his mind another suicide attempt. He was observed pulling the linen cords
    from the mattress and collecting metal clips removed from magazines. These materials were removed from
    the cell immediately before Graham had an opportunity to use them in any way."

through the single window, Graham could see the yard where the mentally ill prisoners were allowed to exercise and, in the distance, a tower manned by an armed guard. Looking through the bars at the front of his cell, he could see the large mirror mounted at an angle that allowed the guard at the end of the hallway to observe him. The furnishings in the cell were virtually identical to those at the Denver County Jail, and there was one other similarity—LeRoy Leick was in the adjacent cell.

Colorado State Penitentiary booking photograph. (Photograph courtesy of Museum of Colorado Prisons)

Unlike Graham, Leick—who had already won one appeal—wholeheartedly endorsed the appeal his attorney was about to file. The other two men on death row—Frank Archina, who had killed four members of his family with a shotgun, and Besalirez Martinez, who had gunned down the owner of a Red Cliff tavern—had already filed their appeals and were now anxiously awaiting the Colorado Supreme Court's rulings.

Charles Vigil and Paul Weadick were also awaiting a ruling from the Colorado Supreme Court. After Judge McDonald had refused to tell them how to proceed, the two lawyers had filed a special petition in the Supreme Court asking the seven justices "whether a person of definite psychopathic characteristics—like Graham—should be permitted to abandon his appeal in a capital case when the attorneys believe there is merit to the appeal. . . . As court-appointed counsel, we seek to protect the rights of the defendant. We will be guided by and will proceed in accordance with the law and directions as to our duties and obligations as the supreme court may direct." In closing, the two lawyers pleaded with the high court to clarify their dilemma "as promptly as possible."

They did not have to wait long for an answer. On Monday, May 21, the justices issued their unanimous ruling refusing to address the petition. The attorneys would have to decide how to proceed on their own.

The next day, Charles Vigil traveled to Cañon City and met with Graham. Afterward, Vigil told a reporter that Graham was "in a little different state of mind" and that, as a result, he and Paul Weadick had decided to file an appeal.

However, when Gibbons went to see Graham on Thursday, Graham "was hostile . . . [and] concerned about published reports he was now less adamant against an appeal." According to Gibbons, Graham had told him, "If the jury had given me life, I would have forced you to appeal [and seek a death sentence.]" Gibbons also said that Graham had apologized for the way he "fouled up his defense" by not letting them present more evidence. "He doesn't want this case to drag on until his kids are old enough to know he is in the pen and fighting for his life," explained Gibbons. "He has definitely made up his mind." Gibbons said he himself had also made up his mind and had decided not to help Vigil and Weadick with the appeal.

On Friday, Graham wrote a second letter to Judge McDonald:

> I would like at this time to acquaint you with the fact that I don't believe these attorneys are acting in my interests as they have no regard for my wishes, but obviously they do what they please. I have no desire to appeal this conviction and I see no reason for the supreme court to be passed the buck. I have talked to Mr. Gibbons and he's agreed to abide by my wishes and let the matter follow its course.
>
> Mr. Vigil made a rather caustic remark saying he would appeal because I have definite psychopathic characteristics. Surely he is overlooking the fact that I was found sane by five doctors who are better versed in these things than Mr. Vigil.
>
> I was found guilty under this assumption, and I assure you I am well aware of the verdict handed down. I hope after reading the above you will accept absolutely no appeal from anyone on my behalf, as I am the only one who has any right to do this.
>
> I hope you will consider this matter. I believe that a person, even when convicted as I am, should have the right to excuse any attorney with whom he cannot get along and who seem[s] to be after only more personal satisfaction.
>
> I'm sure the people of Colorado are satisfied and don't wish to spend any unnecessary money either for attorneys or for another political rally for the district attorney's office.*
>
> Yours truly,
> Jack Graham

---

* A few days before, the district attorney had officially launched his campaign for reelection, urging the voters to "Keep Denver Clean With Bert Keating."

Graham sent a similar letter to the Colorado Supreme Court. However, Vigil and Weadick were not dissuaded. "We were appointed to defend this man and use whatever legal means are available," Weadick reminded the reporters. "Why should the people of this state permit him to commit legal suicide?"

In early June, Graham wrote another letter. The recipient, Victor Riesel, was a reporter for the *New York Daily Mirror* whose column was syndicated in hundreds of newspapers, including the *Denver Post*. Riesel wrote about a variety of subjects, but his main area of expertise was the infiltration of labor unions by organized crime—a choice of topics for which he had paid a very high price. On the morning of April 5, 1956, after Riesel had finished a radio broadcast in which he had identified a Long Island labor union as being under mob control, a man had walked up to him on the street and splashed sulphuric acid in his eyes. The outspoken writer was blinded, and his physicians concluded that it would not be possible to transplant the corneas Graham had offered.*

Most of Graham's other letters were affectionate ones addressed to Gloria. But after she returned from her first trip to Cañon City, Gloria sat for an interview with Zeke Scher and revealed that her feelings had changed:

> You know, I've discussed this over and over with my family and close friends, but I still don't understand why he would do such a thing. I feel sorry for him. I don't hate him. In fact, I have no feeling at all now. Love went out some time ago. To survive this thing I've had to make myself just numb. . . .
>
> When . . . the FBI agents began testifying and telling us all those things that Jack didn't tell us I became convinced. If I weren't convinced, I would fight with everything I have to get the guilty verdict reversed. He had as fair a trial as possible. There was just too much evidence. They said he was guilty. If it would do him any good, I'd want him to appeal. But if Jack doesn't want it, what should I do? The sooner this is all over will be best for all concerned. . . . I intend to start a new life. I don't intend to let this ruin my life or my children's lives. If it is going to be, it is going to be, and let's get it over with. That's Jack's attitude too.

When at the prison for her hour-long visit, Gloria had given her husband a picture of herself and the children and, for the first time, had asked him why he had done it:

---

* In August 1956, the FBI arrested two ex-convicts with ties to organized crime and charged them with orchestrating the attack and murdering the acid-throwing assailant in order to cover up the crime.

He said "I don't know," but we didn't discuss that very [long]. It's not a pleasant thing to discuss. The only thing that hurts him is what this has done to the kids and me. Jack is a very strange person. I didn't really know him and the type of life he had led until we had been married a year and a half. I believe Jack has convinced himself that there was no one else on that plane but his mother. The whole thing is so completely fantastic. The only reason I'm not in the mental hospital at Pueblo is I make like it is all happening to someone else. I've got two little kids, and I just keep going day to day doing what has to be done. Someday it might hit me between the eyes. . . .

Jack had so much—the home, the children, the business—and then he does this. I believe that no one will ever know why he did it. I'm baffled why he did it. To me, there's no explanation. You don't do things like that.

Even though she said she no longer loved him and thought he was guilty, she could not turn her back on him entirely, telling Scher, "I hope to visit him about every two weeks until the end."

In late July, a week after President Eisenhower signed into law a bill authorizing the death penalty for anyone convicted of causing the loss of life by damaging a commercial aircraft, Graham signed a letter addressed to the governor of Colorado—"Big Ed" Johnson. In his letter, Graham complained that he had received no response to the correspondence he had sent to Judge McDonald and the Colorado Supreme Court, and he demanded to appear in person before the justices to voice his objection to the appeal. Graham lashed out at Vigil and Weadick, alleging that when he first met with them they had "intimated the only reason they accepted the appointment was the money and publicity."

At another meeting with them, I was told that if I didn't plead insanity, they would give the District Attorney information of a confidential nature that was given to them in a lawyer-client relationship. I was interviewed again on a Friday afternoon about a month after my return [from the Colorado Psychopathic Hospital]. At this time, using the previous threat, I was told to make a false suicide attempt that evening so as to be returned to the hospital for further examination. I had no choice but to do it. At this time, I was instructed as to what to tell the doctors who might examine me. This was supposed to insure a finding of legally insane.

In making this charge, Graham emphasized that "Mr. John Gibbons advised me against the insanity plea. . . . He didn't know about the suicide attempt."

According to Graham, the "only reason" Vigil and Weadick were appealing was "for more publicity and money, [and] also the fact they wish to have the high tribunal relieve them of responsibility." Graham asserted that, due to "these circumstances," Vigil and Weadick should "be stopped from representing me in any further matters" and should be replaced by John Gibbons, "who has been the only one to try and help me."

Governor Johnson forwarded the letter to the Colorado Supreme Court and publicly stated his own suspicions. Although admitting he had "no proof," Johnson pointed out that the letter "certainly is peculiar [and] worded too legalistically for a man like Graham to have composed it without help. . . . It looks to me like Mr. Gibbons may actually have helped Graham in the composition of this letter. . . . There is a feud that's going on between the defense attorneys and Graham is trying to help one side against the other. It's very probable Mr. Gibbons did help write the letter. I've seen other letters written by Graham, and this one is pretty well constructed." Johnson vouched for Charles Vigil, saying he was "not a man who dodges anything," and commended him for having given "all his talent and effort" to Graham's defense.*

Gibbons flatly denied the governor's charge. "The kid studied law at Denver University and he can write anything. He never discussed this with me. He's very bitter against Vigil." Gibbons also disavowed any advance knowledge of the suicide attempt. "I never did . . . hear Vigil and Weadick say anything like that. I was never apprised of anybody attempting to tell him to attempt to commit suicide so that the doctors would find him legally insane. I never wanted the plea of insanity in the first instance. . . . That was the major difference of opinion between counsel."

Bert Keating stepped into the fray and defended his former adversaries:

> This ingratitude on the part of Graham, while a bit surprising, seems to bear out his general attitude toward people and life. I saw Graham after he attempted suicide, and it didn't look like any fake to me nor did the doctors think it was a fake. His attempt was genuine, and it was motivated by an overwhelming sense of guilt after the psychiatrists at the Colorado Psychopathic Hospital had declared him sane. At no time did any lawyers in this case ever tell me anything. Mr. Vigil and Mr. Weadick are men of integrity and are conscientious lawyers. They ably defended Graham and spent many weary hours and days on the trial.

---

\* Johnson and Vigil were longtime friends. Before becoming governor in 1955 (a position he had previously held from 1933 to 1937), Johnson served as a United States senator. While a senator, Johnson was instrumental in obtaining Charles Vigil's appointment as the United States attorney for Colorado.

Speaking out on their own behalf, Charles Vigil and Paul Weadick both angrily denied Graham's allegation as an "outright lie." "This establishes the fact that he is psychopathic," said Vigil. "Someone may have told Mr. Graham to fake a suicide attempt, but it wasn't Mr. Weadick or I. We didn't see him that day, and I was out of town making a speech."* Vigil said he was "sure" Graham did not write the letter alone. "Look at the language of the letter, Graham doesn't know anything about lawyer-client relationships." However, Vigil declined to speculate as to the identity of the co-author.

Putting aside their personal feelings toward their ungrateful client, Vigil and Weadick continued their work readying the appeal. On August 6, they filed their petition in the Colorado Supreme Court, an act that automatically resulted in the issuance of an order staying Graham's execution while the appeal was pending. After the attorney general filed a brief urging the justices to affirm the conviction and death sentence, both sides agreed that the case could be decided based on the written briefs, without any oral argument. On September 6, Chief Justice Wilbur Alter announced that he had scheduled the matter for an expedited disposition.

On the evening of Friday, September 7, Besalirez Martinez—whose appeal had been denied the month before—was sitting on his bunk listening to a boxing match on the radio when Warden Tinsley and the guards entered his cell. Neither Graham nor either of the other two condemned men said a word as they watched the guards lead Martinez away for the short walk up the ramp to the gas chamber located on the third floor of the building.

In the weeks after Martinez was executed, Graham and LeRoy Leick began speaking about their mutual predicament through the metal partition separating their two cells.† One day, Graham complained about the unsolicited religious material he was receiving, saying, "I wish just once that someone would send me a letter saying let's go out and get drunk instead of saying don't do this, and don't do that. If I get any more of these Bibles, I'll start selling them."

---

* According to the records of the Denver County Jail, Graham did not have any visitors on February 10, 1956, the day of his suicide attempt. However, he did meet with Charles Vigil and Paul Weadick the day before.

† Frank Archina, the third death-row inmate, was unable to participate in these conversations because he spoke little English.

"Why don't you keep one and read it?" asked Leick.

Graham laughed at the suggestion. "What do I need with that kind of stuff where I'm going? It won't do me any good in hell."

Leick—who had found religion after murdering his wife—read several Bible passages aloud. Graham was not impressed:

> If you want to live that kind of life, it's okay I guess. But me, I always be-lieved this was the only life and I was going to live it while I could. . . . [H]ave all the fun you can, take what you want any way you can get it. My ambition was to drink all the whiskey and love all the women, and I sure did make a dent in both. So now I'm ready to go. I just don't want to fool around about it any more.

"You know you don't really feel that way. There's plenty of good in you if you'd let it come out."

"Like hell. I'm not worth a damn."

"Gloria must have thought an awful lot of you."

At the mention of his wife's name, Graham softened. "Yeah, she sure had a lot to put up with."

On another occasion, Leick heard Graham singing *When the Saints Go Marching In*. "You're in fine voice today," he said.

"Glad you think so," answered Graham. "If I thought it could get me out of here I'd start beating the tub for every church in the country."

"There may not be much chance of our getting out, but at least we can prepare ourselves to meet God. Only He knows where we will go when we leave."

"I don't give a damn where I go," replied Graham. "I just want to get gone."

At other times, when Graham was in a more reflective mood, Leick would hear him crying and lamenting his fate:

> Where does the time go? It never did go this fast outside. I guess it's be-cause we haven't got much of it left. Candy always tastes best when you only have one piece left. You don't really know what life is until you reach the end.

"The end hasn't come yet, Jack."

"No? It's so damned close I can already smell the gas."

"It's not funny to me. I've found a lot in life to live for—things I never would have found but for the grace of God."

"God isn't going to help you none when that gas hits you," Graham retorted.

Eventually, Warden Tinsley concluded that Leick's proselytizing was upsetting Graham. At the warden's direction, Leick was relocated to another cell out of earshot of his unreceptive neighbor.

A month after losing his bid for the Democratic nomination in the Third Congressional District, Charles Vigil suffered another defeat. On October 22, 1956, the Colorado Supreme Court issued its opinion rejecting all of the arguments he had made on Graham's behalf.* At the end of their lengthy written ruling, the justices summarized their view of the trial:

> We have painstakingly examined and studied the entire record in this case, and from it we are impelled to the conclusion that the verdict of the jury was based not upon conflicting evidence, but upon uncontradicted, competent testimony, properly admitted exhibits, and the confessions, oral and written, of the defendant. No other verdict than guilty of murder in the first degree could have been returned with due regard to the evidence before the jury, and defendant must suffer the penalty provided by law, he having been accorded every constitutional guaranty.

In a highly unusual move, the justices also added an editorial comment remarking on the extraordinariness of Graham's crime: "Nowhere in the reports of criminal cases have we found a counterpart to this case, and we doubt if anything approaching it can be found in fiction."

Shortly before 11 A.M. on the morning the Supreme Court issued its ruling, Warden Tinsley had the guards bring Graham to his office. "John," he began, "I have received word by phone from the attorney general's office that the Supreme Court has upheld your conviction in district court. The execution has been set for the week ending January 12, 1957." According to Tinsley, Graham showed "no emotion of any kind," saying only that he had "been expecting this."

So had Gloria. Answering the door in a cotton skirt and striped polo shirt, she learned the news from the reporters gathered on her steps. She invited the men inside and spoke with them in the kitchen as her daughter played on the floor. "It's no surprise. It was cut and dried. The man wants to die." Reflecting on the scheduled date of the execution, she lamented that her husband was being put to death two weeks before his twenty-fifth

---

* Justice O. Otto Moore concurred in the result but wrote a separate opinion expressing his belief that Graham's request to abandon the appeal should have been granted.

birthday. But she was also relieved by the timing. "I'm glad they set the date after Christmas. It wouldn't have been very nice around then."

When asked how the situation was affecting the children, Gloria said Suzie was too young to be aware of her father's absence. However, her two-and-a-half-year-old son had noticed, and he occasionally asked, "Where's Daddy?" Gloria had developed a standard response to deflect the boy's inquiries. "I just tell him Daddy is 'bye bye.' At Allen's age, he drops the question."

For the first time, she talked about the letters she had been receiving from Cañon City, revealing that her husband had displayed "as much remorse as he can show." "No one can really want to die if he's normal," Gloria told the reporters. "But you wouldn't say Jack is exactly a normal person. I just can't explain it. I definitely won't be there at the end. I have some fortitude, but not that much."

## CHAPTER FOURTEEN

# *"I expect to see her tonight."*

B Y DECEMBER OF 1956, Morey Engle had left the *Rocky Mountain News* for a career as a freelance photographer.* As one of the most respected cameramen in Colorado, he had no shortage of clients. However, Engle relished a challenge, and he was determined to get a profitable piece of film out of the Graham case before it was over.

Initially, Engle planned to do another filmed interview with Graham, and that was how he explained the proposal when he offered Gloria a percentage of the proceeds in exchange for her assistance. However, after flying Gloria down to Cañon City in a small plane and obtaining Graham's consent, Engle learned that Warden Tinsley would allow only an audio recording of the interview. On December 4, 1956, Engle returned to the prison with a Magnecord reel-to-reel recording system and an ex-convict he had hired as an assistant to work the equipment. Sitting in an office above the prison laundry, Engle and Graham spoke for nearly four hours as the quarter-inch tape rolled from one spool to another.

Engle asked Graham about the persistent rumors that others had been involved in the bombing. "You might say I wasn't hired exactly," Graham boasted, "but I was paid to cause accidents on several United Air Lines planes." Without directly claiming responsibility, he implied that he had played a part in the United Air Lines disaster on Medicine Bow Peak three weeks before the bomb exploded on Flight 629. However, Engle—who had climbed Medicine Bow Peak and photographed the wreckage for the *Rocky Mountain News*—became annoyed and told Graham he had not seen

---

* Not long after he filmed Gene Amole's unsaleable interview with John Gilbert Graham, Engle was fired for punching a city desk editor in the mouth during a newsroom brawl. According to Engle, the overbearing editor deserved the drubbing.

Morey Engle interviewing Graham on December 4, 1956. (Courtesy of Morey Engle)

any evidence of a bombing. "I'm trying to get a story good enough I can sell, Jack," he snapped. "Level with me!"

But Graham continued with his fabrications, telling Engle that the bomb on Flight 629 had been wired to an altimeter so "it wouldn't blow up" before the plane achieved sufficient altitude. However, when Engle reminded him that the cargo hold of the DC-6B was pressurized, Graham quickly changed the subject.

Graham insisted that he had bought all of the dynamite from the Illinois Powder Company, "the same place where they came up with that wire [at trial]." And his outrage over Lyman Brown's testimony sounded sincere. "I don't know whether Brown maliciously testified I bought dynamite up there, or if he had some reason for doing it, or what, but I never set foot in his goddamn store!"*

---

\* It was subsequently confirmed that, on October 20, 1955, the Illinois Powder Company had sold a case of dynamite to a representative of the Colorado-Texas Pump Company (the fictitious business name Graham had given when purchasing the timer). Curiously, during the trial the prosecutors implied that Graham had purchased blasting caps attached to yellow wires from the Illinois Powder Company without ever introducing evidence to prove such a sale had occurred. In an equally puzzling omission, neither the prosecutors nor the defense attorneys ever asked Lyman Brown to describe the type of wires attached to the blasting caps he claimed to have sold to Graham.

Returning to the issue of the coconspirators, Engle told Graham that "Gibbons thinks someone else was in on it." Graham did not dispute having told his attorney as much, explaining that "one of the primary reasons for having that trial was so we could find out how much they knew." However, Graham's descriptions of his collaborators were as vague as his earlier accounts of "Karl" (a figure he told Engle he had "made up" because "I didn't want to tell where I got the dynamite"). "I knew these fellows before. I knew one of them from living up in Alaska, he was on probation up there from California. I knew the other one from Texas. . . . This one guy seemed to know all about United Air Lines' schedules, when and where they flew, and the habits of individual pilots. . . . I think they're so scared now they won't do it again."

Engle wasn't buying it. "I don't believe two-thirds of this, Jack, it's so screwed up. . . . Do you feel any remorse, any sympathy for the other passengers?"

"I feel sorry for their families. As far as the people on the plane, how can I feel for them? . . . I'm not sure in my own mind that dynamite caused that son-of-a-bitch to crash."

When Engle asked Graham why he had wanted to kill his mother, Graham said that her presence on the plane was an unfortunate coincidence, pointing out that if he had really wanted to kill her, "I could have shot her, could have said it was a hunting accident, could have said I thought I saw a grouse or a deer and got manslaughter, not first-degree murder."

Engle expressed disbelief that Graham could have built the bomb without thinking about the dozens of people who would be on the plane.

"I shouldn't say it didn't bother me," Graham admitted, "it did. I don't know how to explain it. I felt like someone walking on a two-inch plank over a thousand-foot hole."

Although Engle's questions were primarily focused on the bombing, it was his inquiry about Graham's childhood that elicited one of the stranger revelations. Recollecting his teenage years, Graham casually mentioned—with no apparent appreciation for the happenstance involved—that he had once worked in a sugar beet field during the harvest.

After Graham was returned to his cell, Engle packed up his equipment, drove back to Denver, and set the four unmarketable reels of tape on a shelf in his basement, alongside the metal canisters containing the film of the interview he had nearly sold to NBC. It had been another frustrating experience, but the intrepid photographer had one more idea for a way to cover the plane bombing story—an idea not dependent upon Graham's cooperation.

For the first fourteen years following its statehood, all executions in Colorado were conducted by public hanging. In 1890, the legislature—disgusted by the public spectacles—passed a law requiring that all hangings be carried out at the state prison in Cañon City. However, officials at the prison objected to the responsibility, a protest that bolstered the lobbying strength of death-penalty abolitionists and ultimately resulted in the elimination of the death penalty in 1897.

In 1902, capital punishment was restored, and executions resumed using the "Do-It-Yourself Hanging-Machine," a Rube Goldberg–like contraption designed to eliminate the need for an executioner. A condemned man would step onto a platform with a noose about his neck and activate a mechanism that hoisted the noose by releasing three hundred pounds of weight attached to the other end of the rope. In theory, the machine would swiftly snap the condemned man's neck. In actuality, the results were often gruesome, and only two of the forty-five men put to death in the device died as intended. Many of the men languished for as long as ten minutes before dying of strangulation. In one particularly ghastly case, the condemned man had to be hung a second time after the rope broke. When word of this botched execution spread beyond the prison walls, the public demanded a less cruel method of execution.

The idea of using hydrocyanic gas for executions had originated in Nevada in 1921 when the citizenry of that state voiced similar objections to the electric chair. Initially, Nevada prison officials planned to install a pipe to pump gas into the cell of a condemned prisoner while the inmate slept. However, when they realized that this would endanger the guards and other inmates, they built an airtight room in an old stone shed instead.

It did not work well. Several of the witnesses to the first execution were overcome by escaping gas and ran from the area coughing and clutching their throats. The next time the room was used, so much gas leaked out that a reporter fainted. In 1929, Nevada prison officials replaced the "airtight" room with the first metal gas chamber.

Responding to the outcry in Colorado over the hanging machine, in 1933 the state legislature passed a law authorizing the construction of "a suitable and efficient room or place, enclosed from public view, within the walls of the penitentiary . . . [with] all necessary appliances requisite for carrying into execution the death penalty by means of the administration of lethal gas." After traveling

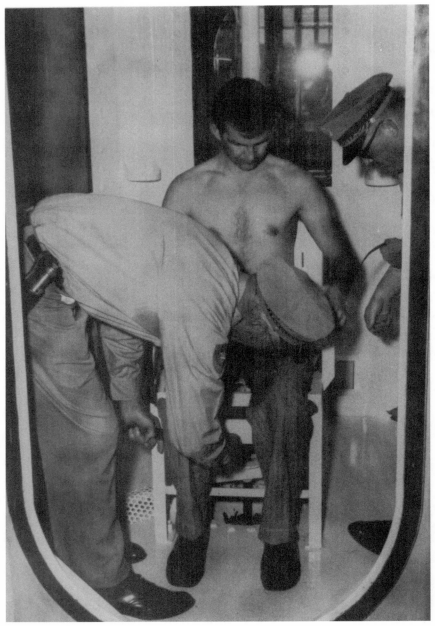

Prison guards practice gas chamber execution procedures. (Courtesy of Museum of Colorado Prisons)

to Nevada to inspect its gas chamber, Warden Roy Best returned to Cañon City and announced plans to have a gas chamber built by the Eaton Metal Products Company, a north Denver manufacturer that had fabricated several components for the Nevada gas chamber.* "The Colorado chamber will be an improvement over the one in use there," promised Best. To fulfill this pledge, Best—a notorious showman—directed the Eaton Metal Products Company to build a three-seat chamber capable of carrying out triple executions.

The company's engineers set to work and designed a large rectangular chamber with a fan that would ventilate the poisonous gas after an execution to make it possible for prison guards to safely enter, verify the death, and retrieve the body (or bodies). Working from these plans, metal workers at the company constructed the chamber with panels of quarter-inch-thick steel, windows made of thick bulletproof glass, and a heavy door with a revolving latch resembling that found on the hatch of a submarine. Before shipping the chamber to Cañon City, a worker with a morbid sense of humor scrawled the words "Roy's Penthouse" on one of the steel walls.

The name stuck. At Best's direction, "Roy's Penthouse" was installed on a hill behind the north wall of the prison. Enclosed in brick and surrounded by barbed wire, it looked like a well-fortified garden shed.

On June 22, 1934—after testing the device by executing a pigeon, a dog, and a crated hog—twelve cyanide pellets dropped into a pot filled with sulphuric acid beneath the lap of William Cody Kelly, the only man to be executed in Colorado without an appellate review of his conviction. The physicians in attendance declared the execution a success, unanimously agreeing that Kelly had died in less than a minute.

Over the course of the next seventeen years, twenty more men were put to death in the three-seat chamber, the last being John Berger Jr., who died on October 26, 1951. There never was a triple execution.†

Although "Roy's Penthouse" worked as intended, it had one drawback: the location. Because the condemned men had to be walked across the yard

---

*When it was founded in 1919, the Eaton Metal Products Company produced metal barrels for use in the oil industry. By the 1950s, the company was making a wide range of metal items, including silos for intercontinental ballistic missiles and home fallout shelters designed to protect against the Soviet Union's atomic weapons.

†On May 31, 1935, Louis and John Pacheco, brothers who had been convicted of murdering a Larimer County farmer, were put to death simultaneously. In the days before the execution, a third condemned man, Leonard Belognia, sent a letter to "Big Ed" Johnson asking the governor to allow him to die alongside his two friends. "There is no use wasting that extra chair," Belognia wrote, "some of my happiest days have been in here with the Pachecos, and it will be hard to wait and go later." Governor Johnson refused the request, concluding that he did not have authority to advance a prisoner's execution date. Belognia was executed the next month.

A guard closes the door of the gas chamber. (Courtesy of Museum of Colorado Prisons)

in full view of the other prisoners, the ritual developed into a heroic procession. Thus, it was decided that the gas chamber would be better located above death row in Cell House 3, the maximum-security building slated to open in 1955. Because "Roy's Penthouse" was too heavy and bulky to be mounted on top of the new building, the State of Colorado ordered a new one from the Eaton Metal Products Company.

By this time, the Eaton Metal Products Company had developed an improved gas chamber—for which it later obtained a patent—used by seven of the nine other states then conducting executions with lethal gas. The new Colorado chamber, a single-seat model, was delivered and installed on the uppermost level of Cell House 3—literally a penthouse location. Once the new chamber was in place, "Roy's Penthouse" was moved to the warden's ranch, where it was converted to a grain storage bin.

The new gas chamber was used for the first time on September 7, 1956, the night Graham watched Besalirez Martinez walk up the ramp. Four months later, Warden Tinsley directed the guards to test the chamber before its next scheduled use—the execution of John Gilbert Graham on Friday, January 11.*

On Sunday, January 6, Gloria visited her husband for three hours. Although she had brought the children with her the week before, this time she came alone. It was to be her last trip to Cañon City. "It's too hard on both of us," she explained.

After she returned to Denver, Gloria told a reporter, "Naturally he's frightened, but he didn't break down." While nervously tapping her husband's wedding band on the kitchen table, she looked at her children. "Someday I'll have to tell them," she said with a tremor in her voice.

On Wednesday, January 9, Deputy Warden William Kinney assigned guards to begin observing Graham around the clock. Kinney told reporters not to misinterpret the precautionary measure as an indication that Graham was suicidal. "His attitude is good. He is not depressed. He seems resigned to his fate and we don't expect him to change." Kinney said Graham was sleeping well. "In fact, I had to wake him up when I visited him the other afternoon." He also said Graham had been exercising regularly by playing handball in the yard with Frank Archina, a fellow resident of death row.

---

* Pursuant to statute, the Colorado Supreme Court set a week-long period for each execution and left the selection of the actual date to the warden. In this case, the court had ordered that Graham be executed during the "week ending January 12, 1957" (a Saturday). Over the years, a succession of wardens had developed a practice of conducting executions on Fridays to allow the condemned men to live a few extra days. (However, Saturday executions were deemed cost-prohibitive because the guards would have been entitled to overtime wages for working on the weekend.)

When Kinney asked Graham to select a member of the clergy to be present for the execution, Graham, a Protestant, surprised the deputy warden by asking for the prison's Catholic chaplain, Reverend Justin McKernan. The decision also came as a surprise to Father McKernan. Although McKernan had attended several executions, all of those prisoners had been Catholics. "It's the first time this has happened in my thirteen years as Catholic chaplain at the penitentiary," said the gray-haired priest, emphasizing that he would not be able to perform last rites for a non-Catholic. "I will be appearing strictly as an official witness and as the clergyman required by law—not Graham's minister."

Asked why he thought he had been selected, Father McKernan told reporters he had met with Graham frequently during the previous seven months. "I don't talk religion or his case with him. We talk about books he is reading, about sports, about chess—he's sharp at that. Still, Graham is an enigma to me. I can't get to the bottom of his thinking."

Graham had several visitors that day. Dr. Earl Miller came to say farewell with Graham's two aunts, Helen Smith of Missouri (Daisie's sister) and Myrtle Walker of Denver (Daisie's sister-in-law). Graham also met with John Gibbons, who later emerged from the prison carrying his client's civilian clothing and two Bibles. One of the Bibles was a gift to Gibbons that Graham had signed with his date of birth and his expected date of death. The other, which Graham had asked Gibbons to deliver to Gloria, was inscribed to his family: "I give this to my wife and children, who have given me the only happiness I have ever known."

Graham's other visitor on Wednesday was his pastor, Reverend Kellams of the Lakewood Community Methodist Church. Graham told Kellams of his decision to have Father McKernan escort him to the gas chamber and asked the minister to be with Gloria on Friday night. Kellams said he would.

After his meeting with Graham, Reverend Kellams granted an interview to Zeke Scher in order "to remove any doubts that might remain anywhere about this man's guilt." Kellams told the reporter that Graham had first confessed to him three days after the suicide attempt. "He admitted he faked the suicide hoping the doctors would change their finding that he was legally sane," said Kellams. "After he confessed the crime to me, I asked him why he hadn't shot his mother and spared the lives of the forty-three other persons aboard the plane he dynamited. He told me he just couldn't shoot her."

Describing his most recent meeting with Graham, Kellams said, "I honestly believe he is not one bit afraid to go. He told me, 'I don't think it's so bad to die.' He asked me why others are afraid to die and said he thinks it is a very pleasant thing. 'I've shot deer and rabbit and seen them die,' he said. 'I don't think death is so bad.'"

"I am told by relatives that Jack hated his mother with a passion," Kellams said. "I think he had a mental maladjustment that prevented him from realizing what he was doing. I don't believe any kind of psychiatric treatment would have prevented him from doing what he did."*

Graham slept little on his last night. "It's the first time he's been restless," said Warden Tinsley. "I asked him if he had any special requests—anything special to eat or anything new in the way of reading material. He told me he'd just as soon have the same food as the other prisoners. He seems to have an inner calmness, indicating he realizes the situation fully and has neither hope nor expectation for a last-minute reprieve."

After nibbling at his breakfast, Graham granted his final interviews. He was unrepentant when speaking to a reporter from *Time*. "As far as feeling remorse for those people, I don't," he said. "I can't help it. Everybody pays their way and takes their chances. That's just the way it goes." "I don't mind getting the gas," he told a *Newsweek* reporter, "but I would like to make my last request. And that is to have Zeke Scher sitting on my lap when I go."

When the reporters were gone, Graham smoked a cigar, a habit he had developed after receiving a box of them as a Christmas present from one of his aunts. He was not expecting any more visitors. However, in the middle of the afternoon John Gibbons made a surprise appearance at the prison.

Sitting on the bunk with his lawyer, Graham told Gibbons that Reverend Kellams was mistaken. "I have a very strong feeling for my mother. I expect to see her tonight. There is no truth to the story I had any bitterness to her." He also disputed the report of his confession to the minister, telling Gibbons,

---

*After the story was published on Thursday, Reverend Kellams received numerous phone calls from readers criticizing him for disclosing the confession of a parishioner. The next day, Kellams issued a statement indicating that Graham had given him permission to release the information. However, Kellams also said he thought his interview with Scher would not be printed until after the execution, and that he had failed to notice the Thursday dateline on the advance copy of the article Scher had given him to review.

"I have told you seven or eight different stories. I have told other people other stories concerning the case. Only I know what the truth is, and that's the way I want it." For the remainder of the time, the two men spoke about things unrelated to the bombing, such as the many new buildings being constructed in Denver. When Gibbons stood to leave, Graham asked the attorney to communicate his final regards to Gloria. "Be sure you call her when you get back."

Speaking with reporters afterward, Gibbons took the newsmen to task for their sensationalistic portrayals of his client. "If I had believed Graham was the heinous killer—the mad-dog killer—would I have sat two hours with him in a locked cell?" He also told the reporters that Graham had found faith in his final hours. "He believes there is a Creator who predestines everything and every thought. He believes there is a heaven, and he has made his peace with his God. He is willing to meet his Maker."

At 4:15 P.M., a guard delivered Graham's final meal. Pursuant to Graham's request, the food on the tray was the same as that which would be delivered to the other prisoners later that evening: steak, fried potatoes, a tossed salad, a cup of fruit cocktail, and a bowl of ice cream. Graham ate only the ice cream and returned the rest, asking the guard to "take the steak to one of the boys"—which the guard did.

Father McKernan arrived just after 7:00. The two men talked about the many books Graham had read while on death row, including the thesaurus McKernan had given him the week before. "He read it all the way through," the priest would later recall. "He wanted to get to the roots of words. Words had a fascination for him."

At 7:45, Warden Tinsley, Deputy Warden Kinney, and two guards approached the cell. "Well," Graham said to the priest, "I guess it's time." Pressing the last of his cigars into Father McKernan's hand, Graham asked the cleric to accept the gift. "Take these, Father, I won't have much use for them tomorrow." McKernan pocketed the cigars. "I'll smoke one of them later for you, Jack."

On the other side of the steel bars, Warden Tinsley looked pale and haggard. "How are you doing, Jack?"

"Just fine, Warden. I feel good," Graham replied.

Tinsley was flustered. As Father McKernan and Graham stood in the cell waiting, the warden searched in his pockets for the key to open the door.

"You wouldn't want to lose that key now, would you, Warden?" Graham asked jokingly.

Tinsley finally found the key and unlocked the door. Stepping inside the cell, he formally read Graham the death warrant from the Colorado Supreme Court.

"Do you understand, Jack?"

"I understand, Warden."

"Then you may go now, Jack."

Graham did not hesitate, striding purposefully up the ramp with such long, rapid steps that Tinsley and the guards had to hurry to keep pace. Father McKernan followed behind, saying a prayer: "Have mercy on me, O God, according to Thy great mercy. In thee O Lord have I hoped. Let me never be confounded. Incline unto my aid, O God. O Lord, make haste to help me."

Without prompting, Graham entered a small changing room and removed all of his clothes. Tinsley handed him a pair of white shorts that had been made in one of the prison's factories. "Here, don't forget to put on these." Graham donned the shorts and slid his feet into a pair of slippers.*

The official witnesses required by law had already been assembled. In addition to Undersheriff Charles Rudd and Captain Logan Ketchum from the Denver Sheriff's Office, there were five doctors and thirteen other men selected by Warden Tinsley.

Tinsley had also granted nineteen reporters access to the execution, including representatives of all three national wire services, the major national news magazines, and several Colorado newspapers. The warden had only one condition—no photographs of any kind could be taken inside the prison.

In the late 1800s, it was not uncommon for public hangings to be photographed. But in the modern era, there had been only two instances in which cameras had been smuggled into executions. In 1928, a reporter named Tom Howard attended the execution of Ruth Snyder at Sing Sing prison in New York wearing a small plate camera strapped to his ankle with a cable shutter release running up his pant leg. As the electricity was being applied to the body of the young woman convicted of bludgeoning her husband

---

* The requirement that men put to death in the gas chamber wear only shorts was necessary to prevent poisonous gas from becoming trapped in the condemned man's clothing, a potential hazard to the guards charged with removal of the body.

to death, Howard lifted his cuff and captured a single grainy image. The photograph was enlarged to fill the front page of the *New York Daily News* and created such a sensation that the newspaper sold an extra 750,000 copies. In November 1949, Joe Mignon of the *Chicago Herald-American* repeated the feat by hiding a Minox* camera in his shoe and snapping a photograph during the electrocution of James "Mad Dog" Morelli, a notorious Chicago criminal. That photograph had created an equivalent stir.

Morey Engle did not own a miniature camera. However, when *Life* magazine offered him $2,000 for a photograph of the Graham execution, he rented a Minox from a camera shop and set out for Cañon City with Bob Ajenian, a reporter for the Time-Life Corporation. On the way, the men stopped for dinner and Engle bought a package of Viceroy cigarettes. Using a pocketknife, the photographer carefully cut out the center of the letter "o" from the word "Viceroy" printed on the side of the package, creating an opening for the lens of the small camera. After slicing around the top of the package to make a flap, Engle removed a few cigarettes and slid the Minox inside. It fit perfectly.

When they arrived at the prison's security checkpoint, Engle emptied his pockets and placed the pack of cigarettes on a small wooden shelf as Ajenian went through ahead of him. When the guard wasn't looking, Engle slid the cigarettes forward on the shelf. Ajenian collected them with his other possessions and proceeded inside. As they were heading upstairs, Engle asked his friend for a cigarette. "Here," said Ajenian, handing Engle the Viceroys, "keep 'em, I have another pack."

When Engle joined the other reporters waiting to go into the viewing area, he was surprised to see Jack Foster, the editor of *Rocky Mountain News*. Foster was equally surprised to see Engle, and he knew the photographer never went anywhere without a camera. Moments later, Warden Tinsley—apparently tipped off by Foster—unexpectedly instructed the reporters to go back through the security checkpoint.

When it was Engle's turn, the guard picked up the cigarettes and bounced them in his hand. "These are mighty heavy," he said. "Well," said Engle, realizing he had been caught, "I'm a heavy smoker." The guard was not amused.

Nor was Warden Tinsley, who confiscated the camera and berated Engle for the smuggling attempt. Nevertheless, after delivering the reprimand,

---

* Developed in 1938 by a Latvian photographer named Walter Zapp, the original Minox miniature camera was not much larger than a pack of chewing gum. During the Cold War, CIA and KGB agents often used the tiny cameras for espionage missions.

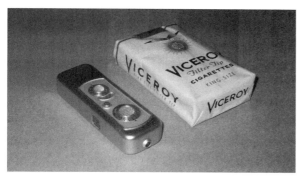

A 1950s Minox camera and a pack of Viceroy cigarettes from the same era. (Photograph by D. Scott Young, Minox Historical Society)

Tinsley offered to let the photographer view the execution. Engle wasn't interested. "I came here to do a job," he said, "not to see a man die."

Graham entered the execution room, nodded toward Charles Rudd and Logan Ketchum—two of the men who had guarded him throughout the trial—and stepped through the oval-shaped doorway of the light green metal chamber. By the time the eighteen reporters were allowed into the execution room to take up their positions behind a railing near the rear glass windows, Graham was already seated in the metal chair.

One guard tied a three-inch-wide black blindfold around Graham's eyes as another guard fastened the thick leather straps to secure his arms and legs to the chair. The two guards then positioned a stethoscope listening piece over Graham's heart and attached it to a thin rubber tube that extended out of the chamber to a pair of earphones.

Once the final leather strap was fastened across Graham's chest, Warden Tinsley patted him on the shoulder.

"God bless you."

"Thank you, Warden."

The next man to enter the chamber was Father McKernan.

"May God forgive you all your sins," he intoned.

"Thanks," said Graham.

Finally, Deputy Warden Kinney stepped inside.

"Goodbye, and good luck," he whispered.

"Thanks," replied Graham.

A guard quietly entered the chamber carrying a metal scoop containing the cyanide pellets, leaned down, and poured the pellets into a bracket located beneath the metal chair.

At 7:56 P.M., the guards swung the heavy door closed and spun the wheel to seal it tightly against the rubber gasket lining the opening. One of the guards flipped a switch and activated the fan within the chamber as another guard watched the manometer and waited for the air pressure inside the chamber to fall below the pressure in the surrounding room.

At 7:57 P.M., a guard cranked a metal handle connected to a rod and turned the bracket under the chair. Graham was visibly startled by the sound of the white pellets dropping into the vat of sulphuric acid. Thirty seconds later, when the vapors reached his face, Graham gasped for breath. His head dropped forward, snapped back, and then came to rest on his chest.

At 7:59 P.M., Graham gulped, strained against the restraints, and let out a loud groan that lasted almost two full seconds. It was a harrowing sound, and at least one of the spectators looked as if he might become ill.

After Graham fell silent, the prison physician listened to his heart through the stethoscope until it stopped beating. At 8:08 P.M., the doctor officially pronounced Graham dead.

The execution had taken eleven minutes—the same length of time Flight 629 was in the air before the bomb exploded.

After it was over, the witnesses filed out and the reporters walked across the moonlit grounds to the warden's office for the traditional post-execution press conference. While they were waiting for Tinsley to arrive, one of the guards pulled out a pen and corrected the prisoner population figure on the bulletin board, changing the number of inmates from 1,572 to 1,571.

Tinsley appeared a few minutes later and told the reporters that Graham's final outburst was highly unusual, an unconscious "reflex shriek" that had occurred because "Graham had a tough heart." In a clarifying remark, Tinsley made clear that his statement concerning Graham's heart was not a figurative description. "He was one of the best prisoners we ever had, cooperative and always agreeable. I hope he is better off."

One of the reporters asked Tinsley what he planned to do with the fifty dollars he was statutorily entitled to receive for carrying out an execution. "I'm going to split the money among the five or six guards who participated in the execution," the warden replied. "I don't want that money."

Tinsley refused to identify the man who had turned the handle to drop the pellets. "We do not want to point the finger at any one executioner. Every citizen in this state is an executioner, since this is the law." When asked about his own views of capital punishment, the warden struggled to find some meaning in what had just occurred. "If there is any justification for the execution of Graham, it is this: with him dead, his wife can establish a new life . . . for herself and her children. As long as he lived, that would not be possible."

Gloria Graham had spent the evening at a friend's house holding a quiet vigil with Reverend Kellams. "She held up very well," the minister said later. "She was calm and composed. There was no official notification that Graham had died while I was there. We sat and talked quietly for about two hours. That was all. Along about 9:30, before I left, we joined hands and I offered a word of prayer. That was what Mrs. Graham requested."

At 10 A.M. the next morning, Graham's body was delivered to the Fairmount Cemetery in Denver, where, in accordance with his wishes, it was cremated. Reverend Kellams presided over a simple ceremony attended by Gloria, John Gibbons, Graham's aunts, and two friends of the family.

When the service concluded, the cremated remains of John Gilbert Graham were buried in the Walker family burial plot, near his mother's grave.

Headstone marking the grave of Daisie E. King (first name misspelled, maiden name engraved as middle name).

# Epilogue

ALL OF THE MAIN PARTICIPANTS in the trial are gone now.

Judge Joseph McDonald stepped down from the Denver District Court bench in 1959 and moved to Washington, D.C., to serve as chief counsel to the Senate Judiciary Subcommittee on Administrative Practice and Procedures in Government Departments and Agencies. He was killed in a car accident in 1969.

Max Melville died three years after the trial at the age of sixty-seven. At the time of his death, Melville was writing his third treatise on Colorado criminal law. Bert Keating helped complete the book, published it, and donated the proceeds to a memorial fund in Melville's name at the University of Colorado School of Law.

Keating went on to serve many more years as district attorney. He was midway through his fifth consecutive term of office when he died of lung cancer in 1967. His nineteen-year tenure is longer than that of any other district attorney in the history of Denver (a record that cannot be eclipsed unless the voters of Denver repeal a term limits provision enacted in 1995).

Greg Mueller succeeded Max Melville as Keating's assistant district attorney. Three years after Bert Keating passed away, Mueller left the District Attorney's Office to become a Denver County Court judge. He retired in 1987 and died in 1992.

Paul Weadick also became a Denver County Court judge. He retired in 1985 and died the following year.

Charles Vigil continued practicing law for more than forty years, dividing his time between law offices in Trinidad and Denver. In 1988, at the age of seventy-five, he was the Democratic Party's nominee in the Fourth Congressional District, a race he lost to the Republican incumbent, Representative Hank Brown. Vigil died in 1999.

John Gibbons's career as a practicing attorney was interrupted in 1965 when the Colorado Supreme Court suspended his law license following his federal convictions for perjury and income tax evasion. Although Gibbons was later reinstated, he was disbarred in 1984 for engaging in a sexual relationship with a young female client while representing the woman's husband as a codefendant in the same criminal case. He died in 1989.

Roy Moore held several senior positions at FBI headquarters in Washington, D.C. In 1964, he was sent to Jackson, Mississippi, where he established an FBI office to investigate racial violence, including the murder of three civil rights protestors. Before retiring in 1974, he worked on many other high-profile cases, including the kidnapping of Patty Hearst.

Roy Moore's work on the Graham case was featured as the lead story in *The FBI Story: A Report to the People,* a 1956 book about the agency's history and its most famous cases. In 1959, the book was made into a movie starring Jimmy Stewart, with J. Edgar Hoover making a cameo appearance portraying himself in a segment of the film that showed him on the phone coordinating the nationwide investigation of the airplane bombing.

Several relatives of the victims filed lawsuits against United Air Lines claiming that the company was negligent for failing to detect the dynamite. James Fitzpatrick, who lost his wife and infant son on Flight 629, was represented by Melvin Belli, the nationally famous San Francisco lawyer known as the "King of Torts." The case was dismissed by agreement of the parties in 1958; the terms of the settlement are unknown. Similarly, the lawsuits filed against United by the children of Virgil and Goldie Herman, and that filed by the widow of John Des Jardins, were also dismissed by agreement of the parties with undisclosed settlement terms.

In 1959, United prevailed at trial in a case brought by a representative of the three Lipke boys. The following year, United won a second trial in a case filed by Alma Winsor's husband.

William "Pat" Patterson retired as president of United Air Lines in 1963.* He continued to serve the company as director emeritus until his death in 1980. Through an endowment, he established the Patterson Chair in transportation studies at Northwestern University.

---

* "United Air Lines" changed its name to "United Airlines" in 1974.

Sally Hall did not sue United Air Lines. Instead, the pilot's widow sued the Mutual Benefit Health and Accident Association and attempted to collect on the $37,500 insurance policy Graham had helped his mother purchase naming him as the beneficiary. She did not succeed.*

Gloria Graham changed her last name, as well as that of her two children. With the help of John Gibbons, she won her fight to keep the City of Denver from collecting the costs of the trial. However, it took her two more years to get the city to remove the lien against her house. As soon as that was accomplished, she sold the house, in part due to the large number of curiosity seekers who were drawn to the infamous address. Although she later remarried, the marriage ended in divorce. She died in 1992.

Helen Hablutzel spent the rest of her life in Alaska. When her children were grown, she worked as a cook in several remote labor camps that were established during construction of the Trans-Alaska Pipeline. She died in 2004.

The next man to die in the gas chamber after Graham was LeRoy Leick, who lost two more appeals before his execution on January 23, 1960.

Frank Archina, the other man who lived on death row with Graham, won his appeal and was granted a new trial. The jury at the second trial found Archina insane. He was briefly committed at the State Hospital in Pueblo before being deported back to Italy. In 1961, he was convicted for the murders he had committed in Colorado under an Italian law prohibiting "murder in a foreign land." He was released from prison two years later.

On June 2, 1967, the Colorado gas chamber was used for the last time to extinguish the life of Luis Jose Monge. Monge was also the last man to be executed in the United States prior to an unofficial nationwide moratorium on executions that lasted until 1972, when the United States Supreme Court declared the death penalty unconstitutional in the case of *Furman v. Georgia*. In 1976, the United States Supreme Court revisited the issue in the case of *Gregg v. Georgia* and ruled that the death penalty is not unconstitutional provided that the jury's discretion is guided through aggravating and mitigating circumstances focusing on the particularized na-

---

* Ironically, before Graham was executed Mutual Benefit Health had paid him $500 to sign a release dropping any potential claims his estate might have under the policy. Graham used that money to make up the past-due premiums on a $10,000 life insurance policy he had purchased as a teenager through the United States Coast Guard. Upon her husband's death, Gloria received the death benefit from the Coast Guard policy.

ture of the crime and the character of the offender. Following the *Gregg* decision, Colorado reinstated the death penalty and changed its method of execution to lethal injection. The gas chamber in which Graham, Leick, and Monge died is now an exhibit at the Museum of Colorado Prisons in Cañon City.

Harry Tinsley served as the warden of the Colorado State Penitentiary until 1965, and as the Colorado Chief of Corrections until 1971. Tinsley was one of several prison wardens who filed a friend-of-the-court brief opposing the death penalty in the United States Supreme Court case of *Furman v. Georgia*. He died in 1984. An annual award established in Tinsley's name is the highest honor bestowed by the Colorado Criminal Justice Association, an organization of corrections officers.

Zeke Scher's work on the Graham case was dramatized in "The Big Story," an NBC television award program recognizing excellence in journalism. Scher later attended law school at the University of Denver and became a practicing attorney. In 2000, he was inducted into the Denver Press Club's Hall of Fame.

Scher's competitor, Al Nakkula, worked at the *Rocky Mountain News* until his death in 1990. During his years with the paper, Nakkula broke many other big stories, including a scandal in the 1960s involving a group of Denver police officers who were committing burglaries throughout the city. After he died, the Denver Press Club established an annual award in his name recognizing outstanding accomplishment in police reporting.

Morey Engle produced films for the Atomic Energy Commission and the Martin Marietta Corporation before opening his own motion picture and television production company. A 1994 book of his photographs, *Denver Comes of Age: The Postwar Photography of Morey Engle,* includes a foreword written by Engle's longtime friend, Gene Amole.

Gene Amole launched a second radio station—KVOD, "the classical voice of Denver." Although Amole won numerous awards for his work in radio and television, he is best known for his twenty-five-year stint as a columnist for the *Rocky Mountain News*. In 1995, Engle and Amole collaborated with Denver newsman Don Kinney to produce *Murder at Mid-Air*, a film documentary about the Graham case narrated by Amole, which included segments of film footage from the Graham trial and portions of Amole's 1956 interviews with John and Gloria Graham. After Amole died in 2002, the City of Denver renamed a stretch of Elati Street bordering the entrance to the *Rocky Mountain News* building in his honor.

By 1965, every state except Colorado and Texas had adopted some version of the American Bar Association's ban of courtroom photography. However, in the mid-1970s, the trend began moving in the other direction. Despite the advent of *Court TV,* or perhaps because of it, cameras are still not allowed in federal courtrooms.

Justice O. Otto Moore received an award from the National Press Photographers Association for his "open-mindedness in reception of evidence supporting the news photographer's constitutional right to report court proceedings." In 1969, Moore stepped down from the Colorado Supreme Court upon reaching the mandatory retirement age of seventy-two. From 1973 to 1985, he served as the assistant district attorney in Denver. He died in 1990 at the age of ninety-four, a passing marked by a statewide lowering of flags to half-mast.

At the time it occurred, the bombing of Flight 629 was the worst single incident of mass murder committed by one individual in the history of the United States.* During the following two decades, there were several insurance-related airplane bombings and attempts, most notably in 1960, when a heavily insured passenger detonated a bomb on a National Airlines DC-6B and killed himself along with twenty-eight other passengers and a crew of five, and in 1962, when another well-insured passenger detonated a bomb in a Continental Airlines 707 and killed himself, thirty-six other passengers, and a crew of eight. For many years, the Air Lines Pilots Association campaigned vigorously to have coin-operated flight insurance machines removed from the nation's airports, characterizing the presence of the devices as an "incentive to commit murder for economic gain." Although the insurance companies successfully resisted the pilots' lobbying efforts, the machines began to disappear when banks started offering free travel insurance for airplane tickets purchased with a credit card.

---

\* On May 19, 1927, Andrew Kehoe killed forty-four persons, mostly young children, in the town of Bath, Michigan (Kehoe, who was bitter about an increase in his property taxes resulting from the construction of a school building, detonated a massive dynamite bomb inside the structure that was the object of his anger). Although the Kehoe and Graham bombings are sometimes referred to as involving the same number of victims, one of the forty-three persons who died in the 1927 bombing was the perpetrator (and the forty-fourth person killed, Kehoe's wife, was actually murdered at home in a separate bombing earlier that same day).

The tragedy left an indelible impression on the land northeast of Longmont. Literally. The following spring, a farmer who planted alfalfa in a field where several of the victims had landed noticed that the seed would not take hold in the areas of earth that had been compressed by the falling bodies. The phenomenon caused the crop to grow in eerie outlines of the deceased.

For many years thereafter, cows that grazed in this area would occasionally die for no apparent reason. Postmortem examinations of the carcasses revealed the cause: intestinal blockages resulting from consumption of small pieces of plane wreckage that had risen to the top of the soil.

In 1957, United Air Lines named a second DC-6B the "Mainliner Denver." The aircraft was retired from service in 1968.

United stopped using the "Mainliner" trademark for its aircraft during the 1960s. However, the airline continued using the term as the name for its in-flight magazine until the early 1980s. Today, there are several non-profit "Mainliner Clubs" located throughout the country "to organize, promote and supervise social and sports activities for employees of United Airlines."

United still uses the number "629" as a flight designation. Currently, Flight 629 is an evening flight between Washington, D.C., and Chicago.

Stapleton Airfield was later renamed Stapleton Airport and, after that, Stapleton International Airport. It closed in 1995 when Denver International Airport opened. The site of the old Stapleton Airfield is now being redeveloped into a community of homes, shops, offices, parks, and schools.

In 2005, detection systems were installed at Denver International Airport to scan all checked luggage for explosives.

# APPENDIX A

# *The Victims*

Fay E. "Jack" Ambrose, 38, Seattle, Washington

Samuel F. Arthur, 38, Seattle, Washington

Bror H. Beckstrom, 48, Seattle, Washington

Irene Beckstrom, 44, Seattle, Washington

John P. Bommelyn, 53, Seattle, Washington

Frank M. Brennan, Jr., 36, Seattle, Washington

Louise D. Bunch, 61, Forest Grove, Oregon

Horace Brad Bynum, 32, Sherwood, Oregon

Carol Bynum, 22, Sherwood, Oregon

Thomas L. Crouch, 23, Wichita, Kansas

Barbara J. Cruse, 23, Aurora, Colorado

Carl F. Deist, 53, Hillsborough, California

John P. Des Jardins, 42, Overland Park, Kansas

James Dorey, 58, Whitman, Massachusetts

Sarah Dorey, 55, Whitman, Massachusetts

Elizabeth D. Edwards, 57, Providence, Rhode Island

Gurney Edwards, 58, Providence, Rhode Island

Helen Fitzpatrick, 42, Batavia, New York

James Fitzpatrick II, 13 months, Batavia, New York

Lee H. Hall, 38, Seattle, Washington

Vernal Virgil Herman, 69, Vancouver, Washington

Goldie Herman, 59, Vancouver, Washington

Elton B. Hickok, 40, Seattle, Washington

Jacqueline L. Hinds, 26, Eugene, Oregon

Marion P. Hobgood, 31, Hatfield, Pennsylvania

John W. Jungels, 57, Aurora, Illinois

Daisie E. King, 53, Denver, Colorado

Gerald G. Lipke, 38, Pittsburgh, Pennsylvania

Patricia Lipke, 36, Pittsburgh, Pennsylvania

Lela McLain, 81, Portland, Oregon

Suzanne F. Morgan, 40, Wilmette, Illinois

Frederick Stuart Morgan, 48, Wilmette, Illinois

Peggy Ann Peddicord, 22, Seattle, Washington

James W. Purvis, 45, Tacoma, Washington

Herbert G. Robertson, 43, Rutherford, New Jersey

Dr. Harold R. Sandstead, 50, Silver Spring, Maryland

Sally Ann Scofield, 24, Denver, Colorado

Jesse T. Sizemore, 24, Munford, Alabama

James E. Straud, 51, Lansing, Michigan

Clarence W. Todd, 43, Tacoma, Washington

Minnie Van Valin, 62, Newberg, Oregon

Dr. Ralph Waldo Van Valin, 72, Portland, Oregon

Donald A. White, 26, Seattle, Washington

Alma L. Winsor, 48, St. John's, Newfoundland, Canada

# APPENDIX B
# *U.S. Aviation Security, 1955–2005*[*]

**November 1, 1955**
John Gilbert Graham perpetrates the first confirmed act of sabotage against a U.S. commercial aircraft.

**July 14, 1956**
President Eisenhower signs a bill authorizing the death penalty for any person convicted of committing an act of aircraft sabotage that results in death. The new law also provides for prison sentences of up to twenty years for acts of aircraft sabotage not resulting in death.

**July 25, 1957**
Saul Binstock, a sixty-two-year-old retired jeweler, purchases $125,000 of flight insurance on his own life and then detonates a dynamite bomb in the bathroom of a Western Air Lines Convair aircraft flying from Las Vegas to Los Angeles. Although Binstock is blown from the plane and killed, the pilot succeeds in landing the plane without injury to any of the other passengers. Only one of the two policies purchased by Binstock contains a provision stating that payment will not be made in the event of death by suicide.

**August 23, 1958**
President Eisenhower signs the Federal Aviation Act and thereby creates the Federal Aviation Agency (which later becomes the Federal Aviation Administration)(hereafter referred to as the FAA). The new agency, which takes over the personnel and functions of the Civil Aviation Administration, is charged with enforcement of air safety rules for all military, commercial, and private aircraft.

**January 6, 1960**
Julian Frank, an attorney whose life is insured for more than one million dollars, detonates a bomb while traveling as a passenger aboard a National Airlines DC-6B flying near Bolivia, North Carolina. All thirty-four people aboard the Miami-bound flight are killed.

---

[*] This timeline is intended to provide the reader with a general overview of events and developments in aviation security during the last fifty years. It is not comprehensive.

**January 22, 1960**
FAA Safety Chief E.R. Quesada concedes that, "in light of recent headlines," his agency may not have devoted sufficient resources to preventing criminal attacks against domestic aviation. Although Quesada acknowledges that the FAA could institute luggage inspection procedures, he does not indicate whether such measures will be implemented.

**April 1, 1960**
FBI Director J. Edgar Hoover calls for the x-raying of all passenger baggage. The FAA and the airlines oppose the idea on the ground that the devices will alert to other metal objects and cause unnecessary flight delays. Hoover also calls for the installation of fireproof tape recorders in all commercial aircraft (recently enacted FAA regulations only require the recorders in jet airplanes).

**May 1, 1961**
Antulio Ortiz, a Cuban, becomes the first person to hijack a U.S. aircraft and take it out of the country when he uses a steak knife and a gun to force the pilot of a National Airlines twin-engine Convair to fly to Havana.

**July 24, 1961**
Wilfredo Oquendo, a Cuban, uses a gun to seize an Eastern Air Lines Electra turbo-propeller aircraft traveling from Miami to Tampa. Oquendo forces the pilot to fly the plane to Havana. The following day, the crew and the other thirty-two passengers return to the United States. Oquendo remains in Cuba (along with the Electra aircraft, which Fidel Castro later exchanges with the United States for a Cuban patrol boat that had been taken to Key West by a group of defectors).

**August 3, 1961**
Leon Bearden and his teenage son seize a Continental Airlines 707 carrying sixty-seven passengers from Phoenix to Houston. After holding the pilot at gunpoint and ordering him to fly to Cuba, Bearden and his son surrender at the end of a nine-hour standoff when FBI agents cripple the plane by shooting at it during a refueling stop in El Paso. Coincidentally, the pilot of the aircraft, Byron D. Richards, was also the pilot of the first plane ever to be hijacked (in Peru, in 1930). Bearden is sentenced to twenty years imprisonment; his son is placed in a juvenile correctional institution.

**August 5, 1961**
Airline officials and leaders of several unions representing airline employees speak out in opposition to an FAA proposal requiring pilots to carry handguns. A second FAA proposal that would require the posting of armed uniformed guards within passenger cabins is met with mixed reactions and is eventually shelved.

**August 9, 1961**
Alberto Cadon, an Algerian, uses a handgun to hijack a Pan American DC-8 flight and then forces the pilot to land in Havana. Over the objections of the airlines, President Kennedy orders that armed federal agents begin flying as passengers on certain undisclosed flights. Two days later, Pan American Airlines fortifies the cockpit doors on all aircraft it uses for its Latin-American routes.

**September 5, 1961**
President Kennedy signs a bill passed in response to the recent wave of hijackings. Under the new legislation, the hijacking of a commercial aircraft carries a maximum penalty of death. Assaults and threats against crew members are punishable by imprisonment for up to twenty years or, if a deadly weapon is used, twenty years to life. Providing false information about a hijacking attempt (i.e., hoaxes) becomes an offense punishable by imprisonment for up to five years. In addition, the bill provides that carrying a concealed weapon on a commercial aircraft is punishable by a fine of up to $1000 or imprisonment for up to one year.

**May 22, 1962**
Thomas Doty purchases $275,000 of flight insurance on his own life and detonates a dynamite bomb while traveling as a passenger on a Continental Airlines 707. The plane explodes over Centerville, Iowa. All forty-five people aboard the plane are killed.

**October 12, 1964**
The Air Lines Pilots Association steps up its campaign to remove flight insurance vending machines from airports. FAA officials oppose the idea.

**October 15, 1964**
The ChemAlloy Corporation urges the FAA to order machines it has developed which use electric and magnetic waves to detonate explosives hidden in passenger luggage.

**August 21, 1965**
FAA officials announce that a contractor hired by the agency is on the verge of developing a "Snifter," a mechanical device capable of scanning luggage and "smelling" odors emanating from dynamite or other explosive substances.

**August 12, 1968**
The Air Transport Association, a group representing the major airlines, indicates that its members will consider installing magnetometers to screen passengers for weapons.

**December 31, 1968**
Twenty-six U.S. aircraft are hijacked during the calendar year.

**September 5, 1969**
The United States formally ratifies the Tokyo Convention of 1963, a treaty requiring the safe return of any hijacked aircraft, and all persons who are on board, if a hijacked plane lands in a signatory country.

**October 31, 1969**
Raffaele Minichiello, a Marine armed with a M-1 carbine, hijacks a United Air Lines flight in Fresno, California and forces the pilot to make a seventeen-hour flight to Rome with stops in Denver, New York, Bangor, and Shannon, Ireland. Italy refuses to extradite Minichiello who, after serving a short sentence in an Italian prison, becomes a minor celebrity in that country.

**December 31, 1969**
More than thirty hijackings or attempts are made on aircraft operated by U.S. airlines during the calendar year. In addition, more than fifty hijackings or attempts occur on aircraft operated by non-U.S. airlines.

**June 4, 1970**
Arthur Barkley, an unemployed truck driver embroiled in a tax dispute with the Internal Revenue Service, hijacks a Trans World Airlines (TWA) airplane and demands 100 million dollars ransom. FBI agents raid the plane when it is on the ground at Dulles Airport in Washington, D.C. Although all 51 passengers escape unharmed, the pilot is shot in the abdomen.

**July 24, 1971**
FBI agents at LaGuardia Airport shoot and kill Richard Obergfell after he hijacks a Chicago-bound TWA jet and forces the pilot to return to the terminal. Although the handgun Obergfell was carrying had set off a magnetometer, a gate agent had allowed him to board because the agent did not want to delay the flight by summoning a U.S. Marshall to conduct a search. Soon after this incident occurs the government increases the number of U.S. Marshals assigned to provide aircraft security from 100 to 230.

**November 25, 1971**
A man identifying himself as "D.B. Cooper" displays a bomb to a flight attendant while traveling on a Northwest Airlines flight bound for Seattle. After securing $200,000 in ransom and four parachutes while the plane is on the ground in Seattle, "Cooper" releases the passengers and orders the pilot to fly at low altitude to Reno, Nevada (Cooper's request for multiple parachutes was apparently intended to convince the authorities he planned to force the crew to jump with him and thereby ensure that the parachutes provided would be functional). Somewhere along the way, "Cooper" lowers the rear exit stairs and parachutes from the plane. His fate is unknown.

**February 6, 1972**
After failing to persuade the airlines to use magnetometers for passenger screening, the FAA institutes a new rule making magnetometer screening of all passengers mandatory.

**April 7, 1972**
Twenty-nine-year-old Floyd McCoy, Jr., uses a pistol and a hand grenade to hijack a United Air Lines Boeing 727 flying from Denver to Los Angeles and forces the pilot to land in San Francisco. Mirroring the earlier hijacking of "D.B. Cooper," McCoy demands and obtains $500,000 and four parachutes. After parachuting from the plane over Utah, McCoy is soon arrested at his home in Provo by FBI agents who recover all but $30 of the ransom money. The McCoy hijacking is the seventh incident in five months in which a hijacker has made a demand for ransom and a parachute. Two days later, yet another hijacker, Stanley Speck, threatens to blow up a Pacific Southwest Airlines Boeing 727 and demands ransom money and a parachute. FBI agents arrest Speck when the plane lands in San Diego.

**May 8, 1972**
To prevent additional "jumper jackings," the FAA orders U.S. airlines to rewire the rear exit door mechanisms on all Boeing 727s to prevent the doors from being opened while an aircraft is in flight.

**August 30, 1972**
American Airlines and TWA announce they will begin inspecting the carry-on luggage of all passengers (under existing FAA regulations, the airlines are only required to search the carry-on luggage of passengers meeting a hijacker profile).

**November 10, 1972**
Three fugitives hijack a Southern Airways DC-9 flying from Birmingham Alabama. Before they are arrested in Cuba, the hijackers ask to speak with President Nixon (who refuses) and threaten to crash the plane into the nuclear reactor at the Atomic Energy Commission's plant in Oak Ridge, Tennessee.

**February 23, 1974**
Samuel Byck shoots and kills the co-pilot of a Delta Air Lines DC-9 and an airport police officer before using the gun to kill himself. The incident is the first attempted hijacking involving a weapon since the FAA instituted mandatory magnetometer screening of all passengers (and the second U.S. hijacking in which a crew member has been killed). It is subsequently discovered that Byck had planned to crash the aircraft into the White House.

**August 5, 1974**
President Nixon signs the Anti-Hijacking Act permitting the suspension of U.S. air service to any country that does not meet minimum security standards designed to thwart hijackings.

**December 29, 1975**
A bomb explodes in the baggage area of New York's LaGuardia Airport. Eleven people are killed and dozens more are seriously injured.

**March 15, 1976**
After conducting a year-long study in response to the LaGuardia bombing, the FAA adopts regulations requiring the inspection of some checked baggage (although the agency does not disclose the percentage of luggage to be searched, it is estimated to be 2% or less).

**September 10, 1976**
Six hijackers take control of a TWA 727 on a New York-to-Chicago flight and force the pilot to fly to Montreal. The hijackers, calling themselves the "Fighters For Free Croatia," force the pilot to fly to Newfoundland and, after an exchange of aircraft, on to Paris. The hijackers eventually surrender after TWA arranges airdrops of "Croatian Independence" leaflets over Chicago, New York, Montreal, and Paris (in addition, several U.S. newspapers comply with the hijackers' demand to publish a statement of their grievances).

**March 13, 1978**
During a refueling stop in Denver, the flight crew of a hijacked United Airlines Boeing 727 escapes by leaping from the cockpit window (the hijacker, who said he was suffering from terminal cancer, had previously released the passengers after forcing the plane to land in Oakland).

**June 12, 1979**
The FAA reports that, although a total of 187 U.S. aircraft have been successfully hijacked since 1961, "only" 36 attempts were made between 1973 and 1978.

**September 30, 1979**
An American Airlines DC-10 is diverted to Denver after a man with a knife wounds three fellow passengers.

**November 24, 1979**
Eighteen year-old Gerald Hill uses a knife to commandeer an American Airlines Boeing 727 in El Paso, Texas, and demands that the pilot fly the plane to Iran. After four hours, Hill surrenders to FBI agents without a struggle.

**August 14, 1980**
For the third time in a week, a U.S. jet is hijacked and forced to land in Cuba. FAA officials meet with airline executives and discuss the possibility of reviving the use of behavioral profiling of passengers.

**February 2, 1981**
Bowing to industry objections, the FAA abandons a proposal that would have required commuter airlines to screen passengers and carry-on baggage for weapons.

**November 16, 1990**
In response to the 1988 terrorist bombing of Pan American Flight 103 over Lockerbie, Scotland (in which 259 passengers and 11 people on the ground were killed), the "Aviation Security Improvement Act of 1990" is enacted. The Act establishes a Director of Intelligence and Security within the office of the Secretary of Transportation who is charged with developing improved transportation security procedures. In addition, the Act requires the FAA administrator to develop a counterterrorist strategy for aviation and stipulates that heads of intelligence agencies must ensure that information concerning terrorist threats is made available to others in the intelligence community.

**September 11, 2001**
Nineteen Al Qaeda terrorists simultaneously hijack four commercial jet aircraft and kill nearly 3000 people.

**November 19, 2001**
President Bush signs the Aviation and Transportation Security Act which transfers the responsibility for aviation security from the FAA to the newly-formed Transportation Security Administration (TSA). In addition, the legislation broadens the Federal Air Marshal Service and requires that detection systems to screen all checked baggage for explosives be installed in all U.S. airports by December 31, 2002.

**November 25, 2002**
President Bush signs legislation authorizing the TSA to grant extensions to airports that are unable to install detection systems by the deadline specified in the Aviation and Transportation Security Act.

**December 31, 2002**
The TSA grants extensions to approximately thirty airports that have not installed detection systems and allows these airports to substitute a combination of explosives-sniffing dogs, manual searches, and matching of bags with passengers.

**September 24, 2004**
A report issued by the Inspector General of the Homeland Security Department reveals that, when tested, TSA screeners are doing a poor job of detecting knives, guns, and explosives at airport checkpoints.

**October 15, 2004**
During his unsuccessful campaign for the presidency, Senator John Kerry repeatedly emphasizes that only a small portion of the cargo shipped on passenger airplanes is currently screened for explosives.

**January 5, 2005**
Officials at Denver International Airport announce that all checked baggage will be automatically screened for explosives beginning in February 2005.

# Appendix C
## DC-6B Diagrams

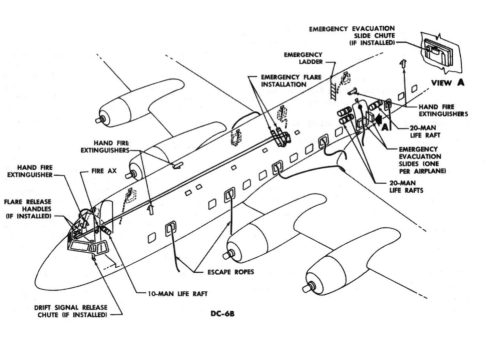

EMERGENCY EVACUATION
SLIDE CHUTE
(IF INSTALLED)

EMERGENCY
LADDER

EMERGENCY FLARE
INSTALLATION

VIEW A

HAND FIRE
EXTINGUISHERS

20-MAN
LIFE RAFT

EMERGENCY
EVACUATION
SLIDES (ONE
PER AIRPLANE)

20-MAN
LIFE RAFTS

HAND FIRE
EXTINGUISHERS

HAND FIRE
EXTINGUISHER

FIRE AX

FLARE RELEASE
HANDLES
(IF INSTALLED)

ESCAPE ROPES

10-MAN LIFE RAFT

DRIFT SIGNAL RELEASE
CHUTE (IF INSTALLED)

DC-6B

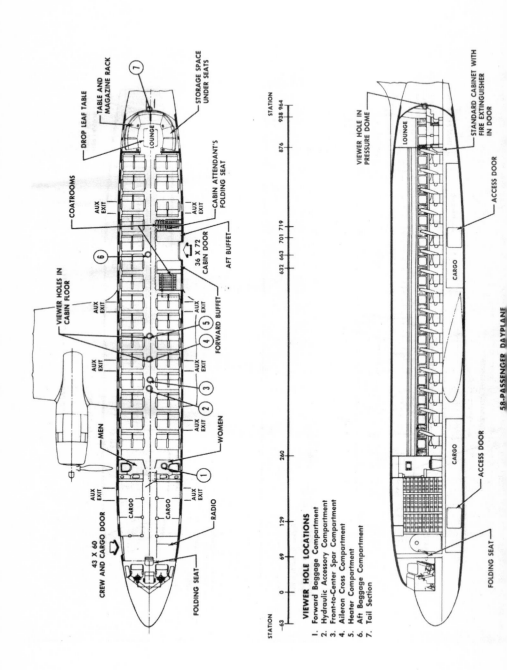

VIEWER HOLE LOCATIONS
1. Forward Baggage Compartment
2. Hydraulic Accessory Compartment
3. Front-to-Center Spar Compartment
4. Aileron Cross Compartment
5. Heater Compartment
6. Aft Baggage Compartment
7. Tail Section

58-PASSENGER DAYPLANE

# Bibliography

**Books**

A.W. Bowen & Co., *Progressive Men of Western Colorado,* 1905.

Barber, Susanna, *News Cameras in the Courtroom: A Free Press-Fair Trial Debate,* Ablex Publishing Corp., 1989.

Denver Foundation for Architecture, *Guide to Denver Architecture, With Regional Highlights,* Westcliffe Publishers, 2001.

*Douglas Aircraft Company, DC-6B Operation Manual,* 1951.

Engle, Morey, *Denver Comes of Age, The Postwar Photography of Morey Engle,* Johnson Books, 1994.

Fant, Kenne, *Alfred Nobel, a Biography.* Arcade Publishing, 1993.

Francillon, Rene J., *McDonnell Douglas Aircraft Since 1920,* Putnam Press, 1979.

Garvey, William & Fisher, David, *The Age of Flight, A History of America's Pioneering Airline,* Pace Communications, 2002.

Goldfarb, Ronald L., *TV or Not TV, Television, Justice and the Courts,* New York University Press, 1998.

Israel, Lee, *Kilgallen: A Biography of Dorothy Kilgallen,* Delacorte Press, 1979.

Kilgallen, James L., *It's A Great Life, My Fifty Years As A Newspaperman,* International News Service, 1956.

Lukas, J. Anthony, *Big Trouble,* Simon & Schuster, 1997.

Miller, Jeff, *Stapleton International Airport, The First Fifty Years,* Pruett Publishing, 1983.

Serling, Robert J., *The Probable Cause, The Truth About Air Travel Today,* Doubleday & Co., 1960.

Smith, P. R. *DC-6: A Production & Pictorial History,* D.P.R. Marketing & Sales, 1984.

Taylor, Frank J., *High Horizons, The Saga of the Main Line Airway,* McGraw-Hill Book Co., Inc., 1958.

Whitehead, Don, *The FBI Story: A Report to the People,* Random House, 1956.

Witzel, Michael Karl, *The American Drive-in, History and Folklore of the Drive-in Restaurant in American Car Culture,* Motorbooks International Publishers & Wholesalers 1994.

**Newspapers, Magazines, and Journals**

*American Bar Association Journal,* May 1957.

*The American Journal of Psychiatry,* June 1959.

*The American Weekly,* Jan. 29, 1956.

*Batavia Daily News,* Nov. 2, 1955.

*Cañon City Daily Record,* Jan 6–12, 1957.

*The Chronicle News,* Sept. 12, 1956.

The Colorado Springs Gazette, January 11–12, 1957.
Colorado Springs Independent, July 18–24, 2002.
Colorado Lawyer, July 2000.
The Denver Post*
Far East Economic Review, July 13, 1995.
Fort Collins Coloradoan, Nov. 2–3, 1955.
The Greeley Daily Tribune, Nov. 2–3, 1955.
Life, Nov. 28, 1955.
The Longmont Ledger, Nov. 3, 1955.
The Longmont Times-Call, Nov. 2–3, 1955.
National Press Photographer, March–May 1956.
Newsweek, Oct. 21, 1933; Nov. 28, 1955; Jan. 21, 1957.
Norriston Times Herald, Nov. 2, 1955.
The Platteville Herald, Nov. 4, 1955.
The Rocky Mountain News*
The Saturday Review, Dec. 3, 1955.
The Seattle Post-Intelligencer, Nov. 4, 1955; April 17–May 5, 1956.
The Steamboat Pilot, Nov. 17, 1955.
The New York Times*
The Oregonian, Nov. 2–3, 1955.
Time, Oct. 23, 1933; Oct. 3–31, 1955; Jan. 21, 1957.
Wyoming State Tribune, Nov. 3, 1955.

**Interviews with the Author**
Morey Engle (Oct. 2003)
Judge Leonard Plank (Oct. 2003)
Zeke Scher (Oct. 2003)
Arlo Boda (Nov. 2003)
Charles Dalpra (Nov. 2003)
Louis & JoAnn Rademacher (Nov. 2003)
Dorothy Heil (Nov. 2003)
Justice William Erickson (Feb. 2004)
Judge John Criswell (March 2004)
Jerry Kessenich (March 2004)
Bernice F. Weadick (March 2004)
Judge Irving Ettenberg (March 2004)
Richard Downing (March 2004)
Edward Lehman (March 2004)
Judge Robert H. McWilliams (March 2004)
Dr. John Macdonald (March 2004)
Richard M . Schmidt Jr. (May 2004)
Conrad Hopp (September 2004)

---

* Numerous issues.

**Court Decisions, Court Records, Statutes, and Government Reports**

*C.A. Dunham Company v. Industrial Comm.,* 156 N.E.2d 560 (Ill. 1959).

*Coates v. People,* 106 Colo. 483 (Colo. 1940).

*Commonwealth Trust Co. of Pittsburgh v. United Air Lines, Inc.,* (D. Colo. 1957 Civ. A. Nos. 5825, 5828).

*Des Jardins v. United Air Lines, Inc.,* (D. Colo. 1957 Civ. A. No. 5833).

*Fitzpatrick v. United Air Lines, Inc.,* (D. Colo. 1957 Civ. A. No. 5566).

*Furman v. Georgia,* 408 U.S. 238 (1972).

*Graham v. People,* 134 Colo. 290, 302 P.2d 737 (1956)(Colo. No. 18058, trial transcript).

*Gregg v. Georgia,* 428 U.S. 153 (1976).

*Herman v. United Air Lines, Inc.,* 157 F.Supp. 65 (D.C.Colo. 1957) (1957 Civ. A. Nos. 5380, 5381, 5747).

*In re Hearings Concerning Canon 35,* 132 Colo. 591 (1956).

*J.E.B. v. Alabama ex rel. T.B.,* 511 U.S. 127 (1994).

*Leick v. People,* 131 Colo. 353, 281 P.2d 806 (1955).

*Loring v. United Air Lines, Inc.,* 19 F.R.D. 322, 323 (D. Mass. 1956).

*Colorado v. Graham,* Denver District Court No. 42604.

*Smith v. People,* 120 Colo. 39 (1949).

*Winsor v. United Air Lines, Inc.,* 153 F.Supp. 244 (E.D.N.Y. 1957).

*Winsor v. United Air Lines, Inc.,* 154 A.2d 561 (Del. Super. 1958).

Section 40-2-3, Colorado Revised Statues 1953 (death penalty).

Section 39-8-1, Colorado Revised Statues 1953 (insanity).

Sections 39-10-18, 48-1-16, 78-1-1, 94-3-14, 94-3-15, Colorado Revised Statues 1953 (jury service).

Sections 39-11-1 to 39-11-8, Colorado Revised Statues 1953 (gas chamber executions).

*Civil Aeronautics Board, Accident Investigation Report No. 257-46,* Jan. 14, 1947.

*Civil Aeronautics Board, Accident Investigation Report No. 1-0097-47,* Feb. 3, 1948.

*Civil Aeronautics Board, Accident Investigation Report No. 1-0092-47,* Dec. 21, 1948.

*Civil Aeronautics Board, Accident Investigation Report No: 1-0050,* Dec. 12, 1951.

*Civil Aeronautics Board, Accident Investigation Report No. 1-0143,* May 14, 1956.

*Civil Aeronautics Board, Accident Investigation Report No. 1-0130,* March 22, 1957.

Federal Bureau of Investigation Case File No. 661187B.

**Miscellaneous**

*Murder at Mid-Air,* Rocky Mountain Reflections (1995).

*Metropolitan Denver Telephone Directory,* Mountain States Telephone & Telegraph Company (Oct. 1955).

*United Air Lines News,* United Air Lines (Nov. 1933).

*The FBI Story,* Warner Brothers Pictures (1959).

# INDEX

**Notes on use:**
  This index includes entries for materials appearing in the main text, footnotes, and captions for photographs; it does not encompass the introductory materials or the appendices.
  Throughout the subentries of this index, the name of John Gilbert Graham is abbreviated as "JGG."

Adamson, Ross, 22, 32–33, 37, 168
aircraft, accidents involving, 4, 9–10
aircraft, bombings of, 29–30, 76, 232
aircraft, reassembly of, 31, 36–37, 52–53,
  94, 165, 177–80
aircraft sabotage, law prohibiting, 72, 206
alienist, 120
Allott, Senator Gordon, 72
Ambrose, Fay E. "Jack," 39
American Aviation Daily, 39–40
American Bar Association, 103, 123–24,
  127, 232
American Newspapers Publishers
  Association, 123
American Society of Newspaper Editors,
  123
American Weekly, 145
Amole, Gene
  interview of JGG, 129
  profile of, 128
  radio station, 172
  subsequent career and death, 231
Archina, Frank, 203, 208, 219, 230
Arthur, Samuel F., 7, 8, 11, 34–35
As a Man Thinketh, 120, 202

battery, 86, 88, 163, 175–76, 179
Beckstrom, Bror H., 23
Beckstrom, Irene, 23
Best, Roy, 200
the Bible, 155, 202, 208–09, 220

blasting caps, 61, 88, 90, 92, 179, 213
bodies
  identification of, 32–33
  recovery of, 16–19, 22, 24–26, 163,
    165, 233
Boeing Air Transport, 9, 38
  See also United Air Lines, history.
bombings, of aircraft, 29–30, 76, 232
Bommelyn, John P., 1, 122, 177
Bommelyn, Martin, 1, 122
Brennan, Frank M., 23
The Bridge of San Luis Rey, 101
Broderick, William, 55, 57, 61
Brown, Lyman
  identification of JGG, 93
  interviews, 89, 94
  JGG's statements about, 136, 213
  testimony, 170–71
Brown Palace Hotel, 2, 70, 156
Buena Vista, 46–47, 196, 200
Bunch, Louise D., 2–3
Burke, Webb W., 32, 38–40, 43–45
Bynum, Horace Brad, 8, 32, 100, 153
Bynum, Carol, 8, 100

CAA
  See Civil Aeronautics Administration
CAB
  See Civil Aeronautics Board
cameras
  Graflex, 128

Minox, 224–25
Rolleiflex, 144
cameras in the courtroom
 *See* courtroom photography.
Cañon City, 47, 200–05, 211–19, 224,
 231
Canon 35, 103–04, 117–18, 123–24,
 139–40
 *See also* courtroom photography
capias, 83
Carroll, Diane, 148, 153, 156–57
Carroll, Congressman John A., 148, 153
Chance, Hugh, 3–4, 160
Christenson, Carl, 166
Christmas gifts
 from JGG, 59–64, 79, 101, 171, 184,
 190
 to JGG, 57, 114, 120, 154, 202, 221
Civil Aeronautics Administration, 33–34,
 36, 72
Civil Aeronautics Board, 28, 30–37,
 39–44
Clayton College of Denver, 47–48,
 113–14, 134
Colorado Psychopathic Hospital, 106–17,
 120, 132, 159, 174, 206–07
Colorado School of Mines, 76–77, 92
Colorado State Hospital in Pueblo, 112,
 230
Colorado State Penitentiary, 187, 200–03,
 215, 220, 231
Colorado Supreme Court
 appeal of JGG, 197–99, 203, 206–10
 Canon 35 hearing, 117–18, 123–24,
 139–40
 decisions of, 80, 141, 153, 179, 203,
 228–29
 *See also* Holland, Justice E. V.; Moore,
 Justice O. Otto.
Colorado-Texas Pump Company, 87–88,
 182, 213
confession, motions to suppress, 162,
 164, 171–73
court reporting, methods of, 82, 158

courtroom photography
 at trial of JGG, 144, 146, 171–72
 history of, 102–04
 special hearing, 117–18, 123–24,
 139–40
Cousins, Norman, 109–10
crash cover, 20
crashes, aircraft,
crash site
 clergy at, 19
 examination by prosecutors, 99
 firefighting at, 20–25, 37
 looting at, 18
 national guard at, 19, 23–26
 photographers and reporters at, 20,
 25–26
 postal inspectors at, 19–20
 police officers at, 18–19
 recovery of bodies from, 22–26
 removal of debris from, 31, 36–37,
 52–53, 94, 165, 177–80
 reporters at, 19–20
 surveying of, 31, 36
 telephone lines, installation of, 22
 United Air Lines personnel at, 19–26
Crist, Oscar A., 68–69, 72
Crouch, Thomas L., 11
Crown-A drive-in
 employees of, 77
 explosion at, 52, 94, 96
 JGG's operation of, 56, 77–78
 menu and opening of, 50
 photograph of, 50
Cruse, Barbara J., 39
Customs House, 60, 68

Davis, Dick, 157, 163, 169, 173, 189, 192
death penalty
 history of, 200, 215–19, 230–31
 public sentiment concerning, 148,
 151–53
 requirements for imposition of, 80
 statutes governing, 80, 200
 *See also* gas chamber.

DC-6
  accidents involving, 4, 9
  history of, 4
DC-6B
  cargo compartment of, 39, 46, 94, 161, 213
  dimensions and weight of, 4, 31
  emergency flares, 33
  fuel capacity of, 9
  photographs of, 26
  scale model of, 162–63, 180
  seating capacity of, 5
  speed and stability of, 4
DC-7, 4
DC-8, 5
Deist, Carl F., 2
Denver City and County Building, 81–82, 137, 145, 147, 154, 179, 190, 194
Denver County Jail
  old jail, 69, 71, 81, 83–86, 93–98, 111, 128–32, 135, 141–42, 208
  mob threats against, 70–72
  new jail on Smith Road, 142, 146, 154, 198
  visitation by Gloria Graham, 79–80, 90
Denver District Court, 75, 81, 104–07, 145, 148, 228
  See also Keating, Judge Edward M.; McDonald, Judge Joseph M.
Denver Post
  articles about JGG, 70–71, 76, 85, 88–90, 92, 108–09, 120, 195–96
  letter to the editor, 109
  photographers at crash site, 20, 25
  photographs appearing in, 50, 104, 107, 166, 169, 178
  See also McWilliams, George; Scher, Isaac "Zeke."
Department of Justice, 29, 174
Des Jardins, John P., 10, 229
Dolliver, Warden Gordon, 70–71, 79–83, 90–95, 128–32, 135–36, 141–42, 149
Dorey, James, 5–6

Dorey, Sarah, 5
Douglas Corporation, 4–5, 34, 38, 42, 162
  See also DC-6; DC-6B; DC-7; DC-8.
Dukes, Gene, 97
dynamite
  invention of, 92
  JGG's experience with, and purchase of, 61–67, 88–90, 93–96, 136, 168, 170–71, 213
  photographs of, 163, 169
  trial, as an exhibit at, 163, 169–70
  See also blasting caps; Nobel, Alfred.

Eaton Metal Products Company, 217–19
Edwards, Elizabeth D., 24
Edwards, Gurney, 24
Eisenhower, President Dwight D., 10, 41, 72, 74, 98, 100, 206
Eisenhower, Mamie, 10, 41
Elson, Gloria Ann. See Graham, Gloria.
Elson, Christine, 59–60, 184–85
Elson, Roy, 184–85
Engle, Morey
  execution, attendance at, 224–25
  photograph of, 213
  photography by, 128–30, 137–38
  profile of, 127–28
  interview of JGG, 212–14
  subsequent career, 231
executions, photography of, 223–25
Eveready. See battery.
eyewitnesses, to explosion, 14–16, 33, 161–62

Federal Bureau of Investigation
  fingerprinting of victims, 32
  interview and interrogation of Gloria Graham, 59, 63–64
  interview and interrogation of JGG, 55–58, 60–65
  interview of Helen Hablutzel, 55
  investigation of airport personnel, 46
  investigation of victims, 44
  search of JGG's house, 62–63

Ferber, Edna, 103
Fitzpatrick, Helen, 6–7, 229
Fitzpatrick, James II, 6–7, 26, 229
Fitzsimmons Army Hospital, 10, 41
flares, 14, 33–34, 37, 161–62, 180
flight engineer, responsibilities of, 7
Flight Engineers Union
  assistance with investigation, 36
  criticism of United Air Lines, 35
  reward offer of, 40
  strike by, 7–9
flight insurance, 11–12, 42, 46, 58, 61,
  65, 72, 160, 180, 232
Flight 629
  as route designation, 119, 233
  crew of, 7–8, 12, 101, 161
  Denver-bound passengers, 45–46
  flight path of, 12
  schedule of, 1, 3, 11, 70, 160, 180
  weather for, 11
Fort Collins, 9, 46, 162
Fort Lupton, 20
Foster, Jack, 224

Galvin, Dr. James, 112, 115–16, 122,
  133–35, 141
Gardner, Erle Stanley, 145
gas chamber
  executions in, 153, 208, 223, 230
  history of, 215–19, 230–31
  photographs of, 216, 218
  three-seat model, 217
  *See also* death penalty; Eaton Metal
    Products Company.
General Adjustment Bureau, 51, 155
Geer, Edward, 131
Gibbons, John J. "Chesty"
  appointment as counsel, 96–97
  closing argument, 187–89
  defense of Gene Dukes, 97
  disagreements with co-counsel, 162,
    207
  examination of witnesses, 160–67, 171,
    178

jury selection, 151–56, 161
leaking of psychiatric report, 120
photographs of, 99, 105, 189
profile of, 96–97
statements to reporters, 97–98, 100,
  102, 131–32, 143–45, 156, 204,
  207, 221–22
subsequent career and death, 227–28
Graham, Allen, 48
Graham, Gloria
  assault by JGG, 115
  children of, 48–49
  death, 230
  interviews, print media, 78–79, 120,
    147, 191, 198, 205–06, 210–11
  interviews, film and radio, 90, 128–29
  marriage to JGG, 48–49, 54, 219
  neighbors of, 67, 152, 184, 198
  photographs of, 105, 138, 192
  statements to FBI agents, 59–60, 63,
    171
  subsequent life, 230
  testimony, 165, 186
  visitation with JGG, 79, 120, 128–31,
    133, 146–47, 154, 177, 184, 190,
    198, 205–06, 219
Graham, John Gilbert
  assaults by, 115–16
  aunts, 120, 202, 220–21, 227
  birth, 47
  children, 48–49, 120, 130
  Clayton College of Denver, time at,
    47–48, 113–14, 134
  Coast Guard, service in, 53–54, 115,
    118–19, 178, 230
  confession, 174–76, 221–22
  Crown-A Drive-in, operation of, 50,
    52, 77–78, 94, 96
  Denver University, enrollment at,
    54–55, 78, 175, 207
  diary of, 153–55
  employment history, 54–55, 214
  execution, 223–26
  father, 47

high school education, 53–54, 114
house, 48–49, 62–63
initial statements to FBI agents, 55–58
insanity evaluations, 112–13, 118–21,
  130–35
insurance claims made by, 52, 56, 94,
  96, 174
intelligence quotient of, 117
interviews (print media), 83–86,
  135–36, 191
interviews (recorded), 127–30,
  212–14
marriage, 48–49, 54
meals, 76, 95, 116
photographs of, 64, 99, 137–38, 173,
  192, 201, 203, 213
prior convictions of, 53
probationer, time as, 53–55
recantation of confession by, 83–84,
  221–22
request to waive jury, 141
request to abandon appeal, 197–208
relationship with mother, 47–48,
  113–16, 129, 133–34, 195–96
relationship with sister, 143, 195–97
relationship with stepfather, 114–15, 178
relationship with wife, 115, 209
suicide attempts, 130–32, 134
testimony, 171–73
weight loss, 146–49
withdrawal of insanity plea, 136, 138
Graham, Suzanne, 49, 120, 130
Graham, William Henry, 47
Grande, Joseph, 87–88, 182
Grand Junction, 48, 54, 156
Greeley Armory, 22–23, 25, 32, 37, 167
Greeley Daily Tribune, 18, 26, 31
Guay, J. Albert, 30, 76

Hablutzel, Helen
  arrest of, 194
  children of, 143, 197
  childhood, 47
  death, 230

photograph of, 105
recollections of JGG's childhood, 143,
  195–97
recollections of mother, 195–97
statements to FBI agents, 55, 115,
  182–83
testimony, 159, 182–83
Hall, Lee H., 7–8, 12, 161
Hall, Sally, 177, 193, 230
Hasman, Lloyd, 60
Hauptmann, Bruno Richard, 103, 145
Hayes, Sergeant George, 137, 192, 201
Heil, Dorothy, 13, 16–17
Heil, Harold, 13, 16
Heil, Jake, 15
Herman, Goldie, 24, 229
Herman, Vernal Virgil, 24, 229
Hickok, Elton B. Goldie, 22
Hilton, Dr. Jack P., 120, 131–32
Hinds, Jacqueline L., 9
Hobgood, Marion P., 24
Holland, Justice E. V., 104, 108, 117, 123
Hoover, J. Edgar, 40, 43, 62, 72, 75, 173,
  229

Illinois Powder Company, 179, 213
information, filing of, 74
insanity,
  evaluations of JGG, 112–18, 133
  plea by JGG, 84, 106, 122
  statutory definition of, 113
  withdrawal of plea by JGG, 136, 138
interference with a national defense
  utility, 67, 69, 162

Johnson, Governor "Big Ed," 206–07, 217
Judicial Canon 35. See Canon 35.
judicial elections, 106–07
Jungels, John W., 24
jurat, 102
jury
  composition of, 157–58
  disqualifications from service, 147
  exemptions from service, 147

gender of, 145, 152
instructions to, 186
investigation of, 161
motion for trial without, 140–41
photograph of, 157
selection of, 130, 145–58
sequestration of, 145–46, 151, 157, 164

"Karl," invention of by JGG, 86–87, 174, 178, 214
KBTV, 127
KDEN, 128
Keating, Bert M.
closing argument, 190–91, 194
cross-examination of JGG, 172
debate with Charles Vigil, 117
election as district attorney, 74, 204
examination of witnesses, 159–72, 179–84
filing of murder charge, 74–75
mayoral campaign, 73–74
opening statement, 159
photographs of, 107, 166, 169, 173
profile of, 73–74
selection of jurors, 148–57
subsequent career and death, 228
Keating, Judge Edward M., 82, 95–106, 116–21
Kellams, Reverend Lloyd C., 76, 100, 220–21, 227
Kelley, Donald E., 67, 69, 73–74, 164
Kelly, William Cody, 199, 217
Ketchum, Logan, 137, 223, 225
Kidera, Dr. George J., 25, 32, 168
Kilgallen, James, 144–45, 191
KIMN, 90
King, Daisie E.
burial of, 55, 227
businesses, 49–50, 56–57, 78
childhood, 46–47
estate of, 56
flight insurance, 11, 46, 58, 65
inheritance, 48
marriages, 46–48, 113

parents, 46–47
personal effects of, 52–53
photograph of, 114
profiles of, 54–55, 77, 116, 134, 195–96
purchase of house for JGG, 48–49
relationship with JGG, 47–48, 113–16, 129, 133–34, 195–96
suicide attempt, 84, 116
suitcases of, 57–64
ticket of, 66, 160
King, Earl, 48, 56, 60, 113, 168
KLZ-TV, 108, 123, 144
Knous, Judge William Lee, 164–65
Kremmling, 53, 78, 89, 93, 170–71

Legg, Jack, 160
Leick, LeRoy
appeals of, 153
execution of, 230
trials of, 93, 100, 104, 142, 153
incarceration with JGG, 142, 203, 208–10
murder of wife by, 51, 97
*Life*, 101, 224
life estate, 48, 56
Lipke, Gerald G., 5, 91
Lipke, Patricia, 5, 91
locus poenitentiae, 187
Longmont, 13–25, 41, 61, 99, 162, 176, 233
*Longmont Ledger*, 25
*Longmont Times-Call*, 21, 25
Lowry Air Force Base, 21, 41, 150

Macdonald, Dr. John, 112, 115–16, 122, 133–34, 141, 159, 185–86
McDonald, R. J. "Little Mac," 161, 198
McDonald, Judge Joseph M.
photographs of, 173, 178
profile of, 122
rulings of, 122, 132, 136, 141, 144–48, 150–58, 165, 171, 179, 183, 186–88, 198–99

selection as presiding judge, 107–08, 118
subsequent career and death, 228
McKernan, Reverend Justin, 220–25
McClain, Lela, 7
McWilliams, George, 89–90
Magee, Dr. J. William, 168–70, 179, 185
Martinez, Besalirez, 203, 208, 219
Mainliner
    as name of aircraft, 5–6
    as trademark in advertising, 5, 233
*Mainliner Denver*, 3, 17–18, 233
Martin, James, 130, 132
Martin, John, 66
Mazzula, Fred, 125, 169
Medicine Bow Peak, disaster on, 9–10,
    36, 42, 55, 70, 86, 180, 212
Melville, Max, D.
    arguments on motions, 105, 183
    profile of, 104–07
    subsequent career and death, 228
Mentzer, William, 30–31, 162–63, 180
Messervy, Lou, 51, 94, 97
Meyer, Jack, 19, 163
Miller, Dr. Earl
    comments regarding JGG, 67
    treatment of Gloria Graham, 66
    testimony, 167–68
*Miranda v. Arizona*, 62
Mischke, Roy, 55–58, 61, 66, 168
mistrial, motion for, 179
Moore, Justice O. Otto
    Canon 35 hearing, 123–27
    opinion in appeal of JGG, 210
    photographs of, 125–26
    profile of, 123
    report concerning courtroom
        photography, 137–40
    subsequent career and death, 232
Moore, Roy K.
    as advisory witness, 159
    interrogation of JGG, 60–65
    photograph of, 45
    profile of, 43
    testimony, 164, 171

Morgan, Suzanne F., 11
Morgan, Frederick Stuart, 11
morgue. *See* Greeley Armory
Mueller, Gregory
    closing argument, 187
    examination of witnesses by, 153, 161,
        170, 180
    photographs of, 107, 166
    profile of, 93, 97
    subsequent career and death, 228

Nakkula, Al "Nak"
    interview of JGG, 84–85
    profile of, 83
    photograph of, 83
    reporting of, 88
    subsequent career and death, 231
National Association of Radio and
    Television Broadcasters, 108, 123
National Press Photographers Association,
    90, 123–26, 232
*Newsweek*, 7, 101, 221
Newton, Mayor Quigg, 1, 74, 122
*New York Times*, 72, 81
Nobel, Alfred, 92
Noland, Judge James M., 82, 104, 124

Oakes, Commissioner Harold S., 68–69
Oschmann, Ed, 144

Packer, Alfred "the Cannibal," 76
Parshall, Jack, 25–31, 37–38, 43, 180
    *See also* Civil Aeronautics Board.
Patterson, W. A. "Pat"
    profile of, 38
    subsequent career and death, 229
    United Air Lines, work as president of,
        8, 34, 38, 40, 68, 70, 75, 102, 177
    *See also*, United Air Lines.
Peddicord, Peggy Ann, 9
Peyton, James, 30–31, 40–44
Platteville, 15, 20
polio, 24
Post Office Building, 68

Pratt & Whitney Aircraft Company, 5
Purvis, James W., 23

Rademacher, Louis, 27
Riesel, Victor, 205
Robertson, Herbert G., 24
*Rocky Mountain News*
 articles about JGG, 76, 81, 83–85, 88,
  95, 116–17, 141, 151, 153–55, 194
 letters to the editor, 109
 photographers at crash site, 20
 photographs appearing in, 105, 128,
  173, 212
 *See also* Engle, Morey; Foster, Jack;
  Nakkula, Al "Nak."
Routt County, 54, 78, 114
Roy's Penthouse, 217–19
 *See also* gas chamber, history of.
Rudd, Charles, 137, 223, 225
Ryall Electrical Supply Company, 87–88

sabotage. *See* bombing, of aircraft.
Sandstead, Dr. Harold R., 10–11
*The Saturday Review*, 109
Scher, Isaac "Zeke"
 disclosure of JGG's confession, 220
 disclosure of sanity evaluations, 120–21
 dynamite, article concerning, 90
 interviews of JGG, 86, 135–36, 191
 JGG's comment concerning, 221
 photograph of, 85
 subsequent career, 231
Schmidt, Richard M., Jr., 126–27
Scofield, Sally Ann, 39, 79, 177
Scrabble, 147, 198
Sebesta, Donald, 60, 171–72, 178–79
sentence, pronouncement of, 200
Ship Tavern shooting, 156
Sizemore, Jesse T., 41–42, 67, 101
Sky Chef restaurant, 1–2
Smaldone brothers, 98
Stapleton Airfield, 1–3, 8, 12, 31, 33, 36,
 38, 45–46, 52, 57, 69, 79, 93, 122,
 142, 146, 154, 181–82, 185, 188, 233

stewardess, history of position, 9
 *See also* Cruse, Barbara; Hall, Sally;
  Hinds, Jacqueline; Peddicord,
  Peggy; Scofield, Sally Ann.
Stratton, Lieutenant Robert, 137, 192
Straud, James E., 2
Strickland, Jerome R.
 at Stapleton Airfield, 69, 185
 representation of JGG, 69, 82, 94–96
sugar beets, 13, 16, 22, 27, 31, 99, 166,
 214
surveying, of crash site, 31, 36

television
 camera at Canon 35 hearing, 127,
  138–39
 cameras at crash site, 20
 camera at trial, 144, 146, 171–72
 *See also* courtroom photography;
  Canon 35; Terry, Hugh.
Tepley, Dr. Leo, 120–21
Terry, Hugh B., 108–09, 123
*Time*, 17, 101, 221
timer, 86–88, 163, 175–76, 182
Tinsley, Harry C., 200–02, 208, 210,
 212, 219, 221–26, 231
Todd, Clarence W., 23
trial
 closing arguments, 187–94
 disruptions, 150–51, 165–66, 170, 173
 exhibits, 163, 166, 169
 jury selection, 143–58
 opening statements, 159, 183
 security, 146, 149
 spectators, 147, 177, 186
 testimony, 159–86
 verdict, 191
Tupperware, 152

union violence, 8, 40, 205
United Air Lines
 accidents, 9–10
 history of, 38
 lawsuits against, 229

men-only flights, 9
recovery team, 19, 21, 25–26, 163
reward offer of, 40, 70
*See also* Boeing Air Transport; Patterson,
  W. A. "Pat"; stewardess.
University of Colorado, 97, 112, 228
University of Denver, 48, 73, 105, 123,
  175, 231

Van Valin, Minnie, 7
Van Valin, Dr. Ralph Waldo, 7
venue, challenge to, 102, 105, 118, 141,
  148
verdict, 191
Vigil, Charles S. "Gangbuster"
  appeal on behalf of JGG, 198, 203–04,
    207–10
  appointment as counsel, 97
  closing argument, 188–90
  debate with Bert Keating, 117
  disagreements with co-counsel, 162,
    207
  examination of witnesses, 160, 164,
    178–82
  exhibits, throwing of, 165–66, 170
  jury selection, 149
  opening statement, 159, 183
  photograph of, 99
  profile of, 97–98
  statements to reporters, 97, 144–45,
    156
  subsequent career and death, 228

Wagoner, James, 60–63, 164, 171, 174,
  178

Walker, Judge Gilbert A., 46–47, 57
Ward, Damon, 181–82
Waters, John, 111
Weadick, Paul
  appeal on behalf of JGG, 198, 203–04,
    207–10
  birth of twins, 150
  comments regarding JGG, 99, 145, 205
  photograph of, 99
  profile of, 98
  subsequent career and death, 228
Weld County, 13, 16, 22, 69, 73, 105,
  118, 168, 183
Westminster Law School, 73, 96, 105
West, Helene, 67, 152, 184, 191–93, 198
West Side Court Building, 74
White, Donald A., 7, 8, 101
White, Maxine, 7, 101
Wilson, Charles, 34, 38
Winsor, Alma L., 24, 229
witnesses
  advisory, 159
  defense, 184–86
  expert, 60–63, 93, 164, 171, 174, 178
  prosecution, 159–84

X-acto tool set, 59–65, 87, 174
X-rays,
  of JGG, 117
  of luggage, 72

Yampa, 47–48, 67, 114, 155
Young, George, 158, 173, 189

# About the Author

ANDREW J. FIELD is a staff attorney specializing in criminal law for the Colorado Court of Appeals. A graduate of Skidmore College and Vermont Law School, he has previously worked as a deputy district attorney in Colorado's Eighteenth Judicial District (Arapahoe County), and as a law clerk on the United States Court of Appeals for the Tenth Circuit and the Idaho Supreme Court.

To contact the author, or to learn more about the people, places, and events described in this book, visit: www.andrewjfield.com